BLACK HOLLYWOOD

From Butlers to Superheroes, the
Changing Role of African American Men
in the Movies

KIMBERLY FAIN

 PRAEGER™

An Imprint of ABC-CLIO, LLC
Santa Barbara, California • Denver, Colorado

Library of Congress Cataloging-in-Publication Data

Fain, Kimberly, 1974–
  Black Hollywood : from butlers to superheroes, the changing role of African American men in the movies / Kimberly Fain.
     pages cm
  Includes bibliographical references and index.
  ISBN 978–1–4408–3190–4 (hard copy : alk. paper) — ISBN 978–1–4408–3191–1 (ebook) 1. African American men in motion pictures. 2. Masculinity in motion pictures. I. Title.
PN1995.9.N4F36   2015
791.43'6521108996073—dc23   2015007051

ISBN: 978–1–4408–3190–4
EISBN: 978–1–4408–3191–1

19 18 17 16 15   1 2 3 4 5

This book is also available on the World Wide Web as an eBook.
Visit www.abc-clio.com for details.

Praeger
An Imprint of ABC-CLIO, LLC

ABC-CLIO, LLC
130 Cremona Drive, P.O. Box 1911
Santa Barbara, California 93116-1911

This book is printed on acid-free paper ∞

Manufactured in the United States of America

For all of those early twentieth-century African American actors who, during an oppressive era, played stereotypical roles, such as slaves and servants, and their efforts to transform limiting depictions of African Americans, as they kicked in the door for contemporary black males to play action heroes, presidents, God, and superheroes.

We thank you!

Contents

Acknowledgments

For a book like this, I hoped to include the major players of each decade. However, for any oversights or intended omissions, I still hope to satisfy those popular culture, film history buffs, and those who recognize the contribution of African Americans in the cinema. Nevertheless, I am grateful to various individuals who have supported this project and offered valuable advice on how to improve the book. During this time, watching classic movies, blaxploitation flicks, gangsta rap films, and movies in the Age of Obama, I have noticed both trends and repetitious themes. I appreciate strangers in the coffee shop, supermarket, and movie theaters who gladly offered their opinion on popular culture and black stars in film. But then there are the scholars, researchers, and writers, who greatly contributed to my knowledge of the topic by recommending books and consulting with me at a moment's notice.

First, I would like to thank my former students at Texas Southern University and Houston Community College. They caused me to ponder the effect of demonized and idealized depictions of African Americans in film. Even more specifically, they assisted me in questioning the problematic representations of black males in cinema. Their introspection and reflection compelled me to address the trifecta of history, popular culture, and film representations. The aforementioned factors work in a manner that creates a comprehensive portrait in Black Hollywood. Similarly, I appreciate the intellectual growth of students who interpreted all film images as benign. For the purposes of academic and cultural value, I now realize that all entertainment does not have to reside in the realm of high art. Since the beginning of my career in literature, I have incorporated cinematic analysis into every course I have taught.

Next, I would like to thank Dr. Ronald C. Samples and Dr. Charlene Evans, two scholars who graduated from Rice University. Yet they chose to give back to their community by teaching at a predominantly African American university. Although Texas Southern University now proudly represents the diversity of the American culture, it was this historically black institution that forced me to ponder African American contribution to literature, history, popular culture, and the cinema. As my graduate advisers, they guided me on interpreting the motive of the artists, African American representations, and their impact on popular culture. Also, I would like to thank Dr. Michael Sollars. As the editor of *World Literary Review: Modernism's Metaphors, Images, and Symbols* (Volume 2), Dr. Sollars offered me the position of assistant editor, due to our mutual understanding of the transforming power of media symbols and representations both stateside and globally. Furthermore, I would like to thank my legal family at Thurgood Marshall School of Law. Professor Edieth Wu and Professor Constance Fain are two legal scholars who forced me to think about the power of politics, policy, and law on early efforts of African Americans in history.

Particularly, in terms of the film industry, without Professor Fain's guidance, who is also my mother, I would not have realized the necessity of including the Jim Crow era, the Hays Moral Code, the McCarthy era, Hoover's FBI blacklist, and the mythical postracial era in the Age of Obama's Hope and Change. By interweaving the social and historical context of the films, the readers will see how politics and social movements impact cultural representations in film. Lastly, I want to thank Professor Fain for the early readings of essays, articles, chapters, and books. By forcing me to clarify portions of my writings, she taught me to question my own intentions. Thus *Black Hollywood* attempts to offer an objective slice of popular culture via the movies.

Lest I forget, my former professor Dr. Elizabeth Brown-Guillory was instrumental in beginning my interpretation of immigrant cultures and minority cultures in terms of American identity. During my teaching, researching, and writing fellowships at the University of Houston Honors College, she was our guide as we questioned the cultural representations in literature and theater productions. Since she has produced over 13 plays on southern culture, she is an expert on her subject matter. Without her contributions to playwriting and expertise in African American studies, I would have lacked the foundation to thoroughly analyze early blackface performance onstage and its subsequent influence in film. Despite her promotion to associate provost/associate vice president for academic affairs at Texas Southern University, she has maintained the rapport we built during my two fellowships at the University of Houston. Eventually, her mentorship led to my being awarded a prestigious honor—the Rice University Center for the Study of Women, Gender, and Sexuality Scholarly Award in 2012. With regard to the intersection of race, class, and gender, receiving this recognition has propelled the continuation of my scholarly pursuits of the aforementioned studies.

Also, I would like to thank Rebecca Matheson, editor at Praeger/ABC-CLIO. After I wrote "Spike Lee: Rise, Success, and Doin' the Right Thing," in *Star Power: The Impact of Branded Celebrity*, edited by Aaron Barlow, and published by Praeger in 2014, I hoped to write an entire book on Spike Lee. However, she suggested that I write a more comprehensive book including various black actors, writers, directors, and producers. As she guided me through my pitch and proposal, I agreed that there should be a text that covered and extended the territory of Donald Bogle in *Bright Boulevard, Bold Dreams: The Story of Black Hollywood* (2005), from the 1910s to the 1950s, and Bogle's book entitled *Toms, Coons, Mulattoes, Mammies, & Bucks* (2013), which covers the period of the 1910s until the year 2000. In 2008, with the advent of the first African American president, it was fascinating to determine whether significant social changes had occurred in terms of cinematic representations. Editor Matheson was continuously patient and attentive, willing to review chapters and offer her immediate critique. Along the way, I never felt as though I was on an island or a lone ranger in terms of this project.

Moreover, I would like to thank Dr. Herbert Fain. Not only is he a fellow graduate of Thurgood Marshall School of Law and a proud seminary professor, Dr. Fain is my father. As my cowriter on "Socio-Economic Status and Legal Factors Affecting African American Fathers," the lead article for the 2012 issue of *Buffalo Journal of Gender, Law, & Social Policy*, I began to contemplate black male fatherhood, black male identity, and the impact of the law and media representations on the surveillance and movement of the black male body. After we discussed movies, television, and commercials in a portion of the article, we realized how black males oftentimes believed that their social interactions and legal destinies were adversely affected by these problematic depictions. Furthermore, I realized that black reproductions on film are congruently influenced by the distorted view of black males in American culture. Not to mention, my father's love of the cinema inspired me to include Bill "Bojangles" Robinson. Who can forget Shirley Temple's famous tap dance with her butler and paternal caretaker Bojangles? His suggestion turned out to be monumental. My father said with paternal love and guidance, "There is no *Black Hollywood* without the contributions of Bill Robinson." I suppose he got his love for the theater and movies honestly. For in the 1960s, his mother, Doris Franklin, and father, Herbert Fain Sr., made sure that despite tight access to economic resources, he saw plays and concerts of performers such as Sammy Davis Jr., who famously recorded "Mr. Bojangles" in 1972, ironically unrelated to the performer by the same name.

With pleasure and appreciation, I would like to immensely thank my husband, Professor Anthony Johnson. As a facilitator for Boston University Metropolitan College and Southern New Hampshire University, he provided consultation of the movie industry in terms of business, marketing, and advertising principles. No doubt, his background in radio and television enhanced his analysis. I am grateful for the extensive conversations on the commodification of black culture and the efforts of black actors and directors to market, profit, and capitalize from their own cinematic representations. Without his expertise in marketing and business practices, I would not have realized how the black body has been a profitable entity since slavery, the early age of blackface, the Jim Crow era, the civil rights era, the booming blaxploitation era, and into the Age of Obama. For purposes of economic gain, his direction has guided me in terms of expressing how the cultural appropriation of blackness has been co-opted by both blacks and whites. For many viewers and some critics, both black and white, they qualify the cinematic depictions of blacks as racist. Professor Johnson insisted that economic components may be more profound than the art and the racism that created the complex black representation. Consequently, he caused me to reconsider artistic choices made by black performers. Instead of strictly deeming early depictions as racist, I explored the monetary benefit for both blacks and whites in the industry. Since the early days of *The Birth of a Nation* and Oscar Micheaux, the black press and black viewers have objected to these negative images. Nevertheless, the desire to transform and profit from one's own image has created black movie moguls such as Spike Lee and Tyler Perry. Professor Johnson insisted that *Black Hollywood* make this connection between black representation, film, and agency for the reader. Thus the story of *Black Hollywood* is one of an American culture cinematically working through tragedy and triumph, in order to earn a rightful and economic position for African American males in mainstream Hollywood.

Introduction: Appropriation, Exploitation, and Agency of Black Performers in Hollywood

Spike Lee and Tyler Perry are two famous actors, directors, writers, and producers whose names are synonymous with the contemporary perception of black Hollywood. Trailblazing the pathway for other pioneering African Americans, both men have found a niche outside of the mainstream studio system. Yet their prolific production and box-office success have surpassed that of any other black directors before them. Lee's production company, 40 Acres and a Mule, is located in New York, Tyler Perry's productions are based in Atlanta. Directors such as Oscar Micheaux during the 1920s–1940s and Melvin Van Peebles in the 1970s operated independently and outside of the social confines of mainstream Hollywood studios. Their films and the actors who performed in them signify how black actors, directors, writers, and producers have learned to make profit outside and inside the margins of Hollywood. Furthermore, famous servant performances such as those by Stepin Fetchit and Bojangles paved the way for self-appropriating negative and monolithic images for personal gain. On the more diverse side of the spectrum, Paul Robeson, Canada Lee, Sidney Poitier, and Harry Belafonte laid the foundation for more in-depth character actors who represent black issues and black themes. Nevertheless, they still transcended the black audience with their complex performances.

Black Hollywood examines the demonized, invisible, and simplistic depictions of black male images from the 1910s into a contemporary era of black males' appropriation of their own representations. African American male images are congruently a reflection of culture and politics, impetus for social progress, and pioneering demonstrations of transformation in cinematic achievement. Although there have been idealized representations of African American actors playing fathers, God (*Bruce Almighty*'s

Morgan Freeman), great orators (*Malcolm X*'s Denzel Washington), military officers (*Officer and a Gentleman*'s Louis Gossett Jr.), and world leaders (*Mandela*'s Idris Elba), the overwhelming prototypes of African American manhood are negative. Pervasively, examples of African American males as criminals, uneducated, hostile, or hypersexual are predominantly featured as universal archetypes. Many of the negative stereotypes that have become a part of the American discourse and culture such as blackface, Mandingo, Sambo, and Uncle Tom have gained popularity due to the public's interest in and acceptance of those depictions. During various eras, how has the public reinforced or rejected those representations? Frequently, these archetypes serve to demonize, demagogue, or differentiate African American males in people's subconscious. But are these images realistic or are they a reflection of society's fears and/or hopes for a pluralistic America? If these antagonistic archetypes stir up so much emotion, why do these controversial depictions continue? Perhaps this problematic paradigm offers not only entertainment for audiences but economic profit for the movie industry. Sometimes change occurs when directors challenge these damaging depictions.

Examination will focus on black male cinematic representations from the last 100 years to the present by black and white directors such as Lee Daniels, Oscar Micheaux, Melvin Van Peebles, Spike Lee, Steve McQueen, Tyler Perry, John Singleton, Steven Spielberg, and Quentin Tarantino. All of these critically acclaimed filmmakers have contributed to the damaging and/or positive cultural perceptions of African American males. Some of their films have featured screen icons such as Idris Elba, Laurence Fishburne, Jamie Foxx, Terrence Howard, Samuel L. Jackson, David Oyelowo, Denzel Washington, and Forest Whitaker who have dominated representations of black males presented by the media. Many of these actors have played chauffeurs, deadbeat dads, drug dealers, pimps, politicians, military leaders, rogue cops, and slaves in a manner that is realistic, human, and sympathetic. Despite the entertainment value, these roles have been a catalyst for political and social change by winning awards, creating a greater African American presence in Hollywood, and inspiring unity among audience members. Black images provide an aesthetic, cultural, historical, and political standpoint in the cinema and society. How have these representations transformed once blacks had more power both politically and socially in American culture? On June 19, 2013, *Newsweek* published an article by President Barack Obama's former spiritual adviser Joshua DuBois. The article, entitled "The Fight for Black Men," generated an immense amount of debate centering on African American fatherhood and the consequences of fathers' absence from the home in the Age of Obama. DuBois insists that it is not healthy for a society "when one single group of people is conspicuously left behind." Do cinematic images of black males represent the alienation, fragmentation, and invisibility that DuBois alludes to? Or are the problematic images reflective of black males' status in American culture? In any case, cinematic black images have the power to transform culture, reflect politics, and invoke social movements that have impacted Hollywood and beyond because African American actors, directors, writers, and producers respond to these relevant political and social issues in American culture.

For the purpose of popular culture, the black male image is arguably the most feared and revered image in popular culture. In a 12-month span, an African American actor, Jamie Foxx, plays an armed and dangerous ex-slave in *Django Unchained* and a black president in *White House Down*. This binary position of demonization and deification is ripe for criticism of contemporary cinematic popular culture images. For instance, the history behind blackface, the earliest known performance of black identity, must accompany present-day analysis of black representations. Furthermore, how do blacks arrive from a position of exclusion to the position of insider? There are modern-day examples who exemplify the appropriation, exploitation, and agency. For the past 20 to 30 years, Spike Lee's 40 Acres and a Mule, Tyler Perry Studios, and Will Smith's Overbrook Entertainment have dominated the conversations and depictions of contemporary African American images, yet they remain profitable. At times their movies have stereotypical and controversial elements, but they are simultaneously revolutionary and triumphant despite prevalent racism in Hollywood and American culture. When actors like Jamie Foxx play a slave in *Django Unchained* (2012) and then a president in *White House Down* (2013), they are demonstrating the evolution of African American images in Hollywood. Furthermore, the success of these diverse roles validates the mass appeal of movies featuring black male leads and movies depicting the complexity of the black experience in America.

In the past, there have been books—such as Donald Bogle's *Bright Boulevards, Bold Dreams: The Story of Black Hollywood* (Random House, 2005) and *Toms, Coons, Mulattoes, Mammies, & Bucks: An Interpretive History of Blacks in American Films* (Bloomsbury, 2001)—that discussed African American images in the movies, their effect on the populace, or their perpetuation of inequality, mediocrity, and/or success in moviemaking and society. Yet Bogle does not focus exclusively on African American male performers. *Black Hollywood* distinguishes itself by specifically speaking to the historical images formerly used to subjugate blacks and how their complexity reflects pioneering achievements of African American males in Hollywood. Furthermore, *Black Hollywood* subverts the images of the African American male as Mandingo, Sambo, or Uncle Tom even though they were essential for the cinematic process of achieving eventual selfhood. Not until the 1970s blaxploitation era will audiences witness black masculinity, sexuality, and societal rebellion that subvert the blackface, Sambo, and Uncle Tom prototypes. By contrast, the 1980s representations of comedians such as Richard Pryor and Eddie Murphy transcend into stardom by capitalizing on black stereotypes. By the 1990s gangsta rap era, hip-hop performers are aware of their artistic worth and fearlessly use their roguish images to act in blockbuster films. Keep in mind how in the twentieth and twenty-first centuries, African American actors, directors, writers, and producers have used these juxtaposed depictions of demonization and idealization to take agency, employ control, and profit from their own cinematic images in pop culture. Various pop culture writers have focused mainly on the marketing and advertising perspective of media misrepresentations and their attempt to program the perception of the inferior black male into the popular culture imagination. *Black Hollywood* acknowledges disparate treatment of black males, yet this book approaches analysis mainly from political and social movement perspectives as the text both reflects and impacts popular culture. Thus emphasis is placed on the transformative power of these black male images to influence the contemporary culture via the cinema.

Moreover, *Black Hollywood* is not a book about black males in crisis, consumed with doomsday rhetoric, or projected demise for the African American culture. Despite the controversial history of black representations at the movies, this book celebrates the success and examines failures of prominent blacks in the industry. How do blacks manipulate degrading stereotypes, gain control, advance their careers, and make profit, while making social statements or changes in culture? Successful black artists create trends, confront complex representations, and explore social injustice and structural racism in politics and entertainment. Furthermore, the historical and contemporary analysis of black representations in Hollywood is a multilayered approach. Examination does not shy away from gangsta rap artists turned actors and their violent images and nostalgic admiration for the 1970s blaxploitation era. Nor does discussion center primarily on the monolithic actor who plays only one artistic role in Hollywood. Rather, this book will focus on the performers who produce, direct, and write some of the roles they play. Thus *Black Hollywood* devotes time to how African American males have revolutionized the way popular culture perceives them. Also, this text will deliberate on how performers who are also social activists, such as Paul Robeson, Sidney Poitier, Harry Belafonte, and Spike Lee, shape political and social movements around their movies. *Black Hollywood* will show the causal links and interconnections between black representations, culture, politics, and social justice each decade since the 1910s. Lastly, *Black Hollywood* reviews the interactions between black and white characters and black actors and their diverse leading ladies to analyze how black males express their heritage, individual identity, and social issues through film. In short, *Black Hollywood* offers a historical, contemporary, and popular culture analysis on cinematic representations of African American males in the movies.

Each chapter is comprised of the actors, directors, writers and producers who had the most impact on black male representations during various decades. *Black Hollywood* delves into the primary pioneers and movers and shakers who kicked down doors and dismantled the barriers that barred equal access and opportunity for African Americans. Frustrated by the racism and segregation associated with Jim Crow, the Hays Moral Code, McCarthy-era blacklisting, and the FBI's Hoover and his contribution to blacklisting, these performers were bold trailblazers. Nevertheless, there are various brilliant and excellent performers who have contributed to the success of the artists mentioned in this book, but they are either only briefly mentioned or not included in this text. To avoid superficial analysis, *Black Hollywood* does not attempt to include every movie production that has contributed to cinematic African American representations. Based on various themes, there are both in-depth coverage and multifarious approaches implemented in each chapter to the most significant black male images and performers of the decade. Each chapter will cover how black artists veer past the emotional, social, and economic constraints to create classic and popular pictures, all while gaining both black and white audiences by taking artistic risks that have a monumental impact on popular culture. Every chapter will discuss the negative and positive images of black male identity, while acknowledging that both blacks and whites have contributed to the destructive representations of black culture. In addition, this book demonstrates how African American performers benefit from the negative images by self-appropriating their own cultural representations for profit. In instances where the social and political climate influenced the character, theme, or artist, *Black Hollywood* presents these multilayered complexities with social commentary and historical facts from the era. In many cases the personal upbringing of the artists, such as Paul Robeson, Stepin Fetchit, and Bojangles, impacted their artistic choices; therefore this information is explored before discussing their movies. For various actors, their personal vices, such as drinking, drugs, gambling, or womanizing, interfere with their artistic reputations and economic status. Then, there are Richard Pryor and Eddie Murphy whose comic antics sometimes overlap with but remain sandwiched between the 1970s blaxploitation stars such as Ron O'Neal and Max Julien and the 1990s gangsta rappers such as Tupac Shakur and Ice Cube. Gangsta rappers strived to transcend rap into the movies and create an even larger pop culture fan base. *Black Hollywood* also covers how the personal beliefs of actors such as Sidney Poitier, Will Smith, and Denzel Washington caused them to accept and reject roles or revise a character's lines. Meanwhile other actors, such as Paul Robeson, Canada Lee, and Harry Belafonte, made artistic choices based on their beliefs of equality and social justice. In other chapters, there is discussion of the racial implications of movies: *Birth of a Nation*, directed by D. W. Griffith; *Within Our Gates*, directed by Oscar Micheaux; *Malcolm X*, directed by Spike Lee; and *Django Unchained*, directed by Quentin Tarantino. Emphasis is placed on the directors' purpose for provoking controversy and their behind-the-scenes methodology for their production choices. Meanwhile, most chapters discuss the cost of production, the profits made, and the awards received by the actors or directors for their films. In actuality, those who survive and thrive in Hollywood are those African American performers who claim agency by writing, directing, acting in, and producing their own films. Consequently, those African Americans are able to capitalize from their own images. Thus the African American artists featured in *Black Hollywood* conquer the movie industry despite racism, and they are undeterred by intraracial jealously that undermines the efforts of blacks who permeate popular culture with their complex yet oftentimes problematic representations.

Structure of the Book

Section 1. Black Images from the Jim Crow Era to the McCarthy Era of Blacklisting

- Chapter 1, "1910s: Whites in Blackface and the Sexually Depraved Black Mandingo—*The Birth of a Nation*": *The Birth of a Nation* was the blockbuster silent movie that came out in 1915. It controversially features white actors performing in blackface. Black characters are depicted as violent rapists who lust for white women; therefore segregation and lynching are deemed necessary evils for the maintenance of white supremacy. Subsequently, discussion continues with the African American William Henry Lane, aka "Juba," who becomes a celebrated blackface performer.

- Chapter 2, "1920s: Oscar Micheaux's Response to Blackface and D. W. Griffith," discusses how Micheaux, the earliest well-known black director of at least 40 films, released the silent film *Within Our Gates* in 1920 as a response to *The Birth of a Nation*. Micheaux's films featured some light-skinned black actors that were fair enough to pass for white and African American actors in blackface for purposes of his story lines. Thus his films are a cinematic response to the racists and demonized images in *The Birth of a Nation*, Jim Crow policies and the rise of the Ku Klux Klan, the Great Migration, and the Chicago Riots of 1919.

- Chapter 3, "1930s: The Hays Moral Code and Jim Crow—*The Emperor Jones* and *Gone with the Wind*": In an attempt to avoid regulation by the government, Hollywood adopted a series of self-governing codes suggested by religious leaders. However, these rules were also written to appease Southerners' concerns over miscegenation in the Jim Crow era. *Gone with the Wind* features dark-skinned blacks as house slaves and their continued loyalty to Scarlett O' Hara and the post–Civil War South. Meanwhile, international actor, singer, speaker, and activist Paul Robeson in *The Emperor Jones* offers one of the first complex portrayals of a black male actor in Hollywood.

- Chapter 4, "1940s: Bill 'Bojangles' Robinson and Lincoln 'Stepin Fetchit' Perry: Black Servants in Musicals and Comedies": Unless they are musicians, subservient stock characters, or extras, African American actors are rarely seen in Hollywood with the exception of black musicals such as *Cabin in the Sky* and *Stormy Weather*. Consequently, black males are seen as unnecessary and inconsequential to the American identity and our cultural milieu.

- Chapter 5, "1950s: McCarthyism and Blacklisting: Canada Lee and Paul Robeson": Due to the radical politics of performers such as Paul Robeson and his friend Canada Lee, who played strong black male characters, they were blacklisted. Both Robeson and Lee were suspected of associating with Communists. However, critics agree that their belief in equality and social justice made them targets for surveillance. Although black male images are more positive and begin to reflect the diversity and complexity of the African American experience, actors such as Lee are often featured as supporting players for stronger white male leads.

Section 2. Black Images from the Apex of the Civil Rights Era to the Age of Barack Obama

- Chapter 6, "1960s: Token Black Actors in the Civil Rights Age: Sidney Poitier and Harry Belafonte": In 1963 Sidney Poitier, the first black to win the Oscar for the Best Actor Academy Award, attended Martin Luther King Jr.'s March on Washington with Hollywood legends such as the award-winning Harry Belafonte, Ossie Davis, Paul Newman, and Marlon Brando—a powerful example of stars using their cinematic power to influence politics and social policy. Meanwhile, movies reflected the social changes of racial integration in film and society.
- Chapter 7, "1970s: Blaxploitation: Preachers, Pimps, Pushers, and Players": Athletes, comedians, musicians, and classically trained actors portray dealers, pimps, and preachers as heroic saviors of urban communities. These groundbreaking movies are widely popular because they are often written, directed, produced, and starred in by blacks who challenge white societal norms and values. Yet blaxploitation movies also received societal backlash because actors exhibited stereotypical and violent behavior and sexually exploited black and white women for humor and entertainment.
- Chapter 8, "1980s: Black Comedians Rule: In the Age of Eddie Murphy and Richard Pryor": *Beverly Hills Cop's* Eddie Murphy and *Stir Crazy's* Richard Pryor ruled the box office with their self-deprecating humor that focused on culture, politics, sexuality, and race in blockbuster films. As the director of the commercial success *Harlem Nights*, Murphy featured three generations of black comics: Redd Foxx, Richard Pryor, and himself. Despite their success, they fall into one-dimensional roles that lack complexity during this era.
- Chapter 9, "1990s: Gangsta Rappers Transcend Music: Ice Cube, Ice-T, DMX, Nas, and 2Pac": During the government's War on Drugs, rappers displayed the multidimensional sides of black males who deal, use, or avoid drugs. They starred as cops and/or criminals seeking to transform and redeem their lives prior to ending up in jail or dead. Movies such as *Boyz N the Hood*, *New Jack City*, *Belly*, and *Juice* feature this transition. Specific attention is paid to the background and multiplicity of Tupac Shakur as both an actor and a human being.
- Chapter 10, "2000s: Black Icons: Control, Agency, and Self-Appropriation: Spike Lee, Tyler Perry, and Will Smith": Lee, Perry, and Smith dominated the depictions of African American males by

taking control of black representation at the movies. All three film-makers featured black male characters who revolutionized the screen with their concerns over family, spirituality, masculinity, and sexuality. Also, this chapter will examine the heteronormative views of masculinity and the use of cross-dressing to diversify black male representations.

- Chapter 11, "2010s "Black Power Hollywood: In the Age of Obama's Hope and Change"": Resurging interest in movies about slavery (*Django*), the Jim Crow era (*42:The Jackie Robinson Story*), and the civil rights era (*The Butler*) often receive critical acclaim and/or box office success, yet they also reflect a sense of nostalgia and regression in human rights. Despite the influence of transformative images, there is also a political and social backlash against viewpoints that humanize the depiction of African American males.

While this book sets out to detail the problematic depictions of black males in history and contemporary film, there is still an effort to create an enjoyable book that will illuminate African American male contributions. Hopefully, readers will enjoy learning more about blacks in popular culture. But also, I believe this book will compel people to see the movies mentioned both briefly and in depth in *Black Hollywood* and that readers will think more introspectively about the ideas, images, and themes that are promoted by media's representations of black males. In other words, the desire to passively enjoy a cinematic experience will be enhanced by a deeper and more profound knowledge of film history and popular culture. In essence, I hope that readers will feel inspired to engage in critical thinking about the films they hated and the films they loved.

Section 1

BLACK IMAGES FROM THE JIM CROW ERA TO THE MCCARTHY ERA OF BLACKLISTING

CHAPTER 1

———— 1910s ————
Whites in Blackface and the Sexually Depraved Black Mandingo—
The Birth of a Nation

In "Making America Home: Racial Masquerade and Ethnic Assimilation in the Transition to Talking Pictures," Michael Rogin refers to blackface as "the first and most popular form of mass culture entertainment" and explains that the practice expresses "both racial aversion and racial desire."[1] The writer Ralph Ellison speaks of the "darky" entertainer as a derivative of American folklore, not representative of the African American tradition.[2] Although there is apparent mimicry of black culture, Ellison asserts that the darky entertainer is white because the art form is popular among whites, not blacks. Ellison's tone reflects the general beliefs of black America in the early 1900s. Since blackface performance defiled African Americans' image, Ellison claimed the practice symbolized both repressed and conscious feelings toward African Americans. Furthermore, blacks were "shackled" to this image whose humiliation was more malignant than the "physical hardships and indignities of slavery."[3] Both whites and blacks performed in blackface for economic gain. Their motives behind the art form differed in terms of available opportunities to perform. Nevertheless, Ellison stated that the racial identity of the performer did not make a difference. The practice had a malignant effect on blacks either way because "its function was to veil the humanity of the Negroes ... and to repress the white audience's awareness of its moral identification with its own acts."[4] As a result, Ellison viewed blackface performance as evidence of the continued degradation of the black culture in America.

During this popular decade of blackface, various Hollywood movies of the 1910s reflect problematic views of black males. Although *Uncle Tom's Cabin* (1914) was based on Harriet Beecher Stowe's abolitionist novel, the story line refuses to reject racial stereotypes. The primary theme suggests a complacent acceptance of racial oppression. The docile Uncle

Tom receives equality in the heavenly milieu, not on earth.[5] Films such as *The Birth of a Nation* (1915) solidify the meek, buffoonish, vulgar, and violent image of black males. Despite the protests, riots, and negative press associated with the film's release, *The Birth of a Nation* was extremely successful. Even though blackface images mock black culture, they have a compelling history that begins on the stage. Early Hollywood perpetuates this cultural art form for profit, while ignoring the emasculating and culturally demeaning aspects. Perhaps the most damaging aspect of minstrelsy is the maintenance of racial stereotypes in Hollywood. Since Hollywood reflects culture and makes culture, the perceptions of black males are framed by limited perspectives. Thus blacks are denied equal entry into the sparkly gates of Hollywood and the ideal American way of life.

Hollywood: The Spectacle of Blackface

Prior to the performance of blackface on film, there was an American fascination with native peoples of this country. Rogin states that "the discovery and appropriation of native peoples, peoples defined by and ripped from their relationship to their land, stands at the origins of the United States" and that this discovery is indigenous to the United States as the "invention of America."[6] In the process of inventing America, the creation of a national culture and identity manifested itself in the medium of entertainment. Rogin argues that for the colonizer, who has discovered this new land and new peoples, power is granted over those already living on the land and that power was maintained when authority was assumed over blacks who toiled the land and served the interests of a developing American culture. This authority over people and the perception of various groups creates a cultural advantage. Hence the cultural myths repeat themselves in print media, on the stage, and eventually in early motion pictures. Since the earliest forms of American culture were "the frontier myth, and blackface minstrelsy," literature about Native Americans and blackface presents "both racial aversion and racial desire."[7] Consequently, this fascination is subverted by undercurrents of disdain. By imitating the speech patterns, dance movements, and musicality of blacks, ethnic whites were able to transition from a place of exclusion to white inclusion.

Blackface or racial cross-dressing transformed Europeans to Americans. The Americanization of European descendants occurs not only in frontier myths but in urban areas as well. Rogin declares that "blackface made white Americans out of Irish immigrants on the 'cultural borderland' ... between the Anglo-Saxon and colored races."[8] According to Rogin, Jewish movie producers, vaudeville performers, and songwriters shared a commonality with Irish immigrants: the status of those aforementioned groups did not occupy a secure and decided position between whites and people of color. Hollywood movies featured the ideal America that "moguls and their immigrant audience aspired to enter."[9] By utilizing racial cross-dressing, these entertainers were acknowledging their ambiguous racial status within American identity. In essence, for the purposes of gaining access into mainstream America, Hollywood movies became a vehicle of entry by displaying the spectacle of minstrelsy. The process of white inclusion mandates a differentiation between whiteness and blackness. Blackface, which is only skin deep, creates a visual distinction between whites and nonwhites. However, blackface is a spiritual miscegenation. Thus, by placing black identity at the forefront of white entertainment, an American identity excluding blacks is forged.

The Significance of Early Blackface Performance Art

Oftentimes, popular culture differs on the significance of blackface performance. Some critics insist upon the benign essence of the early American art form. Meanwhile other cultural critics, such as the literary giant Ralph Ellison, tend to disagree with the benevolent interpretations of blackface. Ellison insists that blackface performance is popular because it mocks black folk culture. Furthermore, blackface art has a malignant effect on the African American culture because it substantiates irrational fears and prejudices of white Americans. Blackface is "a symbolic role basic to the underlying drama of American society" for the purpose of assuming "a ritual mask—the identical mask and role taken on by white minstrel men when *they* depicted comic Negroes."[10] Even blacks whose natural coloration should have exempted them from the practice culturally participated in adorning the mask. Furthermore, Ellison asserts that the practice of "Negro idiom, songs, dance motifs and word-play" is not emblematic of a black comic tradition; moreover, blackface is born out of white imagination in terms of black and white culture.[11] In other words, minstrelsy is more of a cultural misappropriation of sweeping generalizations, capturing the fascination of white culture. Minstrelsy creates a black mask that imprisons the black male within a one-dimensional prism of buffoonery. Consequently, the opportunities of black males in culture and Hollywood are limited by these blackface performances. Since images of blackface were deeply ingrained into the American conscience, Ellison believed that blackface minstrelsy was extremely damaging to white Americans' perception of the Negro. Therefore it was impossible for many whites to perceive black men in terms of their humanity. Due to the disparaging images of blacks in popular culture, white folks are unable to ponder issues of gender, class, national identity, history, or social equality without summoning evil images of black men into consciousness. Thus white American folklore and the field of entertainment thrive on the exploitation of blacks, and the Negro's humanity is transformed into "a negative sign that usually appears in a comedy of the grotesque and the unacceptable."[12] The spectacle of early minstrel shows is reminiscent of an exorcism ritual: choreography lacking in black influence, "ringing of banjos and rattling of bones, ... cackling jokes in pseudo-Negro dialect, ... nonsense songs, ... bright costumes and sweating performers."[13] As a result, blackface performance was a subpar imitation of blackness and functioned as a ceremonial exercise in demonizing the subject. The derogatory "mask was an inseparable part of the national iconography."[14] Consequently, the black male image became a universal symbol of buffoonery and demonization in the public's imagination.

Minstrelsy: The Emergence of Black Images and Black Agency

Whereas Ellison offers both an objective and an African American perspective on blackface performance, Eric Lott explores the motivations behind the controversial art form. As Lott examines the history behind blackface, he delves into the cultural conflicts between blacks and whites. Ironically, the class intracultural conflicts between whites engendered blackface as an artistic outlet for working-class resentments. Additionally, Lott explains why blackface performance became extremely popular with white audiences. Blackface served as a secure means of experiencing black culture without the intimacy of personally engaging with black people. In other words, blackface performance satisfied white fantasies and curiosities of blackness without the social stigma of interacting with African Americans.

In his title *Love and Theft: Blackface Minstrelsy and the American Working Class*, Lott states that "white male workers targeted both employers and black workers, reformers (often wealthy or evangelical whites) and their 'fashionable' black associates" for their animosity toward social changes.[15] Black males became the primary target of blackface performance due to their presence in the public sphere. As early as the 1830s, before Hollywood produced a silent movie, various images such as the "urban black 'dandy' " are conjured by the white imagination and, traditionally, minstrel performers appeared on stage "between the acts of 'respectable' theatrical productions, or as afterpieces to them."[16] They also shared the stage with comic acts in the pleasure gardens, circuses, museums, and vaudevilles and other performance arenas. Due to the rising popularity of this entertainment among the emerging urban population, the American stage reflected this vaudeville demand.

In the early 1840s, P. T. Barnum was faced with both a problematic and economic situation. When his profitable blackface performer Master Diamond abandoned the circus for a better life, Barnum was forced to find a replacement. Barnum searched the dance houses of the Five Points and discovered a boy who was a better performer than Master Diamond. The young boy was literally a Negro, and Barnum feared his audience would be repelled by an actual "negro" performer; for that reason, Barnum smeared black cork on the black boy's face, covered his lips with red coloring, and placed a wooly wig over his head.[17] For white audiences, actual black representation was deemed "offensive or outrageous," which made "the appearance of black people onstage" less palatable than minstrelsy.[18] Lott contends that the blackface impersonations may resemble the 1830s–1840s period of black theatrical self-presentation.[19] However, the white performers set the standard for blackface performers.

Ironically, Barnum's desperate need to profit from the mockery of black culture led to black agency of the art form. Although the picture is uncomfortable for some, a black performer was able to profit from the caricature of black performance. Interestingly, Barnum's hired black boy Juba (William Henry Lane) became "the most famous—and, significantly, nearly the only—black performer to appear in white theaters in the mid-1840s."[20] Like other black minstrel performers, William Henry Lane was able "to offer credible imitations of white men imitating him."[21] The imitation of white men performing blackface is a precursor to black males obtaining agency over their own image. Due to slavery in the South and segregation in the North, blackface imitation of white men is an economic strategy for social gain. In the 1800s, the black minstrel performer is an ironic trickster who navigates from the stage to 1900s Hollywood productions. Eventually, William Henry Lane's success provides him an opportunity to perform in white theaters as a stereotype but without the black cork makeup.[22] Thus, consciously or unconsciously, Juba utilized blackface as a vehicle of economic and social mobilization.

Nevertheless, black agency does not erase the negative impact of dispossessing black males by controlling their image. As a result of whites' attempts to regulate the threat of black performance while profiting from the threat, Lott refers to these white minstrel performers as "counterfeit" since the dances of the whites were "predictably miscegenated"; therefore "whites subtly acknowledged the greater power of the genuine article."[23]

If whites acknowledged that these counterfeit performances lacked authenticity, what purpose did they serve in theatrical production? Lott argues that these counterfeit performances were a "means of exercising white control over explosive cultural forms as much as it was an avenue of racial derision."[24] With this history, minstrelsy becomes a "safely imitative form."[25] But the consequence of a black dancer imitating an inauthentic version of himself results in the revocation of the black performer's control over his own image, economic independence, and cultural reproduction.

At the center of this subversion of black manhood, as a means for economic advantage, is the black male body. In Dickens's record of Juba's stage performance, he "marked the male body as the primary site of the power of 'blackness' for whites."[26] Dickens describes this dance as a dazzling production of "body into fingers, legs into no legs."[27] Instead of admiring the black body and the artistic production that is presented on stage, the black body transforms into a source of danger and perceived vulgarity that must be reproduced for the white cultural imagination. Performers employed sexual exaggeration in the songs and dances performed on stage; therefore the black male body was "grotesquely contorted" even when sitting or extending his arms and legs.[28] At this time, the obsession of the black male image works against African Americans in entertainment and social realms. Due to the roots of minstrel performances by both whites and blacks, some white audiences are consciously or subconsciously unwilling to view black performers outside the parameters of white cultural appropriation.

In "The Good Lynching and *The Birth of a Nation*: Discourses and Aesthetics of Jim Crow," Michelle Wallace speaks to African Americans' attempts at profiting from their distorted public persona.[29] Prior to the Civil War, as Lott has previously stated, minstrel shows were a popular immigrant working-class pastime and assimilation ritual. After emancipation, African Americans formed blackface minstrelsy troupes that "traveled throughout the North and the South, as well as to the Caribbean, Latin America, Europe, Australia, and even South Africa."[30] Therefore black musicians, actors, comedians, and dancers had an opportunity to make money from their artistic talents. Although scholars assert that blacks were forced into these "childlike, comedic, and even absurd" performances, blacks promoted themselves as authentic.[31] As opposed to blacks who could provide an authentic satirical depiction of the African American culture, white minstrels were at a creative disadvantage because their counterfeit performances featured whites farcically imitating blacks. Wallace draws attention to the seventh film production of *Uncle Tom's Cabin* (1914); the movie was released a year before *The Birth of a Nation* (1915). Sam

Lucas, a famous minstrelsy actor and songwriter, was the first black to play Uncle Tom on stage and in film. However, *Uncle Tom's Cabin* portrays blacks as "harmless children" and in need of the "benevolent guidance of whites."[32] *The Birth of a Nation* treated blacks as potentially dangerous in the workforce and as voters.[33] Both movies reinforce the perception of blacks' inferiority to whites. In the early 1900s, this problematic history of whites' profiting from blackface performance and the grotesque distortion of the black male image causes black filmmakers to respond. Inflammatory movies like *The Birth of a Nation* inspire the Johnson Brothers in the 1910s and Oscar Micheaux to challenge the mockery of blackness in the 1920s with their own cinematic productions.

Southern Supremacy: D. W. Griffith's *The Birth of a Nation*

Blockbuster Profits

According to James Monaco, author of *How to Read a Film*, Europeans have been creating epic features since the 1910s with movies such as *Quo Vadis?* (1912) in Italy and *Germinal* (1913) in France.[34] However, D. W. Griffith was the first American to experiment with the feature film form. When Griffith invested $110,000 in the making of *The Birth of a Nation* (1915) and profited $20 million, he set the precedent for the "blockbuster" film. Monaco estimates that the movie may have actually made $50 million to $100 million since "the film was distributed on a 'states' rights' basis in which licenses to show the film were sold outright."[35] Nevertheless, despite the success of the film, Monaco has concerns about the subject matter. Monaco states that "no amount of technical expertise demonstrated, money invested, or artistic effect should be allowed to outweigh the essential racist tone of *The Birth of a Nation*, yet we continue in film history as it is presently written to praise the film for its form, ignoring its offensive content."[36] Although Monaco disapproves of *The Birth of a Nation*'s racist content, he acknowledges that until "the late fifties, racial stereotypes were pervasive in film, then in television."[37] With the advent of the sixties, blacks played nonstereotypical roles in American cinema.

Southern Fears and Blackface Stereotypes

In *Toms, Coons, Mulattoes, Mammies, and Bucks*, Donald Bogle relays a detailed depiction of the racist subject matter that substantiated Americans' fears of the black male.[38] The premise of D. W. Griffith's epic tale is an account of the Civil War, the Reconstruction era, and the destructive results of emancipation and possible integration between blacks and whites.

This propagandized and fictional account is a cautionary tale that ultimately profited from the distorted black male image. Bogle proclaims that "D.W. Griffith's *The Birth of a Nation* (1915) was the motion picture to introduce the final mythic type, the brutal black buck"; Griffith explored every black type in existence, which launched a "wave of controversy and was denounced as the most slanderous anti-Negro movie every released."[39] Perhaps some of the admiration of the film is due to the precedence of being "twelve reels in length and over three hours in running time."[40] Prior to Griffith's feat, movies used two or three reels and lasted no longer than 10 or 15 minutes. By introducing audiences to "the close-up, cross-cutting, rapid-fire editing, the iris, the split-screen shot, and realistic and impressionistic lighting," his epic film enthralled viewers.[41] Most of the time, these distinctions overshadow the melodramatic content.

At the heart of this film was Griffith's bigotry toward nonwhites. Griffith believed that if "the American Negro was kept in his place," whites would maintain their superior status.[42] If moral order was disrupted, chaos would erupt. However, with the delivery of Griffith's content, he was explicitly stating that moral order is present only when blacks are subjugated to whites' domination. Griffith based his classic film on Thomas Dixon's novels *"The Clansmen* and *The Leopard's Spots*, two rabidly racist novels."[43] Dixon was formerly a preacher and his narratives reflected "the most virulently racist and sadistic thinking of the early years of the twentieth century"; hence, both of his novels reflect his obsessive preoccupation "with white genealogical purity."[44] The film is structured around this perception of whiteness as godlike goodness; meanwhile, blackness is depicted as demon-like, to be viewed with trepidation.

At the beginning of the film, the Camerons of Piedmont, South Carolina, are a joyful, idyllic white family who own slaves that are happy to pick cotton, dance, and perform for their gentle masters. But once the Civil War breaks out, racial hierarchy is disrupted by "carpetbaggers and uppity niggers from the North" who move into Piedmont.[45] After emancipation, there are numerous scenes of "phenotypically black actors, along with some in blackface, aggressively groveling and grimacing."[46] If these melodramatic images were not so degrading, they would appear almost semicomical in their ridiculous depiction of blackness. Then, Southern fears manifest themselves in D. W. Griffith's production. Once the slaves abandon the plantations, blacks take over the political polls and deprive whites of the ability to vote. Black congressmen are portrayed as chicken-eating, liquor-drinking, and uncouth non-shoe-wearing fools; basically, as "lustful, arrogant, idiotic" buffoons.[47] One of the main priorities of the legislators is to legalize intermarriage between blacks and whites. Evidently, Griffith is playing on the irrational fears of whites who seek to maintain miscegenation laws. The climax of the film occurs when black Gus is determined to rape the youngest Cameron daughter; rather than be defiled by the black male body, she commits suicide by tossing herself over a cliff. Gus is a compelling and terrifying character. He is "the first black to show aggression toward whites in cinema, behavior considered so provocative that it was not shown again until the Blaxploitation films of the 1960s and '70s."[48] For that reason, Gus has been at the center of Hollywood's depictions of the black images since *The Birth of a Nation* was released.

However, Griffith does not stop there with the horrors of miscegenation. The "reign of terror of the elite mulatto children of the former plantation" is a significant subplot in the movie.[49] Silas Lynch, the mulatto, has a reckless desire for "power and revenge"[50] because he helps to implement the federal government's policy of Reconstruction, which makes him a societal, cultural, and structural danger to whiteness. Hence, Griffith attempts to define the mixed-race African American in the form of Silas, an individual who covets and desires whiteness. Silas wants to marry the white Elsie Stoneman by force. But hope is not entirely lost. Moral men adorned in "white sheets, and hoods, battle the blacks" and "they magnificently defeat the black rebels! Defenders of white womanhood, white honor, and white glory."[51] These vigilantes exist for the purpose of restoring white supremacy: "Thus we have the birth of a nation. And the birth of the Ku Klux Klan."[52]

Perhaps an important element of *Birth* is the clear obsession with the black male as the "other" and as a dangerous threat to white purity. This fear of miscegenation articulates race mixing as an irrefutable stain to whiteness. The white female body and the white female image must be protected and guarded from the perceived trickery of the mixed-raced black. The mixed-race tricksters are such a danger because they may have skin tone, economic, and/or educational advantage over other blacks:

> After slavery, those blacks who were educated tended to advance first. They became the doctors, lawyers, teachers, skilled professionals, and craftspeople in the newly freed communities. Much more often than we care to admit, these blacks, including some of the most militant and politically radical, were partly white and therefore light-skinned, some so light and so mixed that they could pass for white. That some of these blacks were virtually indistinguishable from whites was an important element in Dixon and Griffith's nightmare of race mixing and of mulattoes taking over the United States.[53]

Historically, people with African ancestry bearing fair skin could blend in with whites. Therefore mixed people's potential access to white privilege and white spaces could facilitate vengeance on whites. For whites who seek to maintain dominance and white hierarchal structure, mixed-raced individuals are terrifying. White supremacists, such as Dixon, feared that the mixed-race black or mulatto represented the brute nature of blacks and the ingenuity of whites; therefore they must be exterminated to prevent certain disaster. Although Wallace is not sure if Griffith promoted a "final solution," he did promote the Ku Klux Klan as a savior to whites.[54] Consequently, his propagandized version of pure whiteness and demagoguery of blackness encouraged white Americans to support acts of violence by the Ku Klux Klan.

Mammies, Uncle Toms, Black Brutes, and Black Bucks

As previously stated, Bogle claims Griffith utilized every type in *The Birth of a Nation*. The first category of archetypes are the mammy and the Uncle Tom figures who are blindly loyal servants. In order to defend the Southern way of life, their servants remain faithfully with the Cameron family; paternalism is at the heart of these depictions of jovial, childlike slaves. These dependent souls are lucky to have their masters take care of them and elevate them from their "bestial instincts."[55] The second category of blacks are the "brutal black bucks."[56] Within those archetypes are the "black brutes and black bucks"; the black brute is a savage who seeks chaos.[57] These characters are "sexually repressed. In *The Birth of a Nation*, the black brutes, subhuman and feral ... setting out on a rampage full of black rage."[58] Griffith used black Union soldiers to convey this type of black male; however, the "pure black bucks" are even more dangerous. According to Bogle, "bucks are always big, baadddd niggers, oversexed and savage, violent and frenzied as they lust for white flesh."[59] Although Silas is a mulatto and Gus is the renegade, both characters are considered pure black bucks. Griffith explicitly plays on the complex connection between sex and racism in the United States. In America, the white woman has become a "symbol of white pride, power, and beauty"; thus Griffith plays on the visual contrast between Lynch's character and the blond actress Lillian Gish.[60] According to Bogle, the symbolic imagery of black and white skin causes panic in the audience and unconsciously instills a fear of miscegenation among white patrons. Ultimately, Griffith encouraged the perception of "the bestiality of his black villainous bucks and used it to arouse hatred" and make a profit at the box office.[61]

Societal Backlash against Blackface

Understandably, organizations such as the NAACP launched protests against the propagandized content of the movie. Clearly, Griffith was playing to the fears of white America and he had no concern for the racial violence that may erupt. The black-faced archetypal portrayals of black males and the "superbly lit and brilliantly edited" ending glorifying "the final ride of the Klan" make Griffith's intentions clear.[62] The Boston, New York, and Chicago branches of the NAACP protested against Griffith's racist propaganda; meanwhile, other civil rights and religious organizations protested as well. Furthermore, race riots erupted in various cities and the number of lynchings rose in America. Many publications censured the film and it "was banned in five states and nineteen cities."[63] By the late 1920s, implementation of sound and the rise of a new era of filmmakers failed to prevent people's scorn against the industry Griffith helped create. Although the artistic and technological merit of Griffith's film ensured his success, the societal backlash to the film caused Hollywood to veer away from the black villain type in favor of black males in comic roles. Nevertheless, Bogle claims, "even the great comic tradition of the Negro in the American film has its roots in the Griffith spectacle."[64] One hundred years after *The Birth of a Nation* appeared, traces of caricatures he popularized are still evident.

Blackface provokes feelings of animosity for some; however, it is a historical art form that in a major way influenced how society perceived black men. On the upside, blackface has undertones of admiration. Lott insists that minstrelsy is a "mixed erotic economy of celebration and exploitation."[65] The performance of blackface exhibits a desire to co-opt black culture into American identity. Yet racial discrimination inhibited white performers from appropriating black music and dance into their performance without blackface. Nevertheless, minstrelsy performance exaggerates and mocks black folk culture. This exhibition of cross-racial desire displayed fascination and "self-protective derision with respect to black people and their cultural practices."[66] For white audiences who lacked exposure to blacks, minstrelsy performances formed their impressions of black males. Thus whites may not have perceived these cultural reproductions as inauthentic. Even though there is an element of "absolute white power," minstrelsy is more about controlling the "panic, anxiety, terror and pleasure" associated with "the intercourse between racial cultures."[67] According to Wallace, after the Civil War blacks sought to reclaim their culture and the economic production associated with blackface; therefore black minstrelsy performers promoted themselves as authentic. Nevertheless, Ellison was not the only African American who lacked identification with the blackface images they saw on stage or screen. Prior to the performance of Sam Lucas, *Uncle Tom's Cabin* featured white actors playing blacks in a demeaning but racially complacent manner. With regard to film history, *The Birth of a Nation* was "the only historical epic focused on the fear of so-called Negro domination in the Reconstruction era."[68] *Birth* remains the most dominant fictional account of this post–Civil War era and an "apologia for the nearly one hundred year reign of Jim Crow segregation and white supremacist politics that followed in the South and effectively dominated social policies in the West and North."[69] The production of cultural images and themes distorted by Griffith still captures the public's imagination for both negative criticism and praise. For those reasons, it is not surprising that race films sought to reclaim the distorted image of the black male in the 1920s.

CHAPTER 2

_____ 1920s _____
Oscar Micheaux's Response to Blackface and D. W. Griffith

The book _Oscar Micheaux and His Circle: African-American Filmmaking and Race Cinema of the Silent Era_ discusses how the mulatto is a targeted prototype in _The Birth of a Nation_. Perhaps Griffith chose the mixed-race black male as the focus of white fear because that figure "played a central and pivotal role in Reconstruction politics."[1] Subsequently, Micheaux's films and other race films responded by depicting the mulatto as an upright and dignified individual as a means to elevate the degraded image caused by Dixon's and Griffith's slander. After the mulatto male's heroic peak in race films, he becomes browner in mainstream movies: "He's not an Uncle Tom, but he's not a black brute either." Nevertheless, multiple depictions of the valiant black male will not emerge again "until the 1940s and 1950s."[2] With the exception of Paul Robeson's continuous rise in the 1930s, audiences will have to wait to celebrate "such actors as James Edwards, Sidney Poitier, and Harry Belafonte, some of whom are light-skinned but whose skin color no longer signifies 'mulatto' or mixed-raced parentage."[3] Furthermore, race films were responding to early blackface comedies and the negative portrayals of blacks in the media; their aspirations were politically motivated because they sought to improve the image of blacks. By providing audiences with an authentic portrait of black citizenship, they could offset the negative images promoted by Hollywood. Typically, white characters in race films are played by black actors; therefore the faces of "light skinned actors were further lightened and powdered."[4] Powdered black faces represent what some critics refer to as "white face," which is "a pointed satirization of 'whitey' and at other times an attempt at realistic representation."[5] For the purposes of casting a black actor in a white role, this ingenious reversal creates a white form.

How is this transracial transition even possible? The "one drop rule" determined that mixed-raced individuals were classified legally as black, not white. Generally, due to anti-miscegenation laws, mixed-raced persons married blacks. Thus the lightening of the black population did not occur because of "interracial intermarriage, as some sociologists mistakenly thought, but by intraracial unions as the white blood that was not supposed to be mixed was instead spread further throughout the black population."[6] Directors such as William D. Foster and Oscar Micheaux are largely responsible for introducing a varied depiction of the African American male. Although Micheaux is considered "the father of black filmmakers," Foster directed and produced his first film, *The Railroad porter* (1912), before Micheaux made his first film.[7] Two years earlier, while a sports writer for the *Chicago Defender*, he created Foster Photoplay, which is credited as the first African American independent film company. Foster's movie "paid homage to the Keystone comic chases, while attempting to address the pervasive derogatory stereotypes of blacks in film."[8] As the most prolific African American director in the world, Micheaux's primary themes of racial uplift and middle-class ideology dominated the content of his films; therefore his movies subvert the negative images of the mixed-race and/or black male as a rapist and violent villain who threatens white society.

Oscar Micheaux: The Most Prolific Black Director of the World

Born in 1884, Oscar Micheaux was raised in a rural, working-class, African American family in the Midwest.[9] Micheaux received a modest and basic public school education. All of his life, he experienced "race and class prejudice," yet he was extremely successful "in one of the most sophisticated, expensive, and fragile cultural endeavors of the twentieth century—commercial cinema."[10] Without the economic support of large film industries on the East or West Coast of the United States, he emerged as the first African American film *auteur*. Micheaux lived in the cosmopolitan cities of Chicago and New York; he visited Latin America and Europe for the purpose of creating his own business connections; and he mingled among the successful African American communities in the North and throughout the American South.[11] From the years of 1913 to 1951, "he wrote, published, and distributed his seven novels, and he wrote, produced, directed, and distributed some forty-three feature films—more than any other black filmmaker in the world, a record of production that is likely to stand for a very long time."[12] Micheaux's novel, *The Conquest* (1913), is considered fictional, but it contains autobiographical accounts that provide insight into his actual life. As a Pullman porter for the railroad, Micheaux journeyed through the country, meeting accomplished classes of people, western land-owners, and eastern businessmen in particular; thus he widened his expectations for himself and ignited his vision of opportunity and empire.

Micheaux was not deterred after his farms failed due to debt, drought, and the time, money, and energy spent on trying to win his wife back. According to author J. Ronald Green, his "fortitude and talent would later allow him to become a successful independent writer and publisher and ... the first African American to successfully write, produce, direct, and distribute films from the era of D. W. Griffith's *The Birth of a Nation* up to the eve of integration."[13] Micheaux is distinguished by his content and style; he believed the goal of cinema was to appeal to middle-class values. This may be why authors like Green state that "Micheaux's films and (and some other race movies and independent films) are ... superior to Griffith's."[14] Griffith's style was "pseudo-aristocratically bourgeois" and appealed to the ruling ownership class; whereas Micheaux's movies pursued social "uplift under conditions of racist obstruction—of two-ness (ethnic double consciousness) ... he developed values and artistic forms" that conformed to "his conditions of film production" and "the general condition of political deconstruction."[15] Ultimately, Micheaux proved that middle-class cinema can counter racism and sexism despite market economies and majority politics. Since Micheaux was not a member of mainstream Hollywood culture, he was able to produce numerous films on his terms while deconstructing the mass cultural values promoted by Hollywood.

Micheaux's Groundbreaking Movies of the 1920s

Of the 43 films produced by Micheaux, only 15 of them survive; therefore discussion will begin with his second film: *Within Our Gates* (1920).[16] The story begins with Sylvia Landry who lives in Boston. After Sylvia's failed engagement, caused by her cousin Alma Pritchard, she becomes a teacher at a backwoods black school in the South. Despite garnering funding in the amount of $50,000 from "Mrs. Warwick, a liberal suffragist and anti-racist philanthropist," she has secrets that may ruin her opportunity for a newfound romance with Dr. Vivian.[17] Jasper Landry, a tenant farmer, adopted and raised Sylvia. When a black busybody accuses Jasper of killing a white landowner, the Klan hangs and burns Jasper, his wife, and the snitch for good measure. Green states that "the lynching includes spectacular shots of the Klan riding at night with torches."[18] The brother of the murdered landowner plans to rape Sylvia until he overpowers her, yanks off her clothes, and notices a mark on her breast; this mark reveals to the man that he is Sylvia's father. Micheaux refrains from revealing her mother's unknown status as "one of servitude such as concubinage, droit du seigneur privilege, or even rape."[19] Although the protagonist of this film has a violent and tainted background, the educated and well-dressed leading man, Dr. Vivian, who is also a middle-class practicing optometrist, accepts her completely. Despite the fact that he has few clients, he is positive, solvent, and skilled, which is a typical characteristic of professional African Americans in Micheaux's films.

Micheaux's central themes in *Within Our Gates* are (1) raising funds for the education of black Southern youth, (2) "overcoming a specific racial and sexual oppression in the history of the leading woman, and (3) "the consummation of the formation of a 'perfect' black middle class couple."[20] After all, Sylvia "is an educated, well-dressed accountant, a school administrator, and a successful, respected fund-raiser—in short, a pillar of the black community."[21] To further reiterate the message of middle-class values, Sylvia turns down Larry Prichard who is a sharply dressed criminal who engages in "gambling, cheating, robbery, and sexual harassment, not to mention murder."[22] Also, Sylvia resists the "director of the rural black school" who is a righteous man "modeled on one of Micheaux's real-life heroes, Booker T. Washington, but he is not as sophisticated, as urbane, or as admired in the film as the leading woman or the optometrist."[23] Racism is a primary theme in *Within Our Gates*; however, these issues manifest themselves through "white-on-black rape, white-on-black tenant exploitation, white-influenced conservative black preaching, white discouragement of black education, and even a lynching."[24] Nevertheless, the primary message is uplift, never blatant retribution or vengeance. If blacks are educated and forgive each other for their ancestors' sexual pasts, Micheaux conveys that they can rise above America's racism. Oftentimes in Micheaux's novels and movies, such as *The Homesteader* (1919), *The Exile* (1931), and *The Betrayal* (1919 and 1948), the leading black male falls for a fair-skinned woman whose color leads him to believe that she is white; in this recurring motif, "the perennial object of his desire is finally obtained because of a dramatic reversal of her race, the white racist 'one drop of black blood' formula providing the axle on which the wheel on his fictional fortune turns."[25] In other words, the black male remains loyal to his race and retains his respective position within the black community. By partnering with a black female instead of a white female in the Jim Crow era, he effectively protects himself from prohibitive anti-miscegenation laws and potential alienation within his own community. Green attributes Micheaux's race reversal theme to "his early love affair with a white woman in South Dakota, whom he finally rejected for reasons of practicality and racial loyalty. He probably regretted that decision all his life, and undoubtedly there is an element of obsession" in the consistency of these themes.[26]

The movie *Symbol of the Unconquered* (1920) is Micheaux's fourth film; it has complex racial and economic issues that lead to compelling plot twists. In a subplot, Micheaux uses a horse scam from his novel *The Conquest* "to stage a retributional fistfight between his hero Van Allen and the ethnically disloyal conman Driscoll."[27] Driscoll is compulsively phobic toward blacks because of his fear that his racial identity will be discovered. Cinematically, a fight between a white man and black man was barred in most movies due to post–race riot censorship; therefore the physical encounter between Driscoll and Van Allen was psychologically satisfying for Micheaux. Since Driscoll "looks and acts so much like a white racist, full of discriminatory hate," the audience may forget that he's actually black.[28] Consequently, this fight becomes "a righteous fight between a wronged black and a scoundrel white."[29] The main plot centers on the mixed-race Driscoll who is the leader of "a Ku Klux Klan-type racial terrorist group called The Knights of the Black (!) Cross"; this terror group is comprised of "ethnically mixed rascals."[30] One member is a former clergy man who is also an upper-middle-class Brit; the second member is a British colonial, an Indian Fakir; the third member is an elder cowboy; and the fourth member "is a distinctly African-American-looking cowboy who is identified as a half-breed American Indian."[31] Presumably, Micheaux is suggesting that racial violence is "motivated by economic competition rather than racial ideology."[32] Instead of the Ku Klux Klan saving the day, as in Griffith's *The Birth of a Nation*, Micheaux has the fair-skinned heroine Eve pull off a rescue.

During Eve's supposed absence, Van Allen has transformed into an affluent businessman because oil has been discovered on his land. Within the mixed-raced motif, common to Micheaux's films, Van Allen is shocked to learn that Eve is a proud black woman who received her land and property from her black grandfather. Although Eve fears Van Allen's disapproval, he is elated and fervently envelops her in his arms because there are no racial barriers to their affections for one another. Both Van Allen and Eve exhibit middle-class values since they are "both polite, reserved, and considerate . . . both speak in formally educated English. That and other evidence suggests they are middle class."[33] The primary themes of the *Symbol of the Unconquered* are as follows: (1) "the struggle for possession of mineral resources on the land owned by the leading man"; (2) the pairing of a black man and woman as they fight "against economically motivated, racially rationalized usurpation"; (3) the intensification of a "sexual and economic partnership, despite perceived racial impediment," between the hero and the heroine; and (4) "their eventual elevation to a wealthy class of African Americans."[34] Micheaux promotes the concept that overcoming the racial oppression of the Ku Klux Klan is feasible when successful black middle-class individuals merge and make an entrepreneurial commitment; for that reason, the subsequent "consummation of their partnership, one that is emblematic of uplift for the race" will benefit society.[35]

Body and Soul (1925) significantly contrasts the religious values of blind religious loyalty promoted by *Uncle Tom's Cabin*. The movie exemplifies the ridiculous nature of entrusting "faith in the promise of otherworldly glory, especially glory as represented by all-too-human men and their some-times dubious religious institutions."[36] Furthermore the movie, set in Tatesville, Georgia, warns against "self-appointed men of God or jackleg preachers."[37] The mother, Martha Jane, is obsessed with the idea that her daughter will someday marry the preacher. Since the daughter is opposed to this idea, Micheaux implies that the mother is projecting her "own desire for the preacher, sexual as well as spiritual . . . to her daughter in this mar-riage fantasy."[38] Paul Robeson, "one of America's greatest actors," charis-matically plays the preacher who "is a con man and former convict."[39]

After a careful narrative buildup to this fire-and-brimstone sermon's cli-max (including shots of adoring women, the excited congregation, the showering of money, a comic deacon, and the preacher secretly taking swigs of liquor and strutting around with the heavy Bible on his shoulder pointing to individual sinners), the spectacular sermon, and Micheaux's carefully cre-ated forward momentum are abruptly halted by Martha Jane standing in the aisle pointing the finger of judgment at the preacher. She tells all, bring-ing the preacher's fire and brimstone down on his own head; the preacher is attacked by the congregation and flees.[40] Later, when the preacher appears at Martha Jane's house, she hides him from one of the people chasing him. Before the fallen preacher leaves her house, she forgives him for stealing her money; however, this is a monumental mistake because the preacher ends up murdering, unnecessarily, one of his pursuers. The dying man's "last words are 'Mama' as if he is calling for Martha Jane," verbalizing the con-sequences of her poor mothering skills.[41] At the conclusion of the movie, the audience realizes that "the story of rape, theft, murder, and starvation was literally only a nightmare dreamed by the mother during a nap."[42] Contrary to Martha's nightmare, her daughter has not starved to death; instead, the young woman chooses to marry the leading man, Sylvester, who is the good brother, also played by Robeson. Due to the purchase of his "discovery," the good brother becomes rich; then the happy couple and the mother "move to a middle-class house with upholstered furniture and a piano, an iconic image that closes the film."[43] In addition to a family home and representations of materialism, proper language is a signifier of the middle-class lifestyle.

Within the layered plot structure, Micheaux thrust forward a brief linguistic and social issue denoting class. When Martha calls Sylvester a "nigger," Isabelle objects to the derogatory word because it represents vulgarity and expresses her lower-class values. By employing this debasing word "associated with her lower-class condition in life and with a network of impediments to her advancement," Micheaux validates Isabelle's assertion.[44] Furthermore, Robeson's "double characterization of the bad preacher and the good inventor" becomes the basis of distinguishing a lower-class figure from a middle-class figure in terms of the hierarchal class structure.[45] Green asserts that racism is implied as an impediment to uplift. Essentially, by refuting the use of the word "nigger," Micheaux is establishing a standard for how black men should be treated in the African American community and in American society as a whole. When employing a term used by the dominant culture to demean blacks, Martha is exhibiting self-hatred for her own community and disrespect for the humanity of Sylvester. Consequently, disparaging terms and self-hatred in the African American community function as an obstacle to racial uplift.

Pre–Hays Moral Code: Micheaux's Battles with Censors

Prior to the Hays Moral Code, both Micheaux and Griffith experienced clashes with censorship boards. The attempts to censor *The Birth of a Nation* and *Within Our Gates* symbolize the "overabundance of appeals—too many black bodies with white women in Griffith's film and too much fire and desire in Micheaux's."[46] The combination of volatile bodies on-screen and off-screen, such as depiction of race riots, is potentially explosive. Whereas Griffith's *Birth* exhibited "spectacle, rescue, criminality, vengefulness, impunity, aggrandizement, possessiveness, purity," Micheaux's style and themes reflected "documentation, redemption; retribution, citizenship, justice, responsibility, uplift, mutuality, hybridity."[47] Nevertheless, Green argues that Micheaux's attempts at rectifying the image of blacks reflect "damage already done, a condition in which rescue is already too late."[48] There was an almost universal praise for the NAACP's boycott of *The Birth of a Nation*, yet there is a mixed response to the censorship of Micheaux's films.

In reference to censorship, there was an attempt to "severely scrutinize and restrict *The Birth of a Nation* as well as other films with racial subjects on the assumption that these works tended to 'incite to crime.' "[49] In Micheaux's defense, his films did not represent a "threat to the public order represented by Griffith and Dixon's epic of hate."[50] As evidenced by the censorship boards in New York, Chicago, and Virginia, Micheaux experienced "massive resistance and naked hostility ... when he tried to secure licenses to exhibit nearly every one of his films produced in the 1918 to 1930 period."[51] When the New York State Commission initially withheld a license for *Body and Soul*, they attributed their decision to the minister's theft and the fact that representations of the minister seemed blasphemous and likely to encourage criminal acts. However, Gaines wonders if the "particular deeds (drinking, gambling, stealing, wielding knives)" caused the board's resistance, or was the "all-black-cast action film a nightmare inversion from the point of view of the white censor?"[52] As for the movie *A Son of Satan* (1924), the Virginia board objected to the negative characterization of the mulatto male protagonist, due in part to the criminality of this villainous mulatto as attributable to his white heritage instead of his black heritage. Furthermore, it objected to the impure references to miscegenation and "the representation of race riots 'incited' by the mulatto villain."[53] With respect to Micheaux's film *Birthright* (1925), the scenes that are cut from *The Birth of a Nation* appear "in inverted form in Micheaux's films of the silent era, from the sadistic lynching sequence in *Within Our Gates* to the defiant *Birthright* intertitle."[54] Thus Micheaux attempts to historically correct the images in Griffith's film. But the attempt is not actualized because the censors eliminate the scenes that exhibit Micheaux's response to Griffith.[55]

Generally, censorship board positions were held by white males; still, Gaines urges the reader to consider that whites were not the only voices that advocated censorship of racialized images. Occasionally, there were exceptions, such as the "Harvard educated black conservative Reverend A. J. Bowling" who objected to both *The Birth of a Nation* and *The Symbol of the Unconquered*.[56] Furthermore, Micheaux's *Within Our Gates* caused both black and white ministers to object; however, blacks were mostly concerned with the lynching scene. When George P. Johnson "tried to book it for a second run at the Loyal Theater in Omaha in August 1920," he requested that Micheaux cut the lynching scene because "people had walked out."[57] Even though Johnson had a difficult time distributing the film to various venues around the country, the "militant" *Chicago Defender* did not agree with Johnson's concerns. The paper fully endorsed the film for its critique of racial oppression and lynching. People do not like to admit it, but Johnson's objections reflect the views of the black middle class. Newspapers like the *Defender* reported the real data associated with the practice of lynching. Gaines claims that "reporting lynchings as the southern injustice that it was, Micheaux not only corrected Griffith's fictional representation of Gus's lynching as justice, but indicted the very vigilantes who were going unpunished for lynchings and other crimes against the black community in 1920."[58] In another scene, apparently cut by the censors, the actress Evelyn Preer (Sylvia) recalls taping a different version of the attempted rape by her white father. Preer remembers that her black lover is the hero in the scene; after he kicks down the door, he gives the white man a horrible beating for trying to rape his girlfriend. Undoubtedly, the censors had very little tolerance for this scene of black male bravado. In addition to criticism of his content, there were critics who disapproved of his directing skills and the caption writing in his silent films.[59] Gaines suggests that Micheaux's movies are impacted by racial tension: "Race struggle produced it, rewrote it until it became nearly incoherent, and finally exiled it."[60] Additionally, there were mistakes on the titles in some countries and languages such as in the Spanish language. In essence, Griffith mainly concerned himself with censors and white audiences, whereas Micheaux had the double burden of satisfying mainstream concerns and the worries of the black community who represented his primary viewership.

Critical Gaze: The Power of the African American Press

Since the 1800s, the African American press has existed for the purposes of countering "white racism and to promote self-determination."[61] Six years before the release of *The Birth of a Nation* African Americans spoke against negative representations publicly. There was a dual purpose for criticism from the black presses: they objected to "negative screen representations," and they encouraged blacks to subvert those industry images "by becoming actors, actresses, filmmakers, producers, directors, and technicians."[62] In an effort to transform degrading industry images, such as those promoted by movies like *The Birth of the Nation*, African American newspapers insisted that African Americans must produce their own films. For instance, African American presses encouraged movies that presented middle-class values. In the past, there was an assumption that if middle-class values were adopted by blacks, they would achieve the accompanying rise in social status; however, this presumption has flaws because "white racism was a universal experience for all African Americans and knew no class distinctions."[63] By supporting companies who produced films that engaged black audiences, the black press expanded "the market for black productions by providing reviews, advertisements, behind-the-scenes gossip, and discussion of these films."[64] The flipside to this support was the negative criticism issued by the black presses suggesting how filmmakers could "improve, promote, and distribute their films and, thereby increase their exposure and proceeds at the box office."[65] In the event they considered a film to be subpar, they were outspokenly intolerant of those productions. In terms of African American actors appearing in blackface or comic roles, these race films were negatively criticized, whether they were produced by white- or black-owned companies. Encouraging criticism was reserved for "positive representations of African Americans, representations that were consistent with its own views."[66] Furthermore, there were journalists who provided glowing "reviews based on promotional materials and may never have actually viewed the film praised in their columns"; consequently, audiences had to consider the journalists' and critics' responses with careful contemplation.[67]

The *Chicago Defender* gave white-owned Norman Film Manufacturing Company rave reviews for Richard Norman's film *The Green-Eyed Monster* (1920). Since the film featured black actors in the professional sectors of law, medicine, and banking, the African American press construed these images as evidence of intellectual and economic advancement of black people. When critiquing the directing, writing, acting, and plot of race films, critics must consider the "limited and unstable amount of capital"; furthermore, these films were distributed in fewer theaters because theater owners feared that they would lose profits.[68] By 1923, there were only "three filmmaking companies (the Lincoln Motion Picture Company, the Norman Film Manufacturing Company, and the Micheaux Film Corporation)."[69] African American presses dismissed these economic concerns by suggesting the promotion of well-known black stars such as Sherman Dudley, Evelyn Preer, or Edna Morton. Micheaux was commended for choosing a champion boxer, Sam Langford, to play in his movie *The Brute* (1920); furthermore, the black press insisted that the movie was an economic success for Micheaux because Langford was a box-office attraction. By the mid-1920s, black audiences patronized high-quality productions; thus sound and competition from mainstream Hollywood caused black audiences to see films like Stepin Fetchit's *Hearts in Dixie* (1929).[70]

From the years 1918 to 1929, Micheaux produced his greatest number of films—20 in that 11-year period.[71] Micheaux's mission was to "be an answer to whites' demeaning representations of African Americans, and he sought to present lifestyles African Americans could emulate."[72] Cultural critic bell hooks asserts that Micheaux did not intend to create positive images; he sought to project complex images of blacks on the screen. Consequently, Micheaux "endured a sometimes turbulent relationship with" some writers in the black press; for instance, in the early 1920s, the black press praised *The Homesteader, Within Our Gates,* and *The Brute,* but by the time he produced *Birthright,* reviewers began to "qualify their compliments."[73] The main character of *Birthright* is an African American Harvard graduate who returns home after he graduates. As usual the movie features racial issues, but the critics were dismayed by the representations of race and the racial and class differences. Another critic asserted that *Within Our Gates* was just as dangerous as *The Birth of a Nation* because of the "degrading representations provided of African Americans."[74] The reviewer objected to the depiction of Robeson's character as a rapist and the use of the word "nigger." By the late 1920s, Micheaux decided to cut costs by sacrificing production values, which drew strong and negative criticism from the African American press. In addition to the low-quality productions, the following factors also led to Micheaux's bankruptcy: a reduction of "retakes, using title cards to condense a film's narrative, and paying little attention to editing techniques"; Swan Micheaux's (Oscar's brother) mismanagement of funds; the onslaught of the Depression era; expensive technology; innovative movie techniques; and Hollywood's determination to end race movies.[75]

Uplift: Racial Imitation of White Values

In this contemporary era, reminiscent of earlier arguments launched against black literature and black cinema, there are critics who claim that popular culture is an appropriation of African American culture. During the early 1900s, critics attributed race films' themes, plots, and style as imitative of European culture. Gaines states that these similarities are attributed to the contact and "intermixture" of black and white culture in the United States. W. E. B. Du Bois once stated that "knowing how this commingling of blood and culture works," people should not dismiss black art forms as "merely imitative."[76] Nevertheless, there are assimilation signifiers in race movies that are problematic for critics. By casting extremely light-skinned actors with straightened hair, critics like Donald Bogle reason that race movies are promoting "white-likeness" in "one big advertisement for race effacement"; race movies depict what the African American culture would resemble if the "entire culture . . . were to become racially mixed through breeding and what it could look like if assimilation were taken at its word."[77] However, Gaines offers a counterargument to these harsh criticisms by saying that race films were "not about disappearing into white culture, not at all about incorporation and absorption."[78] For instance race movies, from Reol's *The Call of His People* (1922) to Micheaux's *God's*

Stepchildren (1938), disapproved of passing. Various filmmakers such as Reol and Micheaux celebrated the "visible difference" in black culture despite the "racist exclusions of white society."[79]

Uplift ideology is a paradox in theory and application: there is a desire to uphold the black status quo and there is the social striving for emancipation and freedom for all. In the early 1900s, the racial uplift melodrama was designed to encourage race improvement. Eventually, the narrative of sentimentality transitioned to stories about the achievement of respectability. George P. Johnson wrote the script for *By Right of Birth* (1921).[80] Clarence Brooks stars in the film because Noble Johnson, George's brother, had to resign because of contract issues with Universal.[81] The female protagonist, Juanita, appears Indian to her foster parents. After an African American lawyer helps the "co-ed at a California university," she finds her fortune and long-lost black relatives. Uplift ideology reiterates the hegemonic "dream in which slavery is reversed and negated by a legacy of wealth," enabling the subsequent generation to elevate themselves into the upper middle class.[82] The uplift ideology upholds the educated elite and bootstraps self-help rhetoric as the method for advancement. From one perspective, uplift ideology is emulating a white point of view from a black source; in essence, uplift theory is white discourse appropriated by the black middle class. Since the black middle class enculturated "the dominant culture as its own," they exhibited paradoxical strivings; at times, the black middle class engaged in behaviors that undermined black progress, "while at the same time conscientiously protesting white offenses."[83] This class conflict within the black community was reflected on-screen and disdained by critics.

Increasingly, the black press disapproved of the color consciousness reflected by upwardly mobile blacks. During Micheaux's era, the black press objected to Micheaux's casting of specific skin tones and his use of pejorative types; yet contemporary research suggests that Micheaux did not strictly cast his light-skinned male actors as heroes and his dark-skinned actors as villains. Lorenzo vehemently defends Micheaux by stating that he cast "all the shades of the black race" without regard to stereotypes based on skin tone.[84] Lincoln films featured similar problems with type casting, but economic problems and the departure of their main star, Noble Johnson, signaled an eventual end to the company. Since their films were becoming more popular among black audiences, they were "well positioned to profit just at the point that Noble Johnson resigned" to perform full-time for Universal.[85] After Lincoln films closed in 1923, the black press became more upset with the "depiction of the unsettling behavior he observed and deplored in the black community" than

Micheaux's technique.[86] Furthermore, the black press disagreed with Micheaux's excessive depiction of African American millionaires, professionals, and entrepreneurs. Micheaux contended that the vices and corruption of the middle class needed exposure. Additionally, the black community demonstrated intolerance for disparaging characterization of the ministry. Nevertheless, Micheaux was an incredible promoter for his films; early on, he had a talent for "overstatement, for public show, and for the creation of colorful popular discourse" as a "motion picture exhibitor and press agent."[87] According to Gaines, even his frequent depiction of mixed-race themes demonstrates his films' appeal as a mass-market commodity. Despite the color consciousness displayed in race films, Americans received an alternate view of the African American male that went beyond stereotypical blackface casting as caricatures, rapists, and other criminals. Although the 1920s is an exciting era for black film, censorship in the 1930s results in a skewed depiction of the black experience in Hollywood.

CHAPTER 3

_____ 1930s _____
The Hays Moral Code and
Jim Crow—*The Emperor Jones*
and *Gone with the Wind*

Prior to the Hays Moral Code, religious organizations, politicians, prohibitionists, educators, and other factions of society realized the power of the movies; therefore entertainment films were of universal interest. Since the power of the movies "transcended ethnic, class, religious, and political lines," the cinema became the dominant form of American popular culture.[1] As millions of people enjoyed films at the height of the Progressive reform movement, there were others who were distressed by this burgeoning form of entertainment. Progressives attacked "saloons, dance-halls, houses of prostitution, and equally harmful 'immoral' books, magazines, newspapers, plays—and, of course, movies," because they feared that the "dirty and dingy" theaters were polluting the public's minds; meanwhile, reformers feared that a young generation "would learn their moral lessons at the movies."[2] Soon after "ministers, social workers, civic reformers, police, politicians, women's clubs, and civic organizations" sought to censor movies for transforming core American values.[3] Before the implementation of the Hays Moral Code in 1934, Jim Crow codes of segregation and hierarchy influenced black and white interactions on film.[4] On-screen, African Americans existed within restricted space. But if a black filmmaker or exhibitor catered strictly to African American audiences, the economic consequences were astronomical. Ironically, Hollywood was not comfortable featuring African Americans on-screen, but they were intrigued by their African lineage.[5] Although racial adventure films depicted Africans in a conflictual way, working-class and middle-class blacks appeared to enjoy those films as much as white audiences.[6] Occasionally, blacks were featured as the main characters, but the Hays Moral Code and Jim Crow segregation barred miscegenation in all movies including *The Emperor Jones* and *Gone with the Wind*.

Paul Robeson starred in movies such as *The Emperor Jones* (1933). However, the actress Fredi Washington who played opposite Robeson had to wear blackface due to fears that Southern audiences would mistake the light-skinned woman for a white woman.[7] Then there was the epic *Gone with the Wind* (1939), which "was the most despised example of the status of African-Americans in classical Hollywood cinema."[8] Although blacks represented 10 percent of America's population, they were generally absent from the movies during the 1930s. Nevertheless, Paul Robeson was the reigning African American stage and film star at this time. Robeson was proud of his black identity; hence, he was unwilling to star in films that patronized black audiences by depicting blacks in a pejorative manner. Furthermore, he was an international actor, singer, speaker, and activist who influenced the way movies and American culture perceived African American males.

During the late 1920s, MGM, Paramount, RKO, Universal, Fox, Columbia, and Warner Brothers "controlled vertical monopolies that produced, distributed, and exhibited films" that were eventually shipped to headquarters in New York; meanwhile, those corporations "controlled huge theater chains and forced all other theater owners to buy their product."[9] In January 1922, movie moguls created the Motion Picture Producers and Distributors of America (MPPDA); subsequently, the moguls chose Hoosier William Harrison (Will) Hays as the political spokesman for the "squeaky clean image" that was needed to "combat censorship bills at the federal and state level."[10] As the postmaster general in President Warren Harding's cabinet and chairman of the Republican National Committee, Hays was the ideal choice to redefine the perception of the industry. Hays had an all-American appeal because his "roots were solidly midwestern, his politics conservatively Republican, and his religion mainstream Protestant."[11] Hays "symbolized the figurative Puritan in Babylon" because he brought mainstream midwestern sensibilities "to a Jewish-dominated film industry"; thus Hays sought to maintain the largest possible audiences while attaining management over the content of films. By 1922, censorship bills had been passed in Pennsylvania, Ohio, Florida, New York, Maryland, Kansas, and Virginia. If the movie industry self-regulated itself, he could deter the establishment of any more censorship boards. Hays created the Studio Relations Department (SRD) in 1924; thereafter studios were encouraged to refrain from profanity, nudity, drug trafficking, and white slavery. When presenting mature issues such as criminal behavior, sexual relations, and violence, producers should remain tactful; consequently, the studios varied in their interpretations of the guidelines, causing a lack of uniformity in the application of SRD guidelines.

Before the Catholics successfully influenced the code that censored Hollywood production, the antimovie lobby was championed by Protestants. For years, the Women's Christian Temperance Union (WCTU), the Reverend William H. Short's Motion Picture Research Council, and Canon William Shaefe Chase's Federal Motion Picture Council fought for federal action.[12] The transition from silent films to "talkies" was an impetus for the fears held by moralists; sexy starlets could explain away their scandalous actions; criminals used "hip slang" and boasted about their lawlessness; politicians might discuss "bribery and corruption."[13] Even though opposition groups lacked the effectiveness of their successors, in "1928 the New York State censorship board cut over 4,000 scenes from the more than 600 films submitted, and Chicago censors sliced more than 600 scenes."[14] By 1929, Catholics presented Hays and the movie industry with a method of censoring Hollywood films at the production level. For centuries, the Catholic Church kept a list of forbidden books. Although Catholics were not involved in the antimovie movement of the 1920s, "Catholic laymen and priests were becoming more and more uncomfortable with what they perceived as the declining moral quality of films."[15] Due to the fears of moral depravity, the media felt pressure to publish articles disparaging government censorship.

As the owner and publisher of *Exhibitors Herald-World*, the devout lay Catholic Martin Quigley utilized his influence in the media to reject "government censorship as ineffective"; Quigley suggested that creating films "without censurable material" was the only way to rein in the movie industry; and he agreed with the Protestants' premise "that movies ought to avoid social, political, and economic subjects."[16] Movies were for the purpose of entertainment, not social commentary; subsequently, in the summer of 1929, he began to develop a new code for moviemakers that forced them to evaluate the morality of their films.

Father Daniel Lord, S.J., who was the professor of dramatics at St. Louis University and "editor of the widely read *The Queen's Work*," was chosen to write the moral code for the movies, and his "editorials in *Queen's Work*, in pamphlets, and in Catholic newspapers and journals ... attacked the ultrasophistication of modern living as reflected in literature and drama."[17] After seeing D. W. Griffith's *The Birth of a Nation* as a youth, Lord was convinced that movies had the power to transform thinking and values.[18] Without a doubt, the highly charged racial content of *The Birth of a Nation* instilled a fear of black male sexuality and racial mixing. Thus there is no surprise that a miscegenation clause prohibiting sexual interactions between blacks and whites is included in the code. After performing his duties as a technical adviser for Cecil B. DeMille's *The King of Kings*

(1927), as a young priest he was convinced that movies needed spiritual guidance; thus he was determined to reform the industry.

The Irish Catholic Joseph I. Breen is another important figure in the censorship coalition.[19] After graduating from Philadelphia's Joseph's College, he was a reporter for the Philadelphia *North American*; eventually, he became the Overseas Commissioner of the National Catholic Welfare Conference, and subsequently, the public relations director of the Peabody Coal Company. Breen envisioned no separation between his political conservatism and his deeply held "religious conviction"; for those reasons, he was extremely "opposed to public discussion of such moral issues as divorce, birth control, and abortion."[20] As an intense anti-Semite, Breen's prejudicial views led him to blame the Jewish moguls for the decadence in the movie industry. For months, Breen worked with Quigley, Lord, and a few other priests to refine the proposed code.

In 1930 a Catholic priest, Father Daniel Lord, S.J., joined the crusade against the movie industry. Since Lord believed that immoral movies were corrupting society, he created a "code that prohibited films from glorifying criminals, gangsters, adulterers, and prostitutes," which was referred to as the Bible of film production because it "banned nudity, excessive violence, white slavery, illegal drugs, miscegenation, lustful kissing, suggestive postures, and profanity from the screen."[21] Furthermore, the code promoted family values such as the "institutions of marriage and home," political virtues such as "fairness of government," and respect for religious institutions.[22] The basis of Lord's code relied on the premise that movies are evil; hence, Lord felt a patriarchal and religious duty to protect the masses. At the time, millions of people visited theaters, and Lord argued that "movies cut across all social, economic, political, and educational boundaries"; thus censorship was necessary to curb the powerful influence of the movie industry.[23] Lord's Catholic movie code "was a fascinating combination of Catholic theology, conservative politics, and pop psychology."[24] Ultimately, Lord feared that Hollywood created an irresistible fantasy with "beautiful and glamorous stars"; his patriarchal sense of morality underlay his belief that "impressionable minds of children, the uneducated, the immature, and the unsophisticated" could not resist the temptation of moral turpitude.[25]

Will Hays, the president of the MPPDA, supported Lord's code; therefore the motion picture industry accepted the terms in 1930.[26] Nevertheless, there were Catholics who disagreed with the industry's manner of implementation; as a result, they launched a Legion of Decency (LOD) campaign in 1934. In order to appease religious groups, particularly the Catholic Church, "Hays created a new MPPDA Hollywood censorship office in 1934—the Production Code Administration (PCA)."[27] Next, Hays appointed lay Catholic Joseph I. Breen as director. Prior to issuing a PCA seal of approval, Breen and his staff vigilantly reviewed every script for sexual or political improprieties.[28] From 1930 to 1934, the salacious nature of movies remains evident; however, after 1934, Joseph I. Breen's office successfully transformed the industry under his dictatorial rule. After 1934, if a movie lacked the PCA seal, no major American theater could show the film; these regulatory rules were strictly upheld. The headquarters of the National Catholic Legion of Decency was in New York and any film "considered immoral or dangerous" was condemned by the LOD.[29] Since the LOD reviewed every film, they released ratings to all the Catholic churches in America; Catholics were prohibited from viewing a film that was not approved by the LOD. In this golden era of Hollywood, the powerful forces of Hays's office, the Catholic Church, and the Catholic LOD "struck fear in the hearts of every Hollywood producer."[30] For three decades the code would remain in place. By 1966, most of the advocates for Hollywood censorship were dead; thus the rigid code was replaced by a ratings system.[31]

Pre-Code Hollywood: African Peoples and Culture

In the early 1920s and 1930s, Hollywood's interest in "primitive peoples" peaked.[32] Due to the advent of sound technology and the lack of censorship during the pre-Code era, the widely produced expeditionary films were popular in the West. There were three main purposes of the expeditionary film: (1) elevation of the "Great White Photographer [Who] Brings Back Movies from Savage Land for American Moviegoers"; (2) "the Homeric outline of an odyssey of . . . three-act dramaturgy—departure, adventure, and return"; and (3) "the overt instructional value of the expeditionary film in man, beast, and nature."[33] At best, those films offered a sense of kinship for "whom Americans might delight in and come to know as blood relations," and at worst, Hollywood depicted primitive cultures "with a narrow focus both cultural and cinematic" and with "condescension and racist perspectives."[34] In other words, the cinematic portrayal of the natives created and reinforced limited perspectives held by Westerners. Thus many Americans felt no connection between themselves and the primitives who were "like insects under glass for the paid customers to stare at"; nevertheless, the expeditionary film offered "spontaneous action, a sense of wonder mixed with the adrenaline rush of fear."[35] These types of films are early yet primitive versions of multicultural diversity and global inclusiveness. Audiences could fulfill their hunger for "alternative worlds and primitive lives" by viewing "indigenous peoples (Native Americans, Inuits, Africans,

Asians, Pacific Islanders) and environmentally privileged landscapes (jungles, forests, rivers, and tundra)."[36] However, these films express more about American culture than the primitive cultures that fascinate them. The cultural myopia that is rooted in these films continues in modern-day cinema. This fascination with locales beyond America reflects the "projection of frontier visions onto new worlds in an age of territorial limitations and economic dead ends."[37] In other words, the perception of African American lineage was partly defined by the limited views and exposure of early Hollywood.

Despite the fascination with primitive people in Africa, African Americans were kept at a close distance.[38] Even in the midst of continued reinforcement of Jim Crow, white Americans held an obsessive curiosity with the nature and lineage of African Americans. But the welcoming "embrace extended to American Indians, Eskimos, Asians, and sallow-skinned peoples ... was withheld from Africans and thus, by easy extension, from their sable kinsman on native soil."[39] Due to the tense black and white relations since 1609, Hollywood expressed this interest in black culture with expeditionary films; Africa became a site to engage in "impulses too dark to be released stateside."[40] Even then, America's racial tensions are used to promote Warner Brothers' *Adventures in Africa* (1931); under the supervision of Wyant D. Hubbard, the emphasis was that a venturesome white man is daring travel into the innermost portions of the African wilderness. Another film, *Congorilla* (1932), promised horrific sounds—terrific scenes featuring the remarkable race of grotesque pygmies as they engage in odd rituals. By otherizing Africans and African culture, the perception of white superiority over less civilized subjects is heightened. The pioneering white couple Martin and Osa Johnson were the stars of these films. Their depiction of African wildlife are some of the most incredible images ever filmed.[41] However, this respect for the animals did not extend to the African natives; the Johnson couple treated the natives like servants or children and made snarky remarks behind their backs. Ironically, when the Johnsons play jazz for the pygmies, they refer to it as white music, despite the African roots of this popular musical form. In the Johnsons' "open-mindedness and myopia," they fail to realize that the Ituri pygmies danced rhythmically to the beat because they "recognized in the wild and passionate uproar of the modern jazz the sounds of their shared humanity with the American intruders."[42] Although it may seem harmless that the Johnsons were oblivious to the remote kinship between themselves and the African natives, their marginalization of their cinematic subjects reinforced the negative narrow perceptions of African American identity.

Pre-Code Hollywood: Harlem and Beyond

The intense fascination for the expeditionary film eventually extended to the curiosity of blacks on American shores. Due in part to the artistic explosion of the Harlem Renaissance, the public was interested in stateside black life. In the movie *Strange Justice* (1933), a downtown party girl becomes bored with the "vanilla diversions of a downtown nightclub."[43] In her state of drunkenness, she believes a trip uptown to Harlem will offer a taboo view of the American experience. After all, the expeditionary film offers "symbolic journeys to forbidden zones where" the rigid restrictions of "Anglo-American Christianity might be overturned with impunity."[44] These films are geared toward white audiences who seek to explore black culture while retaining their innate whiteness. Thus the underlying factor behind a high "percentage of the escapist fantasies of pre-Code Hollywood" is white racism.[45] Ironically, many of the racial adventure films that explored the "darkest Africa, exotic Asia, or unchartered islands" were filmed on the backlots of the studio; therefore "the racial adventure film is laughable as ethnography but indispensable as cartography."[46] Actually, these movies failed to enlighten America on African Americans as individuals nor revealed the depth of black culture. In essence, these films expose the lack of meaningful interactions and "the murky regions of American race relations."[47]

Even though Jim Crow-era policies forbade images of "the dread and the allure of racial mixing, cultural and sexual," the predominating theme of the racial adventure film "is the shiver of sexual attraction, the threat and promise of miscegenation."[48] In an issue of *Variety* magazine, the publishers discuss the number of times white women venture into the Australian outback and how white women interact with blacks in Harlem. Hollywood promotes this "lure of miscegenation" by constantly featuring "the violation of the blond by the black, of the purest of white women threatened with defilement by ebony savages."[49] Films such as *Trader Horn* (1930), *The Blonde Captive* (1932), and *Blonde Venus* (1932) feature blond female victims as a symbol of white power that will remain pure if they can resist exposure to blackness. Moreover, racial adventure films reveal a perverted fascination with the virtuous white female body and the untamed black male body. Furthermore, these films reinforce the obligatory duty of white men as self-appointed protectors of white virtue. In the 1930s, when terror against African Americans is seen as extracurricular entertainment for southern white men, these images underscore and justify whites' fears of black men. By highlighting the African savage, white imagination is unable to disassociate their perceptions of Africans abroad from their

African American descendants. If their ancestors are horrible, violent, and animalistic, their descendants are extensions of the inhumanity present in Africa. Thus the discriminatory treatment that blacks receive in the entertainment business and in American culture is deserved because of their projected inferiority.

Paul Robeson: The Early Roots of Artistic Integrity

Robeson strongly believed that his role as a black actor should reflect his sense of personal integrity. Despite the criticism he faced during the McCarthy blacklisting era, politicians in the 1930s sought to use Robeson's stardom in their ploys to gain black votes. In 1936 the national chairman of the Republican Party, John Hamilton, sought Robeson in England to "campaign among Negroes for Alf Landon against President Roosevelt."[50] If Robeson agreed to work against Roosevelt, he could write his "own ticket in regard to future Hollywood contracts and starring productions, since the big film magnates were staunchly Republican and hated the man in the White House."[51] Earlier in Robeson's career, he refused a lucrative 10-year contract because the agent would have taken complete control of his public life. Robeson refused to be led "around by a golden chain or any other kind."[52] Robeson, whose father was the "pastor of St. Thomas A.M.E. Zion Church," taught him that success should not "be measured in terms of money and personal advancement, but rather the goal must be the richest and highest development of one's own potential."[53] These values led Robeson to determine that most Hollywood roles were unsuitable for a black actor with integrity. Robeson insisted that Negro artists should not accept roles simply based on individual interests; instead, the black actor "had a responsibility to his people who rightfully resented the traditional stereotyped portrayals of Negroes on stage and screen."[54] If Hollywood and Broadway producers failed to offer Robeson worthy roles to play, he was determined not to accept any role at all. Unfortunately, this strong social stance with regard to cultural responsibility would brand Robeson as a firebrand and disruptor of the status quo.

Perhaps one of the most fascinating aspects of Paul Robeson is the relationship between him and his father, Reverend Robeson. In 1910, his family moved to Somerville, New Jersey, which was a larger town between Westfield and Princeton.[55] Conservative Booker T. Washington deemed manual training as the best method to educate blacks. Reverend Robeson disagreed with Washington's philosophy. Paul's father trained his children to understand "that the heights of knowledge must be scaled by the freedom seeker"; therefore he exposed Paul to "Latin, Greek, philosophy, history, literature" and read Virgil, Homer, and other classics with his son.[56] Long before Paul Robeson became known as a "class orator and college debater," his father was his "first teacher in public speaking."[57] When Robeson attended eighth grade in Somerville, he was top of his class; later, once he attended an integrated high school, in which he "formed close friendships with a number of white classmates," he still impressed his teachers.[58] Eventually, he won a four-year academic scholarship to Rutgers College.[59] Ironically, Paul was not considered the smartest of the pastor's children; Paul's brother Bill received that designation in the Robeson family. During Bill's enrollment in college, he held jobs as a Pullman porter and a redcap at Grand Central Station.[60] When Bill was home from college, he directed Paul's studies. Once Bill earned his degree, he earned it in the field of medicine. Then there was Pastor Robeson's son Ben, who was a superior athlete and was good enough to play in the major leagues, but baseball was not integrated at that time. Nevertheless, Ben was Paul's favorite brother because he exposed Paul to the world outside of small-town life. Later, Ben becomes the next preacher in the family. Lastly, there was Paul's sister, Marion, who married Dr. William Forsythe; she became a schoolteacher.[61] Since Paul's siblings were adults as he was growing up, he benefited from their education, experience, and wisdom. Consequently, Paul's family had high expectations of him and he was determined to satisfy their hopes and dreams.

Paul Robeson in *The Emperor Jones* (1933)

Paul Robeson was an actor, singer, lawyer, college football athlete, published writer, and activist. To this day, few actors can boast of so many accomplishments. Perhaps this is why he refused a position of submissiveness and designation as an inferior member of American society. As a dynamic actor, Robeson held an "unapologetic stance as a strong black man."[62] In plays and movies, he "raised his booming bass voice not only in Negro spirituals but in radical labor songs and impassioned speeches for civil rights," but unlike "entertainers of any color," he was not afraid "to be disliked and unpopular."[63] During the early 1930s, a false rumor spread that "the silent film actress Lillian Gish, the vessel of undefiled white womanhood in *The Birth of a Nation*, had played opposite Robeson as Desdemona in a production of *Othello*."[64] If the rumor had been true, society would find this romantic coupling unacceptable. In 1924, the Ku Klux Klan warned Robeson of the consequences if he chose to perform in "*All God's Chillun*, in which a white woman will kiss his hand."[65] Unafraid by his detractors, including those who were willing to commit violent acts, his stage acting as Jim Harris was a raving success. Since he refused designation as a second-class citizen on-screen and in life, he was a threat to white establishment and he incited fears with his individual talents and his commanding acting prowess.

When audiences become aware of Robeson's educational and professional background, his personal determination becomes even more apparent. Ironically, discrimination in the legal field led him to heighten his pursuit as an actor. When a "secretary refused to take dictation from him," he quit his job at a downtown law firm.[66] For Robeson, this discriminatory treatment was unacceptable. Since he was no longer practicing law, he accepted the lead in two plays—*All God's Chillun Got Wings* and *The Emperor Jones*—written by Pulitzer Prize winner Eugene O'Neill. London critics declared Robeson "one of the great actors!" after seeing his performance of *The Emperor Jones*; they also exclaimed that he was "one of the great singers!"[67] T. Thompson interviewed Robeson for *The Millgate* in an article entitled "Paul Robeson Speaks about Art and the Negro."[68] Robeson was dressed in a uniform when he spoke frankly about the role of black culture and black performance; Thompson wrote that "Paul Robeson is proud of his race and deeply concerned with its progress."[69] Robeson equated the value of Negro spirituals as having excellent melodies as other folk songs. Exposure to African culture taught him that the "negro in Africa is not tied down to half or quarter tones, or any European musical conventions."[70] As a black musical actor, this knowledge of African musical tradition was liberating. Nevertheless, his natural inclinations as an artist were not limited by his knowledge of Africa; instead, his knowledge of African music explained his range as a singer and the flexibility of Negro spirituals. Robeson declared, " 'In Africa (the true home of the negro, not America) German and French explorers found pieces of sculpture—mainly in wood—equal, if not superior, to anything done by the ancient Greeks.' "[71] Robeson claimed that the Greeks were concerned with bodily perfection, whereas African art is concerned with spirituality because " 'the negro ... did not care whether his carvings looked like human beings or not.' "[72] Robeson's newfound conceptualization of African culture informed his artistic performance in every way. Thompson declared, "Off the stage he is the charming man of culture. On the stage he is the voice of one crying for his people."[73] Apparently, Robeson's proud nature was appreciated more by the British audience than by Americans.

Years later, in May 1933, Robeson returned from England to star in the film version of *The Emperor Jones*.[74] Ironically, England is the country where Robeson discovered his African roots. In the 1920s and 1930s, Robeson was treated with admiration and appreciation for his stage and film performances. Due to Jim Crow-era segregation, England offered more opportunities for black performers.[75] Robeson said the he was "deeply gratified to gain a prominent place in the theatre, in films, as concert singer and popular recording artist."[76] But he mostly appreciated how well English society accepted him; since mostly high society patronized the arts, he traveled in predominantly upper-class and aristocratic circles. By 1923, Robeson held two college degrees, which is still impressive by contemporary standards. England treated Robeson like he was a gentleman and a scholar. By contrast, he felt that his Rutgers education and academic interests were not respected in countries such as "America where bankrolls count more than brains and where bookish people are often derided as 'eggheads' when they are not suspected of being 'subversive.' "[77] Eventually, Robeson claimed to enjoy London even more once he lived among the common people; for Robeson, "London was the center of the British Empire and it" is where he " 'discovered' Africa."[78] In England, as he learned more about Africa from Africans living in England, he no longer considered himself "an adopted Englishman"; he then became proud to deem himself "an African"; and the West African Students Union embraced him and his wife as honorary members.[79] The Africans at the university were mostly of princely origin, yet Robeson also came to learn more about Africa from the seamen in the ports of London, Liverpool, and Cardiff. Eventually, Robeson became fascinated with African art, but he also learned African languages such as "Yoruba, Efik, Twi, Ga and others."[80] Robeson's pride grew even more when he learned that "scholars had traced the influence of African music to Europe—to Spain with the Moors, to Persia and India and China, and westward to the Americas."[81] Eventually, he was compelled "to speak out against the scorners," by celebrating "the real but unknown glories of African culture" in articles he published in the *New Statesman and Nation*, *The Spectator*, and other venues.[82] As Robeson's cultural and historical knowledge grew, his spiritual knowledge of his humanity enhanced his performance as an artist.

In a press release, United Artists declared that Paul Robeson was " 'probably the only person adequately endowed racially, physically, histrionically, and temperamentally to play Brutus Jones in *The Emperor Jones.*' "[83] Because Robeson played the role on stage in New York, London, and Berlin, he was the most obvious film choice. Due to Robeson's personal and family background, he was considered "the only African-American actor with sufficient backstory charisma to embody an emperor on screen."[84] Generally, Robeson worked well with directors and producers on movie sets, but he was uncompromising on one issue.

Consequently, he was labeled difficult by *Variety* press because he refused to film below the Mason Dixon line. If he acquiesced to the will of the director, Dudley Murphy, he would have to submit to Jim Crow segregation laws in terms of transportation and hotel accommodations. Instead of empathizing with the plight of black actors, considering that white actors were not subjected to the same inhospitable working conditions, they referred to Robeson's stance as a flash of temperament. Robeson's demands were considered economically inefficient for producers who would have to build expensive and disingenuous sets to please him. In hindsight, *Variety*'s interpretation of Robeson derived from a limited perspective that lacked an objective understanding of Jim Crow-era policies. Furthermore, *Variety* lacked sufficient comprehension of the social expectations that Robeson experienced from not only whites but blacks as well.

As one of the first performers who refrained from performing under Jim Crow conditions, Robeson was a leader in tearing down societal walls separating blacks and whites. Whites from the most conservative to the most radical misinterpreted Robeson's demands for equal treatment.[85] They perceived Robeson's sense of pride as "ungrateful to the good white folks of America who had given him wealth and fame, and that he had had nothing to complain about."[86] However, Robeson did not measure his human dignity by his monetary gains and artistic achievements. Once, he said that African Americans were aware "that nothing is ever 'given' to us, and ... human dignity cannot be measured in dollars and cents."[87] When Robeson refused to sing in front of a segregated audience, his commitment to equal access for African Americans made headline news. But later, African Americans grew to appreciate his efforts and expressed disapproval "whenever a prominent Negro artist agrees to perform under Jim Crow arrangements."[88] Segregation prevented all Americans from enjoying the multifarious talents of black actors. Thus black and white audiences were both denied an invaluable segment of the American experience during Jim Crow.

For audiences, "*The Emperor Jones* was a black Horatio Alger story for a time of racist exclusion."[89] Like many tragic protagonists of the Depression era, "Brutus Jones is a doomed and deranged self-made man in a society closed to self-transformations."[90] Successfully, *The Emperor Jones* geographically links "a tribe of Caribbean natives thumping tom-toms and dancing in a frenzied voodoo ceremony [that] dissolves into an equally ecstatic gospel service in a Baptist church."[91] Wearing a crisp new Pullman porter uniform, Brutus Jones leaves his loyal girlfriend to begin his personal quest. Jeff, Brutus Jones's friend, introduces him to urban living in Harlem. Jones forgets his girl who remains back home in rural Georgia; then, he begins to enjoy the pleasures of "high yaller" (light-skinned) prostitutes living in the North. In an era of moral movie codes and Jim Crow policies, Fredi Washington, who played Jones's girlfriend, was forced to don a kind of blackface. Since Fredi's skin was so light, she could pass for white; therefore the studio needed to reshoot her scenes "in dark pancake makeup so audiences wood not think Brutus/Robeson was consorting with a white woman."[92]

Brutus Jones's career excels as he is promoted and then "profits from an insider stock market scam. Later, gambling in a more stereotypical manner in a high-stakes crap game, Jones kills Jeff in a knife fight."[93] Soon, Jones is jailed and working in a chain gang. However, in this emotionally low moment, the director frames the shot to emphasize Robeson's powerful and imposing stature; Robeson is "singing, shirtless, astride the landscape, his muscular bare torso and booming voice a picture of dominance and virility in image and sound."[94] When Jones is commanded by a white straw boss to batter another prisoner, he refuses to obey. In the midst of a violent scene, the movie alludes to Jones killing the guard, which is considered an incendiary act of black insurrection; in essence, Jones demonstrates an act of rebellion against an authority figure. After the killing, Jones escapes in a truck and "orders a steam shovel full of rocks onto him."[95] On the steamer, Jones finds an opportunity to jump ship and swim to a Caribbean island. *The Emperor Jones* reverses the master-servant role when Jones rises from the bottom of society and up the economic ladder of success. At first Smithers (Dudley Digges) purchases Jones, but as Jones's status changes in Caribbean society, he begins to order the white men around. During this decade, this power of " 'nerve and brains' " was "never again given to a black man by the Hollywood studio system in the 1930s."[96] The role of Brutus Jones has been compared to Fitzgerald's Jay Gatsby because Jones is "an active agent of his own destiny, the star performer, the black Gatsby"; whereas some critics equate Brutus Jones to Tony Camonte in *Scarface* (1932).[97] Brutus adorns "regal threads" and relishes in "his self-image in the mirror but for a time at least the world really is his"; he becomes lord of the island and "pumps the island dry with taxes and corruption, investing his ill-gotten gains offshore, not in America" with their chain gangs and Jim Crow policies.[98] Despite Jones's internal triumph over the capitalistic practices that plague America, he suffers from the haunting memories associated with his transformation. At the end of the movie, Jones "runs through the island jungle tormented by the sound of voodoo tom-toms"; he remembers murdering Jeff and the guard; and he dies in the final scene when "he collapses at last on the drum, dead, killed by a silver bullet."[99] According to the *New Age*, the movie was received well by both black and white audiences who saw the movie separately at a rare double premiere.

The distributors of *The Emperor Jones* accommodated the Jim Crow polices of the era. Nevertheless, for different reasons, the movie created discord for both black and white audiences. The word "nigger" was said 34 times; therefore it was edited out for "colored theaters" but not for white theaters, yet words such as " 'Lord' and 'God' " were kept in the film because these utterances were spoken by "the Negro" when distressed.[100] As expected, southern exhibitors stayed away from *The Emperor Jones* because of the depiction of Paul Robeson as "a strong black man ordering around a white man"; movies featuring a dominant black male were unpalatable for southern audiences.[101] *The Pittsburgh Courier*, the premier African American weekly, denounced Robeson's use of the word "nigger" by exclaiming that the lowbrow comedy of *Amos 'N' Andy* was preferable; moreover, they declared *The Birth of a Nation* as the only movie worse for black America than *The Emperor Jones*. Obviously, this critique deeply affected Robeson. In an interview with Robeson, Eugene Gordon writes in "A Great Negro Artist Puts His Genius to Work for His People" that *The Emperor Jones* is a wonderful play by one of America's greatest playwrights; nonetheless, the next time Robeson performs it he planned to "eliminate all epithets derogatory to the Negro."[102] Although Robeson's intentions were noble, his subsequent enlightenment did not affect the 1933 film version. Prior to Robeson's stage role in *The Emperor Jones*, Charles Sidney Gilpin played the lead role as Brutus Jones.[103] Instead of using the word "nigger," he altered the dialogue by saying "Negro or colored man."[104] This change angered O'Neill who was already infuriated by Gilpin's incessant drinking. For Gilpin, a successful stage actor but failed movie actor, he felt that the use of word "nigger" negated the achievements of blacks. Nevertheless, Robeson championed the role despite the incessant use of the derogatory language and the black critics who opposed its use.

Even though some Harlem theaters had to "turn away" audiences due to the lack of available seats, *The Emperor Jones* was not successful at the box office. The "black protagonist and black milieu" of *The Emperor Jones* is not the distinguishing factor from other "racial adventure film of the 1930s"; instead, the "integration of white and black life from the black perspective" differentiated Emperor Jones as not "another scheming Kingfish but a man of nerve and brains."[105] Jones navigates through "a hostile world and wears the mantle of authority as his birthright."[106] In the Jim Crow era, the eminence of pride projected from Paul Robeson as the emperor made the film intolerable. Nevertheless, Robeson would be defined by this role. Robeson felt it was important for a black actor to demonstrate a high level of artistic ability. Then, he wanted to perform on stage "or pose before a camera with the same presence as the whites, and sometimes with greater presence."[107] Some American audiences may have been turned off by such pride in a black male. But Robeson knew that in the time period in which he lived, he represented more than himself.[108] This was a burden he was proud to carry on his broad shoulders. As a culture maker, he symbolized necessary racial progress in the minds of everyday Americans.

Robeson and Mitchell's *Gone with the Wind*

Gone with the Wind (1939) remains a cinematic classic despite the political and racial controversy that envelops the movie's legacy. Based on the 1936 bestselling novel by Margaret Mitchell, the movie, starring Clark Gable and Vivien Leigh, "held the record for gross earnings for more than two decades."[109] The book and the cinematic ambitions impressed Robeson along with most audiences. In 1936, six months after the book was published, "1,000,000 copies were sold, 50,000 in one day." By the time Robeson wrote the preface in 1939, sales had mounted to 2 million books in the United States.[110]

Much of the success of the film was attributed to the stars of the film. Molly Haskell writes in " 'Gone with the Wind' Still Raises Fuss after 70 Years" that the movie was "crafted by the geniuses of the studio system."[111] Clark Gable and Vivien Leigh are star-crossed lovers; their romance is tested due to "the agony of war, of economic loss and devastation, the resilience of a woman who won't accept defeat."[112] During the golden era of movies, MGM was known "for its glossy production values and middlebrow subject matter."[113] David O. Selznick produced the picture independently, but MGM released it in typical MGM style; consequently, *Gone with the Wind* was characteristically "romantically melodramatic, expensively produced, with a lush score, [and] it treats epic subject matter while doing relatively little to illuminate its themes."[114] Various studios such as MGM, Warner Brothers, and Paramount had different styles; however, there is very little difference in terms of "the political and social consciousness" of their productions.[115] Based on the studios' history, people should not have expected a fair depiction of race relations in the South. There were those films who portrayed servants and sidekicks with malicious racism. Yet most films treated racial diversity with condescension and indifference. According to the black press and the civil rights community, black characters playing in *Gone with the Wind* represented the most abhorrent characterization of African Americans' position in Hollywood. As previously stated, although blacks were one-tenth of the nation's population, they were "more often just plain missing in action."[116]

Then and now, many audiences are still uncomfortable with the one-dimensional depiction of African Americans in *Gone with the Wind*. But Selznick was open to pacifying the concerns of African Americans, the South, and the studios during production. In an uncomfortable book sequence, involving the Ku Klux Klan, Selznick omitted a racially inflammatory scene.[117] Leonard J. Leff writes in "*Gone with the Wind* and Hollywood's Racial Politics" that in Walker's book, there is a black male who grabs the breast of a white female.[118] Therefore, in the tradition of *The Birth of a Nation*, the KKK is elevated as a necessary evil for maintaining social order. Since the scene uses the protection of white virtue as justification for the white supremacist organization, he chose to omit the controversial scene. One black writer for the *Pittsburgh Courier*, Earl Morris, urged Selznick to refrain from using the word "nigger."[119] Also, Leff writes that Val Lewton, Selznick's assistant, believed that the "absence of the word 'nigger' had cost the picture an ounce of dramatic punch and a pound of comic material."[120] Considering the subject matter of the Reconstruction era, contemplating comedy at the expense of the integrity of the black actors demonstrates the persistent trivialization of the black community and the minimization of their concerns. However, Selznick kept his promise to "negro societies"; he did not want to lose his integrity by using the derogatory term. Despite the epithet's use in Mitchell's novel, Hattie McDaniel (Mammy) also spoke on behalf of editing the word out of production.[121] However, McDaniel is not the only black actor that demanded respect and fair treatment on the set of *Gone with the Wind*.

Lenny Bluett, who played a Yankee soldier in Shantytown and a townsperson, refused to allow his part as an extra to minimize his impact on the set. According to Bluett, who spoke on a featurette for TCM, "Race and Hollywood Black Images on Film," one situation was unfathomable.[122] One morning when Bluett arrived on set, he noticed that there were segregated toilets labeled "white" and "colored." The studio set was private property located in Southern California; therefore the Jim Crow South was not a part of the regional culture. Like his mother, Bluett grew up in Southern California and did not see segregated toilets and fountains growing up. Thus this on-set treatment was an outrage. Also, Bluett had attended integrated schools; therefore, he lacked exposure to this type of segregation. When he spoke to some of the male extras on set, they did not want to speak out; after all, they had families at home to feed.

Bluett reminded them that the studio could not fire them all; it was impossible for the studio to hire 400 Mexicans to look like black people. Despite studio rules that "forbade extras from approaching stars," Bluett was unfettered in his dissatisfaction.[123] Bluett speaks with pride when he says that Clark Gable was the Brad Pitt and Clark Kent of his day. After knocking on Gable's door, Gable spoke with Bluett and then went to see the segregated toilets. Immediately, Gable was enraged and expressed his feelings to the director, Victor Fleming, via telephone and to the property master. Supposedly, Gable said, "If you don't get those God Damn signs down, you don't have a Rhett Butler on this film."[124] After Gable expressed his frustration to the studio, the signs were removed. For the most part, it appears that the studio attempted to make their black actors feel appreciated on the set of *Gone with the Wind*.

None of the outrage associated with *The Birth of a Nation* occurred when screening *Gone with the Wind*.[125] Due in part to the Hays Code, Selznick was ruled primarily, not by racial concerns, but by a sense of politics. The producer "expected a tough fight with the censors over the word 'damn' in Rhett Butler's curtain line."[126] Selznick hoped that "concessions on 'nigger,' a word whose use Breen now adamantly opposed, might soften the Hays Office later on 'damn.' "[127] Selznick was victorious on this issue. Furthermore, the movie removed mention of " 'darkies,' for slaves in rebellion, for indictments of Ku Klux Klan activity and southern lynch mobs"[128]—all of which Griffith promoted, in order to profit from the fear caused by the threat of integration in *The Birth of a Nation*. Under the leadership of its president Walter White, the NAACP urged Hollywood to create better roles for black actors. To Selznick's credit, he hired White as a consultant "either to improve the depiction of blacks in the controversial film or to ameliorate their disapproval of it."[129] Thus moral outrage on all sides was subsided by Selznick's choices during production.

McDaniel did not attend the premiere in Atlanta "because of attitudes in the South."[130] Although Selznick wanted the entire cast, both blacks and whites, there, he did not want "racial tyranny" to ruin the premiere of his movie; thus Selznick was primarily concerned for movie sales.[131] He did not want to lose potentially huge black audiences, and he did not want to offend southern sensibilities. However, McDaniel's efforts in the movie were recognized by Hollywood. Even though she was nominated for the best supporting actress category and beat out Olivia de Havilland, she and her date, black actor Wonderful Smith, were forced to sit separately from the other stars.[132] Other major black roles were played by Oscar Polk (Pork-Servant), Eddie Anderson (Uncle Peter-Scarlett's Coachman), Everett Brown (Field Foreman), and Butterfly

McQueen (Prissy-House Servant).[133] Since leading roles for black actors were rare, "Black Hollywood" considered these servant roles as important.[134] Even Polk defended the monolithic depictions of African Americans in *Gone with the Wind*. Apparently, Polk was happy to appear in a movie; therefore he wrote a letter, which was printed in the weekly *Chicago Defender*.[135] Even if that movie offended members of the community, according to Polk the movie demonstrates the progress of black America since their enslavement in the South. Understandably, Polk sought not to offend mainstream Hollywood if he expected to attain another role in a major production. Nevertheless, Carlton Moss in the *Daily Worker* declares that the movie "offered up a motley collection of flat black characters that insulted the black audience. Hattie McDaniel's Mammy was especially loathsome in her love for a family, the O'Haras."[136] Eventually, most of the African American community supported McDaniel after her nomination in 1940. If McDaniel won the Academy Award, members of a black national sorority claimed this would signal the end of discrimination and racism. Donald Bogle says that Black Hollywood erroneously thought that "McDaniel's achievement seemed to signal a new era for African American actors and actress."[137] But World War II in Europe would have a greater impact on the transformation of Hollywood than McDaniel's accomplishment.

Today, most young people object to *Gone with the Wind*'s depiction of happy slaves and the claim that Reconstruction was a complete disaster.[138] Yet Haskell disagrees with referring to the movie as racially retrograde. She states that the movie reflects the times in which it was made. However, Haskell says, "We can't bear to look at that time and place—itself a mark of how far we've progressed."[139] This statement reflects the misconceptions of white society toward history as it was experienced by blacks. Also, *Gone with the Wind* reinforces placation in black society with low economic status and second-class citizenry. Since the 1600s, there have always been free blacks who lived among various class levels. Furthermore, the movie shows black males as thinking, speaking, and acting in a similar manner, which has never been the reality of blacks or any other culture living in America. The African American culture is complex. Monolithic characterizations are generalizations based on the assumptions of the majority culture. Lastly, the black men in the film relish in helping the whites live and work to maintain the hierarchal system that oppresses them. In actuality, these men were more likely interested in providing for and protecting their families than upholding racial stereotypes. Oftentimes, blacks worked those menial jobs because their options were limited during the Reconstruction era. Similarly, black actors accepted the roles that were available to them in the golden age of Hollywood. Thus the black male roles in *Gone with the Wind* reflect a commercialized ideal that is propagated by Hollywood's imposed fantasy of black male identity.

The danger resulting from *Gone with the Wind* is the framing of how people interpret race relations between blacks and whites. Furthermore, the portrayal of black men's humanity is limited by their low intelligence and low ambition. Consequently, these narrow depictions relegate them to performing only servile functions in movies and society. If movies did not have the power to shape culture, the Hays Code would not have received so much support from religious leaders, social workers, civic reformers, police, politicians, women's organizations, and civic organizations. Despite the objection to the word "nigger," the Hays office was mainly concerned with the dominant culture's values, social norms, religious, and governing principles. There is no evidence that Breen prohibited the use of the word "nigger" because of its offense to blacks. Moreover, the Hays Code protected mainstream society from cultural introspection. By insisting that religious and government organizations appear in a positive light, the code did more to satisfy deeply held beliefs of black male inferiority. Movies have the power to make society question itself and its treatment of its citizens, which was a source of concern from various movie critics. By upholding prohibition against miscegenation, society was prevented from visually evaluating their negative reinforcement of black images and their continued practice of barring blacks from full actualization of their citizenship by marrying or dating whomever they chose.

Gone with the Wind promoted the idea that blacks should stay on the lower rungs of society and socialize with their own people. Even though *The Emperor Jones* was viewed by fewer audience members and profited less at the box office, performers such as Paul Robeson embody a more actualized portrait of the black male experience. The internal conflict imposed by maintaining self-dignity; meanwhile, adjusting to the black community's expectations and the deflection of whites' misconceptions was embodied by the character of Brutus Jones—not to mention, the external conflicts caused by urban exposure to prison culture. Even if there is a desire to walk a straight line, the temptation to fall into a life of crime is perilously tempting for some and complicated for those who operate inside the boundaries of the law. Racial adventure films were not made for the purpose of improving the image of black males. Instead, their exploitation of Africa and its wild animals bolstered the heroic treatment of white males, meanwhile, perpetuating the fear of black males by placating racial desires and mainly white audiences.

Ironically, the Hays Code dominates the production of Hollywood movies from the 1930s to the 1960s; Will Hays retired from the MPPDA in 1945 and died nine years later in 1954; Father Daniel Lord died in 1955; Martin Quigley passed away in 1964; and subsequently, Joe Breen passed away in 1965.[140] A year later, the studios overturned the code system, replacing it with a rating system.[141] By 1966, a strict era of regulation in Hollywood ends. With changing times and the relinquishment of rigid censorship, Hollywood in the 1970s will transform the monolithic treatment of black males and thrust forth miscegenation as a revolutionary signifier of black male liberation.

CHAPTER 4

───── 1940s ─────
Bill "Bojangles" Robinson and Lincoln "Stepin Fetchit" Perry: Black Servants in Musicals and Comedies

For black actors who desired work, playing black slaves and servants in musicals and comedies assisted in the rise to stardom. However, by the end of the 1940s, Americans grew weary of the narrow themes depicting joyful, dancing, and comical servants. The public perceived the Sambo images of actors, such as Bojangles and Fetchit, as a justification for slavery, subservience, and discriminatory treatment. Yet Perry's biographer disagrees with this interpretation. In *Stepin Fetchit: The Life and Times of Lincoln Perry*, Mel Watkins argues that Fetchit's comic image "was not nearly as harmful, deleterious, and degrading as the images projected by many of today's black comedians, rap artists, and even television sitcom stars."[1] Due to the Jim Crow era in which Fetchit lived, in terms of motion picture opportunities his choices were limited. Watkins believes that black entertainers now have vast opportunities, yet they "still often opt for routines or projects that are mired in either salacious or degrading stereotypes."[2] According to *The Black Perspective in Music*, Perry is "one of the black pioneers of Hollywood films and first to receive equal billing with white stars, he appeared in a number of musicals although he was not a musician."[3] Equivalently speaking, Bill "Bojangles" Robinson is mostly known for his tap dancing and roles with Shirley Temple. Because of the nostalgia associated with Robinson's performances with the young American icon, his image does not evoke the same amount of offense as Perry's image. Many African Americans consider Stepin Fetchit's acting roles as far more damaging to the American psyche. Typical of the 1930s and 1940s musicals, Robinson's roles are generally restricted to his singing and dancing talents.

Despite their differences in performance style, scope of talent, and acting range, this chapter juxtaposes Bojangles and Stepin Fetchit.

Their humble beginnings, commonalities, and humongous impact on the entertainment industry are comparable. Bojangles and Fetchit achieved mainstream success, but their legacies have been barraged by negative interpretations launched by the black press and black organizations—primarily, the negative criticism received by Bojangles occurred after his death.[4] Retrospectively speaking, some of the damaging criticism may be attributed to their brushes with the law.[5] Both Bojangles and Fetchit were well known for their notorious tempers. Bojangles's biographer claims "that Robinson's famous, or infamous, temper" was justified because of his upbringing.[6] Nevertheless, Bojangles's funeral was a testament to the personal and professional relationships he fostered. White and black legends in the diverse fields of sports, entertainment, and politics were among his fans and friends.[7] However, Stepin Fetchit died without any celebrities in attendance except for his eulogist Sonny Craver.[8] On behalf of their own careers and at the expense of the black community's interest in racial and social progress, both men were referred to as Uncle Toms for serving the racial desires of Hollywood and for catering to white audiences. Nonetheless, neither Bojangles nor Fetchit wanted the "Uncle Tom" racial epithet associated with their cinematic legacies. Despite their defenders' protests, due to their early stage history as minstrel performers and their typecast roles in musicals and comedies, the tom label continues to define their images. Furthermore, both Bojangles and Stepin Fetchit were highly paid black actors at the peak of their careers, yet they died poor with tarnished screen images.

Mr. Show Business "Bojangles": A Credit to the Human Race

Rosetta LeNoire, who was a stage, screen, and television star, considered Bill "Bojangles" Robinson "one of the most accomplished, creative, famous, and talented dancers."[9] After his death, LeNoire praised his generous nature; Robinson indiscriminately bestowed gifts upon people. Without regard to gender, race, or color, he also shared his talent with others. Although Robinson was well loved by most, LeNoire remained impressed by his cleanliness and his insistence that all of his stage performers keep their dressing rooms immaculate.[10] Robinson opened the doors on stage and film for many actors, but he was considered an "Uncle Tom" by many blacks. Despite this derogatory label, Robinson's talent and professionalism was a "model for all people," as evidenced by the number of everyday people and celebrities who came to his funeral in 1949.[11] The church service held 3,000 of the 13,000 people who attended the celebration of Robinson's life.[12] Some of the honorary pallbearers were Jimmy Durante, Bob Hope,

Louis B. Mayer, Darryl Zanuck, Jackie Robinson, Joe DiMaggio, Duke Ellington, Irving Berlin, Cole Porter, Joe Louis, and Milton Berle. Various other attendees were Danny Kaye, Sugar Ray Robinson, Eddie "Rochester" Anderson, and Ethel Merman, along with other "show business and sports stars" who "sat side by side with famous local politicians." Ed Sullivan, who paid for the "funeral arrangements," and Reverend Adam Clayton Powell Jr. are some of the famous attendees who spoke at Bojangles's service.[13]

However, Robinson's star appeal and reputation would suffer in the future. As time passed, people believed that he should have used his Broadway and Hollywood stardom to oppose racial discrimination in America; people referred to Robinson as an "Uncle Tom and criticized [him] for not having done more to fight segregation."[14] In particular, future black generations tarnished his name. Although the critical perception of his civil rights contribution off-screen is significant, this chapter determines his contribution to the on-screen African American image of black males in Hollywood. Judging by some of the famous and politically influential blacks that attended his funeral, such as Jackie Robinson, Joe Louis, Sugar Ray Robinson, and Adam Clayton Powell Jr., it is difficult to believe that Robinson did not positively influence the lives of black males in Hollywood and beyond. At Robinson's service, Powell addresses the perception of Bojangles as an Uncle Tom. First, Powell spoke of Robinson's legendary impact by stating that he "was a legend because he was ageless and raceless"; Robinson was not selfish with his talents because he taught "anyone, anywhere, how to dance"; and famously, Powell proclaimed that "Bill wasn't a credit to his race, meaning the Negro race, Bill was a credit to the human race. He was not a great Negro dancer, he was the world's greatest dancer. Bill Robinson was Mr. Show Business himself."[15] Why are these distinctions significant? Considering that Reverend Powell was considered a liberal politician by some and a radical activist by others, his approval suggests that Robinson's contribution to America transcends racial boundaries and the invisible walls of segregation. By modeling greatness, Robinson proved that blacks were equal and capable of outperforming white musical performers of his era. Furthermore, considering Robinson's background, he modeled racial and social progress judging by the personal and racial obstacles he overcame to become a Hollywood star.

Bill Robinson: The Early Years

In a volatile era, Bill was born in Richmond, Virginia, which was the seat of the Confederacy.[16] For blacks living in the South, they anticipated disaster once the federal troops evacuated.[17] During the five years of Reconstruction, otherwise referred to as the Union's occupation, blacks saw gains in politics, education, and employment opportunities. Robinson's parents were "Maxwell Robinson, a machinist, and his wife, Maria, a 'choir director' in 1878."[18] Unfortunately, Robinson faced tragedy in 1885 when his parents "died from a questionable accident, rather than of natural causes."[19] Although Robinson was considered a wonderful individual, his temper was legendary. Due to his background, it is clear why this young orphan showed his propensity for anger at a young age. As one would expect of siblings, Bill and his brother were not averse to scuffling. After winning a fight against his brother, Bill shed his birth name Luther and he took his younger brother's name William.[20] From that moment on, Robinson began to refer to his younger brother as Percy.

When Robinson's parents died, he and his brother went to live with his grandmother, Bedilia Robinson; she was a former Richmond slave who had no interest in rearing her two little grandsons. Bedilia's religiosity caused her not to recognize her young grandson's talent; therefore Robinson's grandmother forbade him from dancing or even mentioning the "evil word" in her presence.[21] Since she was elderly and sick, she fought the responsibility of their custody. So John Crutchfield, a white judge who was known for his fairness toward whites and blacks, cared for the boys until a proper guardian was appointed for them. This compassion from a white authority figure, in a racially tense era, gave Robinson and his brother a "healthy respect for the law."[22] Yet these early struggles did not deter Bill's expression of his talents. Bill and his young friend Eggleston enjoyed dancing so much that they performed in front of the Ford Theater; even if they could have afforded the price of admission, blacks were barred from patronizing or performing on stage.[23] At the Ford Theater, minstrel shows were performed by whites who "darkened their faces with burnt cork and played" black characters.[24] Eventually, Eggleston and Robinson performed minstrel shows, but Robinson chose not to perform in blackface.[25] When Robinson was 12 years old, his interests extended beyond dancing. He developed a fascination with the racetrack and a lifelong "preoccupation with gambling."[26] Sadly, Robinson's primary desire was to please his grandmother. Despite his grandmother's stringent disapproval, Bill would fall back on dancing to avoid "stealing the bread and milk" from people's doorsteps.[27] Ironically, a bullet in the knee would not hamper Robinson's dancing skills. In 1898, when Robinson was a drummer in the Spanish American War, "he suffered his first bullet wound"; although he was shot accidentally by a second lieutenant cleaning his gun, he liked to brag that the bullet never exited the other side of his knee.[28] Ultimately, this incident demonstrates Robinson's resilience, fun-loving attitude, survival instinct, and entertainment spirit.

Household Name: Movies That Made Mr. Bojangles a Star

Prior to the advent of the movie industry, the black male image had been distorted and misconstrued in the public's imagination. Donald Bogle, a leading cultural critic, traces black stereotypes to the pre–Civil War days. Consequently, Americans are familiar with these images and unable to accept depictions of blacks that operate outside the parameters of their comfort zone. Hollywood capitalized on these biases in American culture; for that reason, they accommodated their audience by reproducing these inflammatory images on film. According to Bogle's *Toms, Coons, Mulattoes, Mammies, and Bucks*, the black stereotypes reproduced on-screen "existed since the days of slavery and were already popularized in American life and arts"; since the movies "catered to public tastes," they "borrowed profusely from all the other popular art forms."[29] Therefore, when constructing black characters, Hollywood used the traditional stereotypes and in many cases they distorted the images even further.

At different times, Robinson and Stepin Fetchit played the tom or the coon roles for Hollywood. Even though some members of the public were dismayed by the Civil War theme in *The Birth of a Nation*, Hollywood produced more benign Civil War productions starring Robinson: *The Little Colonel* (1935) and *The Littlest Rebel* (1935).[30] During the 1930s, African American actors such Hattie McDaniel, Bojangles, and Fetchit rose to stardom playing slaves and servants. On the other hand, Fetchit popularized the "much maligned handyman, flamboyantly shufflin' and stammerin'."[31] Meanwhile, Robinson garnished his performances with far more grace and class. Bojangles wowed audiences with his "smooth-as-silk butler, calm, cool, and lighthearted as he dances up a staircase with Shirley Temple."[32] Bogle praises Bojangles for his urbanity and self-assurance. Also, Bogle praises Bojangles, as well as other black performers, because they "played their types but played against them"; earlier in the decade, some black actors neglected to individualize or take ownership of their roles.[33] By playing against the type, those pioneers became "nondirectorial auteurs" gaining agency over their roles due to their "unique quality of voice or personality."[34] With their outlandish behavior, the servants tried to outperform one another; "the blacks created comic worlds all their own in which the servant often outshone the master."[35] Since they were determined to break the color barriers in Hollywood, they made the best of the servant roles by infusing minor roles with their personality and individuality.

For instance, Bojangles's performances with Shirley Temple are legendary. Yet when Shirley Temple played in *The Little Colonel*, she had earned a reputation for being "overbearing, outspoken, and forever in charge."[36] Temple's character bossed Lionel Barrymore, her grandfather, and provided advice to her distraught mother, but with Robinson, Temple did not retain her position of dominance. Generally, when she interacted with servants in the movies, there was an occasional element of "condescension or manipulation," yet in her relationship with Robinson, he transformed into the master as "he taught her the staircase dance routines."[37] Including *The Littlest Rebel*, Robinson and Temple starred in a total of four features together. As the character of Uncle Billy, for the first time in history a black actor played the guardian to a white child; therefore, Bogle affirms, " 'Uncle Billy' was the perfect—perhaps the quintessential—tom role."[38] However, by 1935, nobody was surprised that Bojangles continued to play the same type of characters in films. Since Bojangles was the grandchild of a slave, who survived in life by "dancing for pennies in saloons and on streets," the fact that he never received a dancing lesson in his lifetime was quite extraordinary.[39] Bojangles is credited with creating *The Little Colonel*'s dance on the staircase, and Fred Astaire proclaimed Robinson as the greatest dancer of all time.

Robinson's first movie part was in the comedy *Dixiana* (1930). But during his role in *The Littlest Colonel*, his character solidified the perception of him as a "well-behaved, mannerly Negro attendant"; for instance, when Lionel Barrymore's character "fumed and fussed" at Robinson, he remained patient.[40] Thus Robinson was rewarded with more roles because he earned the approval of the audience. In the movie *Hooray for Love* (1935), Robinson sang "Got a Snap to My Finger" and "was formally crowned the Mayor of Harlem."[41] Also, he played Will Rogers's gentle servant in the remake of the movie *In Old Kentucky* (1935); nevertheless, Bogle refers to *The Littlest Rebel* as the tom role that defined Robinson. Prior to the Union soldiers' invasion, Uncle Billy is Temple's favorite slave. Temple's highest joy was having Uncle Billy dance for her. When the Yankees invade the plantations, Temple alters her identity with bootblack makeup, which transforms her into a harmless pickaninny. When Temple's black mask fails to fool them, she eventually needs Uncle Billy to save her from the Yankees. Her mother's death from an illness and her father's imprisonment in the North, by Union troops, results in Robinson taking guardianship.[42] Bogle considers Robinson's roles to be superficial and terribly unvaried, and Robinson sounded often as if he was reading from a blackboard. Robinson's greatest contribution was his "gift as a dancer" because of "his sense of rhythm, his physical dexterity, and his easy-going naturalness . . . to convey an optimistic" and copasetic air.[43] Bogle distinguishes Robinson's prototype from Fetchit's characterizations because Robinson was articulate and dependable, unlike Fetchit; due to Robinson's "urbane cool" persona on-screen, there were rarely complaints about his roles, whereas there was disdain for Fetchit's and Willie Best's performances.

Generally, Robinson's roles are considered respectable, unlike Perry's performances were not. With slight deviation from comedies and musicals, Robinson had a serious role in *One Mile from Heaven* (1937); then he starred in *Rebecca of Sunnybrook Farm* (1938) with Shirley Temple, then *Road Demon, Up the River* (1938), then *Just Around the Corner* (1938). His last film role was in *Stormy Weather* (1943) with Lena Horne.[44] Since *Stormy Weather* "was a thinly veiled dramatization of the life of Bill Robinson," the classic musical was a tribute to Robinson's Hollywood career.[45] Since roles were limited for African Americans, there was always intense competition even for small roles. For African American entertainers who did not play in *Cabin in the Sky* (1943), the all-black production provided another chance for exposure in *Stormy Weather*; jazz musician Fats Waller, Cab Calloway, and the Nicholas Brothers also performed in the film. *Stormy Weather* featured "Negro entertainment from 1918 to 1943, seen through the eyes of its star, Robinson, and told in a series of entertainment sketches with Horne singing, Cab clowning, and Bojangles tapping"; the famous Lena Horne plays Robinson's love interest, but the plot is still "shamelessly illogical."[46] Despite the superficial plot, the dance routines provided satisfaction for audiences. The dancing Nicholas Brothers amazed the audience. Their energy "compensated for the movie's lack of substance"; after all, they were known for "their somersaults, flips, and twirls."[47] Nevertheless, Bogle insists, *Stormy Weather* is not considered one of the best films of 1943. Neither *Cabin in the Sky* nor *Stormy Weather* departed from the general roles bestowed on African Americans in Hollywood; however, *Stormy Weather* symbolized the peak of wartime escapism. Generally, movies with all-black casts were not featured in southern theaters; *Cabin in the Sky* and *Stormy Weather* broke this regional barrier by reaching southern audiences in all-black movie houses.

By the mid-1940s, Americans' fascination with the typical roles of blacks in musicals began to wane.[48] The deterioration in the quality of the performances and the films they worked in caused displeasure among audiences. At the end of World War II, many of the entertainers were overexposed and exploited. Bogle deems Walt Disney's *Song of the*

South (1946) the end of the public's fascination with musicals. Impressively, *Song of the South* featured "animated sequences interspersed throughout"; the setting of the story occurs on an Atlanta plantation; and as a familiar theme, the black servants are happily working on "magnificently photographed Technicolor work fields."[49] James Baskett plays the Uncle Remus character; famously, Uncle Remus is joyous as he sings among animated bluebirds, and butterflies whirl past his smiling face. The 1940s public did not dismiss this film as innocent; instead, they perceived the *Song of the South* as Disney's attempt to capitalize from Old South propaganda. Yet Hollywood never intended for the *Song of the South* to appeal to black audiences. The purpose of the film was to display Disney's specialty. In other words, the movie reflected whites' perception of African American males as inhabited by Uncle Remus. Nevertheless, the movie yielded a profit and Baskett earned a *special* Oscar for his performance.[50] However, two black organizations disavowed the film: the Manhattan Council of the National Negro Congress and the NAACP. The *Song of the South* presented the end of "the Negro as fanciful entertainer or comic servant"; for some time, Hollywood ignored the black servants and songs of African American entertainers.[51] Ironically, the 1940s also signaled the end of both Bojangles's and Fetchit's careers. Bojangles died in 1949. Meanwhile, Fetchit's popularity dissipated in the 1940s, but he appeared in *Harlem Follies of 1949* (1950), *Bend of the River* (1952), and *The Sun Shines Bright* (1953); Fetchit will not appear again in a movie until the 1970s with *Won Ton Ton, the Dog Who Saved Hollywood* (1976).[52] With the disinterest in comical and musical entertainment, Bojangles's and Fetchit's legacies suffer negative criticisms, as does the entertainment business that profited from their famous servile roles.

Stepin Fetchit: First Black Motion Picture Star

Despite his groundbreaking contribution to comedic movies, Lincoln "Stepin Fetchit" Perry died with little fanfare. Perry's wife, Bernice, died in January of 1985, and he died on November 19, 1985. Watkins reveals that "most of the comic's old show-business cronies were either sick, dead, or dying; it was a strikingly sparse and anticlimactic turnout for the funeral of an actor" who paved the way for many black movie stars.[53] During the eulogy, Perry was praised for his generosity; Perry once gave a producer $30,000 because he was having financial problems. Tragically, Perry died broke because he gave most of his money away. Both Robinson and Perry suffered from assaults on their legacy. However, Robinson continued to perform in the latter years of his life. Due to emotional disappointments and ailing health, Perry began to slow down as his popularity declined.[54]

In 1975, during a Ben Vereen performance, Vereen introduced Perry to the audience and they gave Perry a "five-minute standing ovation."[55] Vereen planned to dramatize Perry's life with a cinematic production; however, the project never materialized. Instead of revitalizing his career, Perry "spurned engagements" and preferred "staying at home and turning to his collection of clippings and photographs for comfort." Overwhelmed by the "rancor of his critics," Perry focused on the write-ups that diminished his contribution to Hollywood and he became intensely angry as "he often stormed to the telephone and resumed the dogged attempt to discredit his accusers and revive his reputation."[56] Ultimately, Perry's anger over disparagement against his legacy affected his health. He suffered a massive stroke on April 21, 1976. While Perry was recovering in the Michael Reese Hospital, he received "letters and calls from his fans and admirers and ordinary neighborhood people"; meanwhile, a "stream of entertainers and celebrities," such as Jack Carter, Ben Vereen, Muhammad Ali, and John Wayne, who had been friends with Fetchit for nearly 50 years, visited him.[57] Instantly, Perry was revived, "for an entertainer who had basked in the nation's applause and adulation for almost half a century, then fallen into disgrace and near-obscurity"; later, the flow of visitors died down and only "his wife, Bernice, his sister Marie Carter Perry," and a few other friends came by the hospital.[58] Surprisingly, Perry worried about how his roles were perceived by the public. Yet he never seemed concerned with how his roles shaped American culture's perception of black males and black culture. Fetchit had an alluring screen presence that still arouses more debate than Bojangles.

Nonetheless, Fetchit's humble beginnings are as intriguing as Bojangles's early years. On May 30, 1902, Stepin Fetchit was born and given the birth name Lincoln Theodore Monroe Andrew Perry; born in Key West, he would later say that his father named him after four presidents.[59] Perry claimed that his "youthful self-esteem" was attributed to his Caribbean background. Due to racial tensions in the early 1900s, Perry's family was cautious around whites; therefore they "resorted to a bit of subterfuge and trickery developed in Southern slave quarters as well as the West Indies—a survival tactic that would be sustained long after slaves were freed."[60] In essence, at an early age Perry learned how to manipulate, and he later realized how to profit from the outrageous antics and the racial stereotypes that he perpetrated. Like many contemporary celebrities, "he realized that even bad press sells—that notoriety can and often does confer power."[61] By his own admission, Perry was always in trouble and he frequently stole as a youth.[62] Thus young Perry did not show signs of the Hollywood star he was destined to become. But he did show signs of frequent bouts of real-life drama that would pervade his life as a celebrity. Before Perry became a star in the 1920s, blacks did not expect to succeed in the motion picture business; therefore Perry's ambitions did not reach beyond the New York stage.[63] For in the mid- to late teens, seeking work in the movie business "was about as unrealistic as seeking political office in the South"; yet Perry would elevate himself from performing in tent shows and carnivals to black-circuit theaters.[64] However, Perry's career would progress quickly past the small-time shows that pleased audiences. After Perry lit up the screen in *In Old Kentucky* (1927), his life and Hollywood changed forever.

Stepin Fetchit: The Tom and Coon Everyone Loves to Hate

If Perry was so popular, why does his Hollywood image remain sullied by his critics? Why are younger generations oblivious to his name? Prior to Perry's death, Hollywood attempted to honor him despite his controversial performances and subversive image. In 1976, Perry was awarded a Special Image Award for "his contribution to the evolution of black films" from the Hollywood chapter of the NAACP.[65] Furthermore, while Perry stayed in a convalescent care center, referred to as the Country Home, he was inducted into the Black Filmmakers Hall of Fame. Even that award was a qualified endorsement; the Oakland Museum Association stated clearly that Perry was inducted because he opened the doors for accomplished African American stars of the day. In other words, the Oakland Museum Association acknowledged Perry as a trailblazer, but they disavowed the negative depictions of blacks that he portrayed in his films.

As an elder, Perry barely resembled the "halting, mumbling, perpetually baffled character" or the onstage "wry, laconic, near-somnolent" caricature.[66] Much to Perry's dismay, the public was never able to disconnect the coon image from the roles he played. Nonetheless, Louis Armstrong once declared that "Step was 'born to be a star.' "[67] Also, Flip Wilson was a friend and a fan of Perry; he claimed that Perry's comic act was appropriate for the times and he was an important part of history.[68]

But the image of Fetchit did not grip contemporary African Americans in the same manner as before. In other words, Fetchit's "emblematic status as a symbol of slavery and black America's powerless past—was rapidly expanding" the consciousness of Americans. Fetchit's name symbolized "the era's worst sin: scraping or bowing before the white man"; and it was synonymous with words like "turncoat," "house nigger," and "Tom." These terms reflect "eighties vernacular … for any heretic who did not demonstratively display unquestioned allegiance to black assertiveness and resistance to even the mere appearance of white control."[69] Except for a passing reference, from the 1940s to 1970s most critics chose not to mention Fetchit. By the 1980s, Hollywood attempted to erase his image from most movies that he starred in, and generally his films were banned from television.[70] With the exception of film festivals and his placement in "the Library of Congress or other archival institutions" and now on YouTube, Fetchit is hard to find.[71] Fetchit's image humiliated middle-class Americans; however, a major portion of white America presumed that Fetchit represented the authentic "soul of black men." Fetchit's image was doomed as "filmland's infamous, servile 'coon' image, and for many it became the standard by which that image was measured."[72] Stepin Fetchit made a significant impact on popular culture. Politicians used the term "Stepin Fetchit" as a slur for African Americans who failed to represent the interests of their respective communities, and it was equated with the racial epithet Uncle Tom. Therefore Fetchit's stage and screen accomplishments were tarnished by "racial and political interpretation of his stage and screen character."[73]

But is it fair to diminish the significance of America's first motion picture star because his image is too troublesome? Unfortunately, Stepin Fetchit's image confirmed racist interpretations of African Americans "as, on one hand, slow, lazy, and stupid, and, on the other, as garish spendthrifts."[74] However, Stepin did not create these damaging stereotypes; they existed before he personally benefited from playing them onscreen. Movie stars such as Lionel Barrymore, Warner Baxter, and Will Rogers claimed Stepin "stole nearly every scene in which he appeared"; meanwhile, audiences were mesmerized by Stepin's "tantalizing slow movements, provoking pauses, quizzical expressions, and slurred, molasses-like, almost indecipherable speech, literally forced viewers to watch him."[75] Sadly, Stepin was a victim of his own success. He was typecast and locked into a character type despite changing times. Hollywood had a formula for success by utilizing Fetchit as the model coon caricature. Once his popularity began to subside in the 1940s, he appeared in only a few films in the early 1950s. Furthermore, Stepin demanded that he receive star treatment equal to his contemporaries; he wanted "better roles, and a salary equivalent with that of white actors."[76] This pompous behavior displeased studio executives, and ironically, Stepin's off-screen persona labeled him as a troublemaker or outright uppity Negro. Fox and other studios failed to support him once the critics zeroed in on his screen image even though the studios "reaped huge profits from the films in which he appeared."[77] Erroneously, Perry believed that Hollywood valued his worth as a performer. In no manner was Perry subservient to whites when the cameras were turned off. Instead, Perry's off-screen persona was more a firebrand than a tom or coon.

Basically, Perry was unlike the character type he played. The contrast between his on-screen and off-screen images proves that he was an incredible actor. Perry's genius was the charisma that he exuded on screen. Audiences wondered whether he was playing himself or a character.[78] Based on Perry's off-screen antics, his "cow tipping" performance was an act to please white audiences and studios. Off-screen, he was not afraid to speak up for himself when demanding better roles and more money. Quite honestly, Fetchit's professional and personal legacy is the double consciousness or the duality of the African American man living in America. Stepin's coon caricature was emblematic of the DuBoisian theory of white mask-black skin. Subsequently, in an effort to self-profit by appealing to white desires, Perry maintained the unapologetic archetype of a stereotypical tom and coon. Due to his desire to maintain white approval and love from the masses, his life's work was denied the proper placement in motion picture history during his life and at the time of his death. Perhaps if Fetchit had distanced himself from his past roles and evolved as an actor, he would have received his proper due in motion picture history.

Lincoln Perry: Proud Member of the Black Press

James Baldwin abhorred the character of Stepin Fetchit, according to Charlene Regester who writes about Perry in her essay entitled "Stepin Fetchit: The Man, the Image, and the African American Press."[79] Baldwin likened Fetchit to other characters portrayed by Willie Best. Baldwin insisted that Stepin failed to resemble any black person that he knew; however, Stepin's character was created to appeal to white audiences. As previously stated, Stepin mastered his self-deprecating humor to amuse whites and "soothe their fears and insecurities regarding the African American."[80] Ironically, late in Fetchit's life, the character and the man became inseparable; eventually, Fetchit's characterizations consumed him. What resulted is an "imitator who became his own imitation; the Fetchit who attempted to deceive audiences, ultimately became the Fetchit who deceived himself." Due to his inability to decipher his characterizations from his own identity, he became in real life the buffoon he brilliantly played.[81] As a journalist prior to his screen career, Perry was an advocate for positive film roles for blacks. Furthermore, he disparaged black actors who placed self-promotion over their responsibility to the community, while simultaneously praising studios for their fair treatment of black entertainers.

In the 1920s, Lincoln Perry served as an entertainment reporter for the *Chicago Defender*.[82] The name of his columns were "Lincoln Perry Writes," and "Lincoln Perry's Letter." Prior to Perry's contribution as a film critic, he was a stage performer in a duo act called "Step and Fetchit Act." In his articles, he often applauded the treatment that blacks received from Hollywood; furthermore, he noted how the producers, actors, and crew sat together without regard for color. But then Perry would add that the South could learn something from the level of integration he witnessed in Hollywood. Meanwhile, as Perry performed his duties in the black press, major studios were courting him as an actor.

Although Perry condemned various black performers for their stereotypical depictions, he later capitalized on playing these demeaning roles as Stepin Fetchit. One interesting internal conflict of Fetchit is on the issue of segregation. While he was limited to "dehumanizing portrayals on screen," he continued to voice his grievances off-screen with respect to discrimination.[83] To some critics, Fetchit's public face and personal choices were in deep conflict. Undoubtedly, this dichotomy caused many to doubt his sincere commitment to positive screen images for blacks. Fetchit's duality presented itself with his first major screen performance. Fetchit's breakout role was in the film *In Old Kentucky*.[84] Initially, Fetchit complained that he and his costar Carolyn Snowden were not given star credit for their groundbreaking performances; then Fetchit later praised Hollywood for the star treatment he received at the premiere for the movie. The *Chicago Defender* praised Fetchit and Snowden for opening the door of Hollywood for other race actors; after his role as High-Pockets, he received many offers to perform in motion pictures. Therefore he no longer had time to write his columns for the *Chicago Defender*. When Perry was a journalist, he was concerned about African American images on-screen. As an actor, he singularly cared for earning stardom and big money. The *Chicago Defender* published an article entitled "Actor Too Proud to Work in Films with Own Race.'"[85] Determined to respond to his critics, Perry chose to defend himself in the *Pittsburgh Courier*. Perry claimed that he had no problem working with an all-black cast, but there was less competition for him in terms of dialect and character when he worked with a white cast.[86] Therefore, if he was the token black actor in the film, his opportunity for recognition was heightened. Perhaps Perry should not have responded in this manner. He succeeded in confirming those who disparaged his self-serving performances and his negative role as a Hollywood sellout. Not only did Perry portray black males in a distorted way, he did not want other blacks to steer the spotlight away from him. Perry demonstrated no interest in helping other blacks gain entry or rise in the movie industry.

Another motion picture hit for Fetchit was *Hearts in Dixie* (1929).[87] This picture featured an all-black cast. Regester believes that money motivated his change of heart. Perry's salary was $1,500 a week, which made him one of the highest-paid black actors by the end of the 1920s. The black press fluctuated back and forth between positive and negative praise; nonetheless, they became concerned with his off-screen behavior because he was a "role model of sorts for black success in motion pictures and was criticized for self-indulgent behavior"[88]—for instance, having a public brawl with Bubbles of the famous team Buck and Bubbles. Antics such as this created a negative perception of black performers and their ability to get along with one another.

Another time, Perry once requested that the Cotton Club build a "special dressing room containing a bath and kitchen."[89] Despite Perry's off-screen temper tantrums, the *Chicago Defender* referred to Perry as natural-born comedian in the film *Fox Movietone Follies* (1929). But then the *Pittsburgh Courier* reported in 1930 that Perry was headed to court due to an arrest for drunk driving.[90]

Since the studios were aware of the negative news printed in the black press, these articles hurt Perry's image with the Hollywood studios. These public spectacles eventually escalated into bad behavior on the set. In 1931, he was fired from his role in *Lover Come Back* (1931) because of temperamental arguments with the director; after filing for bankruptcy in 1930, Perry disappeared from films from 1931 to 1934; and in 1930, Fetchit was facing two lawsuits, "one for breach of promise, the other for overdue rent."[91] The next year was a personal blow for Fetchit. Even his home life was placed in jeopardy because of his hot-tempered attitude. In her divorce suit, Fetchit's wife accused him of abuse.[92] Even though Fetchit had countless issues on-screen and off-screen, a film producer once said, "Although Fetchit portrayed a lazy character on the screen, he was indeed quite intelligent."[93] Simply put, Fetchit's undeniable talent resonated with each film performance despite his public and private persona.

Bill "Bojangles" Robinson and Lincoln "Stepin Fetchit" Perry wowed audiences with their talents and mass appeal. However, they witnessed their popularity subside in the 1940s. If Bojangles had not died of a heart attack in 1949, he probably would have kept performing on stage and television. At the age of 61, Robinson celebrated his "birthday publicly by dancing down 61 blocks of Broadway."[94] Bojangles's showmanship was a major part of his appeal as an artist. Sadly, Bojangles's reputation suffered because of the numerous subservient roles that he played. Although Robinson was celebrated by Hollywood, in his 14 films he "was not able to transcend the narrow range of stereotypical roles written for black actors at the time. By accepting these roles, Robinson was able to maintain steady employment and remain in the public eye."[95] Perhaps it is not fair to judge Robinson for the servant roles he played. Robinson's acting parts mirror America's perceptions of blacks in the 1930s and 1940s. Prior to the civil rights movement, Robinson's stardom exhibits the limitations placed on black stars in Hollywood. Some critics may consider Robinson to be the token Uncle Tom, but Perry occupies those shoes with less space for argument.

Among other black tokens in the industry, Robinson and Perry were often considered for the same roles; this caused competition and eventually animosity. According to the studios, Fetchit, Robinson, Clarence Muse, newcomer Jeni Le Gon, and Willie Best "were running neck and neck as fan favorites among Negro audiences."[96] Nevertheless, Perry continued to play roles that solidified his tom and coon image. Fetchit's role in *David Harum* (1934) is particularly demeaning because Will Rogers's character sold him along with the horse he owned.[97] But Perry was a mastermind in terms of his career. Perry understood black agency because he fostered his relationship with the powerful entertainer Will Rogers. When Perry fell out of favor with studios, "Stepin Fetchit's comeback and newfound acceptance in Hollywood was largely due to Rogers's taking the actor under his wing."[98] Once Fetchit returned to Hollywood, he received parts in four films starring Rogers. Ultimately, their on-screen chemistry translated into box office success in terms of white and black audiences. As expected, once Rogers died, Perry was up to his old antics as he complained "about hearing problems and headaches" on the set of *The Littlest Rebel* starring Shirley Temple and Robinson.[99] In actuality, Perry was content to be the token black actor in each film. Fetchit's problems on the set of *The Littlest Rebel* were caused by his rivalry with Robinson; Perry could not bear to share the spotlight with another black actor.[100] As Robinson's popularity increased, Perry's on-set tantrums "reflected the egocentric, star-fixed side of Fetchit's personality."[101] Perry was unable to see that there was room for more than one black star. Despite Robinson's and Perry's talents, fame, and money, neither performer was able to transition into acting roles that demonstrated acting range or latitude. Thus the tom and coon label will remain; neither man spoke out publicly against the limitations placed on black actors. Bojangles and Stepin Fetchit fought happily to maintain their token status. Persistently, they played their typecast subservient roles with little deviation. Quite frankly, both actors achieved heights that were not foreshadowed based on their humble beginnings. But despite their passion for the entertainment industry, their popularity declined. Ultimately, in the 1940s, white and black audiences lost interest in the musicals and the comedies that presented the same old types, performing the same old song and dance and comic routines. With the 1950s, America was ready for black character actors, such as Canada Lee and Paul Robeson, but society was not ready for their activism.

CHAPTER 5

——— 1950s ———
McCarthyism and Blacklisting:
Canada Lee and Paul Robeson

Before Sidney Poitier graced the screen in the 1950s and 1960s, the magnetic radio and Broadway star Canada Lee was a rising black star in Hollywood. In terms of the public's readiness for an emerging yet outspoken black star, a decade makes a significant difference. Poitier and Lee would cross paths both personally and professionally. But according to Mona Z. Smith, the author of *Becoming Something: The Story of Canada Lee*, he vigorously confronted his critics who focused on his politics rather than his artistry. With a small role in *Keep Punching* (1939), Lee played a boxer in his first movie.[1] Also, Lee played the Rev. Stephen Kumalo in *Cry, the Beloved Country* (1952), which was Poitier's second film.[2] Due to his untimely death, Lee never had the opportunity to impact the film industry the way he influenced Broadway. Perhaps years of stress caused by the blacklisting efforts of Hoover's FBI, McCarthyism, and the House Un-American Activities Committee (HUAC) led to his early death at the age of 45, in 1952. With great effort, Lee incessantly tried to clear his name with the public via the media.[3] However, Lee's efforts failed to lift the veil of suspicion from his name. Since 1943, the FBI maintained a file on Lee and contemplated "custodial detention as well as prosecution on charges that he had violated sedition laws."[4] The FBI firmly believed that Lee was either a Communist or a Communist sympathizer; therefore they were determined to keep a close watch on his activities. According to HUAC, Lee had been involved with "twenty-one organizations cited as Communist fronts by either the Attorney General or congressional committees on un-American activities."[5] Many of Lee's supporters believed that the government's persistent surveillance of him resulted in health problems that led to his death.

Although his doctor stated that Lee's kidneys failed, his death was attributed to a heart attack; however, a few "papers linked Canada's illness and death to the blacklist."[6] Furthermore, the media also discussed how "Lee had been Red-baited ... for his links to alleged Communist fronts, his stands on civil rights and First Amendment issues, and his attacks on the Un-American Activities Committee."[7] Various activities of Lee received scrutiny from HUAC, such as the Freedom Train controversy and his objection to the HUAC spy hearings. Moreover, Lee's opposition to "the arrests of Ben Davis and other Communists; a speech at an anti-Franco demonstration; his membership in a group of artists and scientists calling for a world conference on peace and international cooperation; and his sponsorship of a rally to end segregation and discrimination" were documented by HUAC.[8] Initially, Lee came to the attention of HUAC in 1943 for starring in a "radio play about racial harmony sponsored by the YMCA."[9] For HUAC, the quest for racial equality and social justice was a threat to the American establishment. Thus social activists were treated with the same suspicion as Communists, who were deemed an extreme threat to American democracy. Nonetheless, there were journalists who warned against equating Communism with left-wing liberalism. Furthermore, they suggested that this overzealous hunt for Communists posed a threat to civil liberties. After the *Times* reported on the famous Coplon spy trial, the newspaper urged caution that well-meaning liberals were being unfairly swooped into the attacks against "dishonest Communists"; and the *Times* urged that "paranoia over Communist propaganda" should not inhibit "freedom of thought and freedom of speech."[10] Nevertheless, Lee's social activism fed into the government's paranoia and he was named as a Communist along with his close friend Paul Robeson.[11]

Lee vehemently denied accusations of Communist membership to "editors of newspapers and influential news and trade magazines."[12] In 1949, the influential Ed Sullivan "picked up the accusations made during the Coplon trial and condemned Canada as a Communist sympathizer."[13] With respect to Ed Sullivan's condemnation, Canada Lee declared to Sullivan that he was not a Communist; instead, he asserted that he was being harassed by anti-Negro groups who were threatened by his fight for social justice. Just as Stepin Fetchit's relationship with Will Rogers proved beneficial to his career, Lee shared a professional and personal bond with Ed Sullivan. Early in Lee's career as a prize fighter and then as a stage actor, Sullivan supported Lee in the media. Needless to say, Lee was shocked and betrayed when his friend publicly denounced their friendship. After all, Sullivan was "a powerful force in shaping public opinion."[14] Lee pleaded with Sullivan in a letter; he was verbally outspoken because he was a voice for blacks and opposed racist groups, such as the Ku Klux Klan.[15] Nevertheless, Lee's declaration in the *New York Times* would seal his fate with conservatives; for instance, Lee insisted that "he would continue to fight for civil rights, regardless of whether the Communist Party was involved or not."[16] For conservatives, Lee's willingness to support causes even when backed by Communists was disloyal and un-American. But Carl Lee, Ben's son, does not view his father's proclamation in the *Times* as unpatriotic to the American government. Ben believes that his father was a proud man who refused to be controlled by the blacklist machine. Thus he had no intention of acquiescing to the demands of his detractors. Courageously, in life, Lee's integrity forced him to battle the blacklist machine. However, the movement surrounding Communist paranoia undermined Lee's civil rights efforts, curtailed his career, and soured the perception of his professional achievements following his death.

Unfortunately, the legacies of both Paul Robeson and Canada Lee have been tainted by the blacklist machine; therefore their activists' roles in life, on stage, in writings, and in the movies have been sullied by their association with Communism. At the time Robeson and Lee first corresponded in the 1930s, Robeson was already an international star and Lee was a stage star on the rise. Perhaps to their detriment, by 1944 their ill-fated alliance would implicate both of them professionally and personally. Both gentlemen "were friends and colleagues, fellow activists and frequent collaborators, not to mention former neighbors at the exclusive Sugar Hill address in Harlem, 555 Edgecombe."[17] Unlike Bojangles and Stepin Fetchit, they were not adversaries or contemporaries and held no animosity or jealousy for each other's achievements. Moreover, contrary to Bojangles or Stepin Fetchit, they were unwilling to play the tom or coon role in life or in film; hence, Robeson and Lee were targeted as un-American and unpatriotic. In this chapter, examination of Canada Lee will determine how his friendship with Paul Robeson and his support of various social causes adversely affected his career, and how his misguided affiliation with Communists, his passion for civil rights activism, and his refusal to play the tom or coon role caused him to remain on the blacklist.

Red Scare Blacklisting: McCarthy, Media, and Hollywood

How did the rabid hunt for Communist infiltration become an era of blacklisting, shunning, and censoring members of the Hollywood community? In February 1950, Joe McCarthy, the Republican junior senator from Wisconsin, pronounced that more than 200 Communists were occupying positions in the State Department. For this sudden pronouncement, he received headlines in the newspapers "and power in his campaign to thwart what he called the Communist infiltration of American life."[18] After he was reelected to the Senate in 1952, he held endless hearings accusing American citizens of disloyalty to their government with little or no evidence to substantiate his claims. McCarthy was not alone in his efforts to blacklist perceived and actual threats to America's democracy. Hoover's FBI conducted investigations into average citizens, government workers, activists, and members of Hollywood from the 1950s to the 1960s. Nevertheless, McCarthy's sphere of influence was widespread in the 1950s. The government, media, and Hollywood were persuaded to convict, imprison, fire, or destroy the careers of the accused; thus McCarthyism can be defined "as a method, a tactic, an attitude, a tendency, a mood, an hysteria, an ideology, and a philosophy."[19] The blacklisting period of the McCarthy era, "in which friend betrayed friend, remains one of the darkest episodes in Hollywood's history."[20] Sadly, during this era people were afraid to associate with others based on unproven accusations. Furthermore, friendships were destroyed because people feared for their economic and physical well-being. Lastly, burgeoning careers were disrupted because performers, like Lee and Robeson, refused to back down from those who mistook the fight for social equality as support for Communism in America.

During this bleak era of the 1950s and 1960s, the Writers Guild of America complacently failed to support their accused members. For that reason, the memory of those careers and lives ruined by the blacklist still torments Hollywood. In an attempt to make amends, 50 years later the Guild announced that they were "restoring the credits on 23 films written by blacklisted screenwriters"; sadly, members of the Guild who were placed on the blacklist received no credit for their work during those years.[21] Oftentimes, artists accused of having Communist sympathies wrote their screenplays under pseudonyms, names of relatives, or friends. Due to the witch hunts and Cold War hysteria, these artists were forced to hide their true identity to aid in their anonymity. Realistically, they could not expect protection from their unions or studios with regard to this government-sanctioned intimidation. Reminiscent of the supporters of the Hays Moral Code era, Hollywood's studio executives played a major role in the censorship of their own industry. Writers, actors, and other members of the Hollywood were coerced by their own studios into cooperating with the House committee to reveal names of Communists and Communist sympathizers. When people refused to participate in the witch hunt, they were fired from their position. People who "flirted with Communism in their youth, or signed petitions [were] considered too left-wing. Careers—and lives—were destroyed."[22] Other than McCarthy, the Hollywood studios, and the unions, who else contributed to the Red Scare in Hollywood? Many people blame the media for their encouragement and support of blacklisting in their newspapers. Initially, very few newspapers had the courage to question the practice of blacklisting or rebuke the harm it caused to individual's careers, lives, and families. Judging by Lee's desperate attempt to clear his name in the newspapers, entertainers were aware that the media had the power to sway the public's tide for or against their professional and personal interests.

As previously stated, most people associate Senator Joseph McCarthy with the Hollywood blacklisting era, but he is not the first and the only person to lead this heinous practice. However, "if not for the first and subsequent blacklists ... McCarthy might have never had the ability to begin his four-year reign of often baseless accusation, which began in earnest in 1950."[23] Oftentimes, people wonder why artists were the main target of McCarthy's Red Scare obsession. More than likely, he realized the power Hollywood wielded to shape public opinion and influence government policy. Consequently, he feared that Hollywood propaganda threatened the stability of America's institutions and infrastructure. Possibly, McCarthy feared the Red infiltration could result in the overthrow of the American government. Various industry giants like "Walt Disney and Ronald Reagan, then the head of the Screen Actors Guild, testified before the committee about the communist menace" within the industry.[24] Did Disney and Reagan sincerely believe that Communists were infiltrating the industry? Was this testimony for the purpose of protecting their careers and legacies? Or were these industry giants simply trying to gain favor with other powerful people? The answers to these questions are unclear. However, there were actors bold enough to oppose the methods and intentions behind McCarthyism. Stars such as "Humphrey Bogart and Lauren Bacall, who were members of the left-leaning Committee for the First Amendment," risked their livelihoods to speak up for civil liberties; Bogart and Bacall boldly "traveled to Washington to stand up for their colleagues, though ultimately" their advocacy lacked success.[25] However, their careers were not harmed by their refusal to name names. Yet the Hollywood Ten would suffer a different fate for their reluctance to cooperate with HUAC.

Perhaps the infamous Hollywood Ten is one of the most disturbing segments of the McCarthy era. This dark episode in American history exemplifies the power of McCarthy and his government henchmen. As part of an investigation, the Hollywood Ten was forced to attend a hearing held by McCarthy's HUAC in November 1947. The investigation sought to determine whether Communists and Communist sympathizers were sub-liminally placing propaganda into their movies. When the Hollywood Ten chose not to testify before HUAC, they were sentenced to one year in prison. Instead of condemning these proceedings as unpatriotic, the president of the Motion Picture Association of America (MPAA), Eric Johnston, released his two-page Waldorf Statement on November 25 condemning the men.[26] Essentially, the Waldorf Statement banned them from working in Hollywood.

On behalf of 48 movie executives, Billy Wilkerson's column in the *Hollywood Reporter* published the Waldorf statement. The publication pronounced "that the 10 Hollywood men who had been cited for con-tempt by the House of Representatives" were banned from the business.[27] Unless the accused Communists purged themselves of the charges and stated under oath that they were not members of the Communist Party, they would not work in Hollywood. Ironically, none of the Ten "is known to have ever worked or advocated for the violent overthrow of the U.S."; nonetheless, some members of the Ten were actually Communists.[28] The *Hollywood Reporter* was not the only entity to create a blacklist: "Red Channels, a pamphlet published by an anti-communist, right-wing journal called Counterattack, included 151 names when it was released in June 1950. The American Legion, a conservative veterans group, distrib-uted a list of more than 100 people to the studios in 1949, and HUAC also put out annual reports that included rosters of alleged communists."[29] The aforementioned list proves that the media, organizations, veterans, the government, and Hollywood worked in concert to root out all of the sup-posed Communist threats to democracy. After decades of reflection, the hys-teria caused by McCarthyism has been deeply criticized. Today, many people question why the media and studio executives participated in the blacklisting made infamous by McCarthy's committee.

Willie, Billy Wilkerson's son, believes that his father, the founder of the *Hollywood Reporter*, blamed Hollywood for "his own failure to set up a studio on the East Coast in 1927"; furthermore, Wilkerson sought retri-bution because he believed that "the Hollywood moguls" ruined "his dis-tribution efforts."[30] Is it possible that Wilkerson's lack of movie success caused him to render vengeance on an entire industry? Perhaps, but there are other compelling theories for Wilkerson's obsession with blacklisting in Hollywood. Blacklisted writers and actors, including Willie, "view Wilkerson as a shadowy, organized-crime-connected figure who ran roughshod over Hollywood and used his column as a bully pulpit to ruin people's lives for his personal gain."[31] Some suggest that Wilkerson's relationships with various gangsters played a part in his vindication against Hollywood; in the past, these crime figures were known to assist in antilabor practices such as busting unions and ending strikes for businesses.

After all, Wilkerson is credited as the pioneering driver of the blacklist; he strived to pay back the movie moguls via accusing their screenwriters of Communist affiliation. Since the 1930s, Wilkerson engaged in onslaught of attacks against the Screen Writers Guild. His primary issue with them was their refusal to pays fees for advertising in his paper; thus he responded by not giving screenwriters their credit alongside the directors in his *Hollywood Reporter*. Nevertheless, the Academy of Motion Picture Arts and Sciences also played a decisive role in blacklisting. Moreover, in the 1950s, the Academy "would be an accessory to the Blacklist by passing a bylaw that made it impossible for those who invoked the Fifth Amendment in front of HUAC to be nominated for an Oscar."[32] Then there are theories that Wilkerson's opposition to Communism was based on the antireligious stance and the atheism of Communism, which he considered to be an insult to his Roman Catholic faith.

Among desires for revenge and religious concerns, as early as November 5, 1947, Wilkerson called for an industry-enforced blacklist against anyone who espoused liberal ideals; anyone who had views to the left of President Harry Truman was referred to as a "commie." In other words, in this Red Scare era, if individuals espoused liberal principals they were deemed outsiders, un-American, and worthy of surveillance. Then there were those who rewarded people for turning against others. For naming names, Wilkerson received payment, and Howard Hughes was one of those individuals who was willing to reward him. Meanwhile, Wilkerson's other ally in the fight against Communism was the FBI director J. Edgar Hoover. Wilkerson claims that McCarthy "dialed his father, asking him how he'd pieced together his data."[33] Apparently, neither Hoover nor McCarthy cared about Wilkerson's criminal affiliations. Wilkerson's complex history with "organized crime figures of the era, from Meyer Lansky and Mickey Cohen to union enforcers such as Willie Bioff and George E. Browne" and "Bugsy Siegel who became his business partner" in terms of the Flamingo they co-owned in Las Vegas was no cause for their alarm.[34]

Imagine the terror caused by the determination of powerful men such as Wilkerson, Hoover, and McCarthy in their efforts to root out Communism. For a time, these men operated with impunity. Ironically, condemning people based on unfounded and unproven accusations was the most un-American practice perpetrated by HUAC and their supporters.

Americans should know that the widespread impact of blacklisting affected thousands of lives; for instance, at least "300 people were formally named to various public lists including Red Channels and HUAC's own official tallies."[35] Unfortunately, others suffered, from "spouses to siblings and secretaries, [who] similarly found themselves crippled by their graylisting— whether through whisper campaigns or unofficial outings in publications like *THR*."[36] People who could not find work in Hollywood chose "to work under pseudonyms (an impossibility for actors) or with fronts (the non-blacklisted, whose clean names were used in place of the damned)."[37] Other performers found refuge by working in Europe. Nevertheless, on the basis of fear or a careless or intentional rumor, Hollywood would sever contracts, and lives were disrupted by the Red Scare.

The reign of terror would not last forever. Once McCarthy attempted to implicate the U.S. Army, Americans began to question the merits of his Communist findings. McCarthy's overreach and domination would no longer continue in America. The Army-McCarthy hearings of 1954 led to the end of his reign; the televised hearings delved into the "set of charges leveled by McCarthy against the Army and vice versa."[38] McCarthy was unable to hide his unstable temperament under the guise of American pride. During the hearings, McCarthy's personality was revealed "as a loudmouthed dissembler and bully, and his popularity plummeted. In December 1954 the Senate censured him."[39] Even though the government would no longer tolerate McCarthy and his false accusations, the era of blacklisting and intimidation would continue in the government and in Hollywood. Under the direction of Hoover's FBI, the government continued to engage in surveillance of its citizens.[40] Unfortunately for Lee, he had McCarthy's HUAC and Hoover trailing him as he took his crusade for justice to Hollywood. In many ways, Lee was ahead of his time. Prior to the civil rights movement, he declared his pride in his African American heritage. Also, he realized that the media and Hollywood were a means to transform society. Yet, as Lee fought for people to "enjoy the full benefits of democracy, the rights and freedoms guaranteed them as American citizens," the U.S. government perceived him as an enemy of the state.[41]

Canada Lee: Caribbean Roots and Boxing Dreams

Clearly, Lee's personal background is the foundation for his pride as an African American and black male. Although Lee had Caribbean roots and money troubles as a youth, his background is somewhat different from Lincoln Perry's upbringing. Lee's father, James, was an activist who helped "A. Philip Randolph organize Pullman Porters and supported campaigns against poll taxes, lynching, and the Ku Klux Klan."[42] Also, Lee's paternal ancestors "survived the dangerous three-month passage from Africa's Gold Coast to the West Indies."[43] Furthermore, Lee's grandfather, James C. Canegata, was a "literate and ambitious man with an entrepreneurial spirit."[44] According to Smith, "he built a fleet of small merchant ships that sailed between St. Croix and American ports, becoming one of the wealthiest black merchants in the Virgin Islands."[45] Based on Lee's strongly rooted Caribbean ancestry and personal history, it is clear why as an adult Lee was unable to accept the second-class citizenship in America. But despite the social obstacles presented in America, the United States held an attraction for Lee's Caribbean father, James.

Once James reached adulthood, he moved to New York; consequently, James's rich father disinherited him.[46] Since Lee's uncle David became a successful doctor and still lived in the Caribbean, Lee's paternal grandfather left everything to David. James was a rebellious soul and was not afraid to defy tradition. When he married a southern black woman, he defied customary practice by not wedding a woman of Caribbean heritage.[47] Leonard Lionel Cornelius Canegata (Canada Lee) was the firstborn child of three. Despite Canada's stable home, he ran away at the age of 14 to become a jockey.[48] Discouraged by the violent discrimination in the field of horseracing, he returned home at the age of 16.[49] Although his parents were warm and loving to their prodigal son, if he wanted to stay in their home now, he was expected to help the family by paying some bills.[50]

Eventually, Lee pursued boxing and made $90,000 in the 1920s. But as a prizewinning boxer, he spent his money by hanging out with "musicians, star athletes, and other celebrities."[51] His eyesight would signal the end of his boxing career. During his twenties, Lee was forced to abandon the ring because he was now half-blind, and he had "an estranged wife and young son to support."[52] Furthermore, he had squandered the funds he made during his boxing career. Therefore he was forced to reinvent himself with a different career. Once Lee transitioned from boxing to the stage, he became a star as the lead in various plays: *Native Son*, *Macbeth*, and *Othello*.

Canada Lee: *Lifeboat, Body and Soul, Lost Boundaries,* and *Cry, the Beloved*

Early on in Lee's career, he realized that his stage success could promote social change. Thus the FBI kept a file on him since 1943. But once Lee began to transition from the stage to the screen, in 1939 with *Keep*

Punching, his sphere of influence had the potential to widen exponentially. After all, Lee had broken "a color barrier by becoming the first black man to produce a straight play on Broadway, and he urged other artists of color to back meaningful projects."[53] Based on Lee's stage achievements, he would have been a major force in Hollywood had he lived past the McCarthy years. Even though most of his movies were filmed during the 1940s, the progressive motivations behind his movies offered unwelcome leftist propaganda. Sadly, Lee appeared in only five movies before his untimely death in 1952. Nevertheless, every one of those films made political statements that surely caught the unwelcome interest of the FBI and HUAC.

Lee is most well known for his film role as Joe Spencer in *Lifeboat* (1944). John Steinbeck, the author of the classic novels *Of Mice and Men* (1937) and *Grapes of Wrath* (1939), wrote the novella and the original screenplay for Alfred Hitchcock's film *Lifeboat*.[54] Nevertheless, Steinbeck expressed disappointment in the changes in terms of Canada Lee's character, and the movie's disparagement toward organized labor. Steinbeck was so perturbed by these deviations from his original script that he wanted his name to be removed from the credits.[55] But the studio refused to adhere to the famous writer's requests for modifications; instead, they promoted the film with posters and flyers featuring Lee in the back of the boat. By positioning Lee behind the other actors, it signaled to the audience that Lee's role was minor and of less importance than the other characters in the film. Along with Steinbeck, Lee was also disheartened by the studio's manner of promoting the film.

In contrast to the original novella and script, Lee "was not as shocked as Steinbeck. Still, he realized Joe had ended up a minor, though hopefully memorable, character."[56] As usual, Lee held his composure of poise and charm in public, but in private he was disappointed. Once Lee made the complete transition from stage to film, he expected that he would play strong characters like he played on stage. Nevertheless, it is unclear how Lee's character transformed into a racist stereotype. Is it because the scenes exemplifying the dynamic aspects of Lee's character were cut or were the scenes never shot by the director? In Hitchcock's defense, he disagreed with Darryl F. "Zanuck over cuts, arguing they would harm the integrity of the film."[57] Negative criticism referred to the film as "anti-Negro, anti-American, or anti-democracy" due to the heroism depicted by the Nazi ship captain; perhaps the public was swayed by these disparaging critiques because the movie had mediocre box-office receipts.[58] Still, Hollywood rewarded Hitchcock with an Oscar nomination for best director. However, when Lee spoke on the radio with Malcolm Child, a film commentator on WABF, Lee's biographer claims that he caught the attention of HUAC and the FBI. When asked about the movie *Lifeboat*, he responded by discussing the power structure, equality, and justice for blacks. For HUAC and the FBI, Lee's left-wing politics made him a model candidate for blacklisting. Clearly, they feared the power he yielded as a powerful black male. Prior to Lee's sudden death, he was in the process of transforming American culture with his activism and performance on film.

Lee was a proud black man. His self-assured nature discomforted the government and members of the establishment. Due to his patriotism and his tenacious "battle against racism, including pervasive stereotyping in arts and entertainment," he blasted Broadway producers and Hollywood studios for their depictions of African Americans.[59] Lee had no tolerance for the "crap-shooting, eye rolling characterizations of Negroes on stage and screen"; consequently, Hitchcock's team assured Lee that as the black sailor Joe (Merchant Marine), his character would be treated as an equal.[60] As previously stated, this statement lacked veracity. At the time of these empty assurances, Lee was preparing for a monologue about black sailors written by the legendary poet Langston Hughes. The performance *Sailor Ashore* occurred "at the anti-Jim Crow 'Negro Freedom Rally' in Madison Square Garden."[61] Because Lee was interested in achieving the same success in movies that he had acquired on Broadway, he was lured into the *Lifeboat* project with specific guarantees. He was told that his character would have dignity and that the story had thoughtful, political themes. Early on, Lee understood the importance of working with accomplished writers and directors. For the chance to perform in a script written by John Steinbeck and a film directed by Alfred Hitchcock, he decided to accept the offer. From Lee's perspective, the final cut of the movie failed to reflect the purported intentions of Hitchcock. Lee felt betrayed once he saw the film; his character reflected submissive values that he could not support. In the end, Joe's dialogue made him sound like a subservient Uncle Tom. Since Lee was an activist and a performer, this portrayal of Joe the steward was entirely unacceptable and left his expectations of screen grandeur a dream deferred.

Despite the professional disappointment, Lee received a personal benefit from his recent movie performance. Behind the scenes, he felt welcome by most Hollywood performers. He found off-screen friendships with almost everyone except Walter Slezak (Nazi U-boat captain).[62] Intentionally, Slezak made incendiary comments as he attempted to remind Lee of his second-class status in America. Yet Lee was never goaded into a verbal or physical confrontation. Despite Slezak's constant lamentations over not having been born in the era of slavery, Lee maintained his class and composure; since he was new to Hollywood, he wanted everyone to remember him as a dignified actor and gentleman.[63] Like Paul Robeson, Lee understood the importance of his on-screen and off-screen image. Thus the same personal pride that made other performers appreciate Lee's grace is the same pride that made *Lifeboat* a professional disappointment.

Jonathan J. Cavallero launches some similar criticisms against Hitchcock's *Lifeboat* in his essay "Hitchcock and Race: Is the Wrong Man a White Man?" The action in *Lifeboat* occurs when Joe Spencer (Canada Lee) is stranded in a German U-boat "with a group of white survivors."[64] Willy (Walter Slezak) is the Nazi captain of the U-boat that causes the shipwreck of the Americans. Cavallero claims that Hitchcock "upholds the dominant culture's widely held beliefs of racial difference even as he questions them."[65] For instance, Joe's comrades are astonished by the fact that he has a family; they seemed surprised that his black identity does not preclude him from living like the average American. When Joe is asked to participate in a vote to determine the fate of the Nazi captain, this action draws attention to the disparities "of American democracy during World War II"; nevertheless, Joe falls into a stereotypical mode of societal expectations when he opts to abstain from the voting.[66] Thus Joe's abstention proves that Hitchcock had no intention of challenging stereotypes; instead, he glosses over issues of race and renders cursory treatment of the subject matter. Hitchcock flirts "with making strong political statements about the place of race and ethnicity in American society and Hollywood film," but he avoids the topic as major theme of this movie.[67]

Even though Hitchcock's treatment of race is superficial and stereotypical in *Lifeboat*, he is not far behind other Hollywood producers who feigned progressiveness on the issue. Various other classic movies failed to enlighten the audience to the level of their initial intentions. John Nickel writes in an essay entitled "Disabling African American Men: Liberalism and Race Message Films" that "the race-disability films illustrate the promises and pitfalls of liberalism during the postwar era: its potential to engender progressive ideas on racial issues and its ability to recirculate demeaning myths about African Americans."[68] From the 1940s to 1960s, movies with race messages often characterized African American men "as disabled or equated" them "with disabled white Americans."[69] Progressive for their era, movies such as *Body and Soul* (1947), *Bright Victory* (1951), *To Kill a Mockingbird* (1962), and *A Patch of Blue* (1965) feature this prominent theme. In the late 1940s, among other issues the country was still plagued by a practice of lynchings, poll taxes, and unfair employment; thus liberals considered the movies to be "a powerful instrument of reform in social conscience films, an opportunity to mix propaganda and popcorn."[70] These movies did not address race from a black authentic perspective. Instead, they approached poignant themes from a white sympathetic perspective.

Whites were the target audience for their race message movies. Ideally, liberal filmmakers hoped to transform America by appealing to the consciences of white Americans. In a racially divided country, white writers, directors, and producers determined this method was the best way to affect social change. Therefore Robert Rosen relies on the disability motif to provoke compassion for black issues of social injustice. Central to Rossen's protest against the practice of lynching in *Body and Soul* is black impairment.[71] In 1946, when United Artists released the movie, six African Americans were the victims of lynching. Perhaps the propaganda in the movies had an effect on the consciences of white Americans.

For the first time in 71 years, 6 years after *Body and Soul*, there was no news of a lynching in America. Although Rossen addresses the subject of lynching indirectly, the boxing movie utilizes the fatal disability of a character to manifest a vicious racial act. At the inception of the movie, "a punching bag at a boxing camp outside New York City is hanging from a tree branch, swaying in the wind. In the next scene, we see Charlie Davis (John Garfield), the white welterweight champion, waking up in bed in a cold sweat, gasping, 'Ben.' "[72] In a series of flashbacks, the audience learns that Charlie suffers from the guilt of beating his former boxing opponent and friend Ben Chaplin (Canada Lee). Unfortunately, as Charlie is aggressively engaging in his fight with Ben, he is not aware that his friend is suffering from a blood clot. Consequently, Charlie's overzealousness nearly kills Ben. To assuage his guilt, Charlie asks Ben to work in his boxing corner for his next fight. However, Charlie's good intentions receive opposition from criminal interests. Mr. Roberts, the same gangster who hid Ben's health condition, wants Charlie to throw his next fight. Ben cannot resist forewarning Charlie, which results in Ben's tragic downfall. When the gangster hears Ben speaking to Charlie, he tries to erode Ben's credibility by telling "Ben his head is 'soft' and threatens to kill him if he does not leave the camp immediately."[73] But Ben is unwilling to abandon his friend. He refuses to go, yet falls and hits his head, but then rises up. With a dramatic flair, Ben "begins shadow-boxing uncontrollably before collapsing and dying on the canvas, surrounded by white onlookers, including Charlie."[74] Instead of simulating a lynching, Rossen invokes the image of a punching bag swinging from a tree. In essence, the symbol of Ben's tragic life transcends him into Christ-like martyrdom status in death. Thus Ben's sudden death offers salvation for Charlie's spirit. Inspired by Ben's sacrifice and devotion to him, Charlie wins the fight that the gangster wanted him to throw. Ultimately, Charlie is rebuking Mr. Roberts, the gangster.

The director Rossen is delivering the message that good deeds prevail over the will of evil men. Symbolically, vicious racists are denied triumph; progressive values are redeemed but at a mortal cost. *Body and Soul* is one of several liberal movies in which the passing or near passing of a black character functions as a spiritual sacrifice for the white race. Once the tragedy or near tragedy of a good black character occurs, the leading white character reflects on his own faults. As a result of this introspection, the white character realizes his inadequacies as a human being. Therefore his individual redemption reestablishes moral order for American society. Even though the liberal propaganda movie has positive intentions, some critics view these progressive attempts to heal racial relationships with a skeptical eye.

After starring in progressive productions, such as *Lifeboat* and *Body and Soul*, Lee starred in *Lost Boundaries* (1949), which claimed to deal with racial issues. This time the producers address the theme of "passing" with a lack of authenticity. But there is a disingenuous element to these supposedly social conscious "passing" movies. For the most part, "passing" as a way of life was not a viable alternative for most African Americans. Generally, most blacks are visually identifiable. Thus, while some blacks may engage in passing, they utilize this option because their visible racial status is ambiguous.[75] To successfully pass, there was an element of secrecy because some states made passing a crime.[76] In other words, individuals had to abandon family, disconnect from their racial heritage, and live somewhere else as a white person. Although there were black actors with racially ambiguous features, Hollywood did not choose actual actors who could authentically pass.

In an effort to satisfy requirements of the Production Code Administration, blacks who had the skin tone and/or features to play these passing roles were passed over. White actors who supposedly had black features won these parts in passing movies. Basically, a progressive movie about fair-skinned African Americans living in white spaces morphs into a movie with white actors imitating their perception of blackness. Thus passing movies fail to combat the racism they advocate against. Hollywood duplicates "racial hierarchy through performance, and industry practices," which effectively maintains discrimination and perpetuates inequality.[77] Ironically, the pervasive racism in Hollywood reflects the disparities in American society. Thus the act of casting a visibly black actor becomes a progressive act, even when the role is stereotypical, monolithic, or minor. Nevertheless, casting visibly black actors of Canada Lee's acting caliber in minor roles while offering major roles to whites demonstrates a historical bias in the industry. Despite the movie industry's desire to appear objective, the hierarchical practices that limited the roles of black actors reveals conscious and subconscious racism. In actuality, Hollywood had no plans of offering blacks major roles; "the industry practice of racial exclusion in passing films shows that Hollywood had no desire to create racial equality in films or hiring practices."[78] In essence, the "hegemonic notions of whiteness" continued Hollywood's practice of "Whites only casting."[79] Unfortunately for Lee, he was ahead of his time by combating the hegemonic practices of Hollywood and he would never live to see racial barriers broken in the industry.

Canada Lee's presence in *Lost Boundaries*, as an exceptional black, manifests a redemptive opportunity for a white character. In other words, Lee's supporting role in this "passing" film bolstered industry intentions to glorify the desirability of whiteness and the trepidation caused by blackness. When the two siblings, Howie and his sister, Shelly, discover they are African American, this new information transforms their temperament, their appearance, and/or their perception of themselves.[80] How does the discovery of black ancestry transform a socially acclimated character into a state of self-hatred? Is the devastation conveyed by the adult children a result of feeling betrayed by their parents? Or are the children exhibiting the shame caused by their blackness? The movie fails to address the issues that result from self-hatred, racial denial, and the social stigma associated with blackness. To some Americans, Howie's response to the revelation of his black identity is nonsensical and melodramatic.

After Howie learns about his African American heritage, he travels to Harlem to study black people. As a result of his encounter with blacks, Howie goes home and has a terrifying nightmare. His ambiguously white-looking family has recently transformed into a visibly black-looking family.[81] To many blacks and some whites, this manifestation of Howie's identity crisis appears irrational. Appealing to white fears of blackness, this vision dissolves him into "a disheveled and disoriented young man."[82] Overcome by sleeplessness, Howie heads back to Harlem for his continued immersion into blackness. When he gets back to Harlem, he encounters negative black behavior, which is expected by white audiences. In an effort to exhibit moral order, Howie tries to stop an altercation. His act of selflessness appears suspicious. When the assailant flees, Howie is left "there with the injured party and the gun"; following the incident, the police take him to the "station for questioning," but he refuses to "reveal his identity."[83] In the tradition of 1940s movies, the "encounter with other exceptional African Americans (Lieutenant Thompson and his friend, Art)" enables Howie to become the man he was prior to his identity crisis.[84] As usual, Lee renders a respectable performance. But Lee is not the hero or protagonist in this passing film that focuses primarily on race.[85]

White hegemony prevails because only the exceptional blacks speak more than a line or two. The other blacks in the film have small parts, but receive more screen time and perform in a more negative light. Ultimately, racism is cast as a personal problem as opposed to a community problem. Instead of addressing the societal factors that cause some fair-skinned blacks to desire passing, Bowdre claims that the movie places the blame of self-hatred onto the parents. Due to the parents lying about their identity, the penalty for their racial denial is the momentary disintegration of their family. Instead of social, policy, or political change, "racism is addressed, confronted, and overcome by a simple Sunday sermon"; the audience is assured that "whiteness is inherently good and fair, with blackness a problem."[86] In essence, by featuring violence among blacks, the industry thrust forth the assertion that racial issues are caused by the behavior of bad blacks. Lastly, Hollywood maintains the "the centrality of whiteness in the film" because "the protagonists are White, with the Black performers in minor roles only."[87] Consequently, *Lost Boundaries* succeeds in making the performance of whiteness a heroic act. Meanwhile, the performance of blackness is a self-inflicting wound that refuses to allow itself to heal.

Perhaps Lee's most triumphant role is his 1952 part in *Cry, the Beloved*. This apartheid-themed movie addressed race in a realistic manner that depicted a black perspective of oppression. *Cry, the Beloved* conveyed the "condemnation of the indignities suffered by people of color living under apartheid."[88] In the film, based on the "best-selling book by South African novelist Alan Paton," Lee plays an older man named Rev. Stephen Kumalo.[89] The older man's life is destroyed when his son kills a young white man. Lee had an opportunity to play Reverend Kumalo because outside of America, producers such as in the British film industry were not negatively influenced by the creators of the blacklist. Stateside, due to the Red Scare domination, *Variety* magazine reported that Lee "lost television, radio, and film roles because of lies and innuendo."[90] Thus he was forced to accept performance opportunities outside of America like other blacklisted actors.

Neither HUAC nor the FBI found evidence that Lee engaged in criminal activities associated with Communism. Yet Lee's constant fight for civil rights was probably the catalyst for McCarthy's and Hoover's interest in him. Their government-sanctioned terrorism failed to bait Lee into abandoning his civil rights and humanitarian causes, such as raising "money for Negro schools in Mississippi and for blind soldiers."[91] Furthermore, he believed that blacks and Jews should be allies in the struggle for equality and he advocated for "the Jewish state of Israel" and "campaigned for black candidates."[92] Lee believed that social activism could work because he used his influence as a successful Broadway actor to end segregated "seating in venues across the country."[93] According to Smith, Lee was determined to make the invisible lives of black people visible to the dominant culture. In an effort to celebrate the achievements of African Americans, "Canada produced, promoted, and performed in plays and programs that unearthed black history and told the stories of Toussaint L'Ouverture, Marcus Garvey, Frederick Douglass, George Washington Carver, Booker T. Washington, Pearl Harbor hero Dorie Miller, pianist Pinetop Smith, and many others."[94] Evidently, some of these historical figures were subversive in terms of racial equality; this surely caught the attention of conservatives who mistook social activism for Communist infiltration. However, Lee's activism extended "beyond the arts and into his community."[95] Lee utilized his "beautiful voice, a magnetic presence, and a flair for oratory" to speak "for Democrats and progressives, labor and civil rights organizations, social and humanitarian causes."[96] Undoubtedly, his appearances, performances, and public stances on liberal left-wing causes kept him in the purview of HUAC and the FBI until his death.

Days before Lee's death, he was supposed to appear before HUAC.[97] Even though other members of Canada's family "died of heart-related illnesses," such as his "mother, father, and sister," those "who admired the man and his work, and those who loved him, were convinced that the blacklist contributed to his illness and death."[98] Like Bojangles, the list of "actors, directors, entertainers, writers, athletes, politicians, and activists" who attended his funeral was endless: Joe Louis, Gordon Parks, Sugar Ray Robinson, Josh White, Walter White, and producer Rod Geiger were a few of the guests.[99] Crowds convened at the funeral as "thousands of mourners jammed the sidewalks ... theater luminaries came to pay tribute to Lee, including Sidney Poitier" and Frederick O'Neal.[100] At the funeral, Adam Clayton Powell Jr. said that "the enemies of America kept the actor from working and broke his heart."[101] Despite the thousands of people who paid homage to Lee, he was for some, and still is for others, "a traitor to his country, a subversive black activist, a man who betrayed his friend and fellow activist Paul Robeson to save his own skin, a Communist dupe or Red sympathizer."[102] But, although under a cloud of suspicion, there is still no substantiated evidence that Lee ever betrayed America or his blacklisted friend.

Upon discovering that the FBI wanted him to implicate Robeson, Lee was determined not to weaken the civil rights movement by destroying the career of another great American Negro.[103] There are those who believe that Lee would have rather died than betray his friend with falsehoods. Additionally, Lee's widow, Frances, and the son of Robeson, Paul Robeson Jr., state that there is no credible evidence to support that Lee betrayed his friend.[104] But like Robeson's, Lee's stage and movie legacy is haunted by an ominous fog of Communism. Nevertheless, Lee was a charismatic black actor whose Caribbean dark-skinned looks and talent would open the public's arms for another black actor with island roots—Sidney Poitier. However, Sidney Poitier would become an even more famous activist and actor than Lee. Furthermore, the Hollywood establishment and the American public would idolize Poitier, and the African American community would revere him as well. In essence he, along with his musician and actor friend Harry Belafonte, would help change the trajectory of the civil rights movement and revolutionize the entertainment industry.

Section 2

BLACK IMAGES FROM THE APEX OF THE CIVIL RIGHTS ERA TO THE AGE OF BARACK OBAMA

CHAPTER 6

———— 1960s ————
Token Black Actors in the Civil Rights Age: Sidney Poitier and Harry Belafonte

During the 1960s, Sidney Poitier and Harry Belafonte were the most powerful black males in Hollywood. These two men of West Indian descent represented the beauty and diversity of black male identity. Belafonte says in his coauthored memoir, *My Song*, that with Poitier's dark brown skin, he emanated saintly calm and dignified presence.[1] Meanwhile, the lighter-skinned Belafonte admits that he felt like an angry black man. Each man defied stereotypes in both life and art. Belafonte was considered a matinee idol, while Poitier was considered "the top black actor in Hollywood."[2] Initially, Poitier believed his dark skin presented a disadvantage to his career; however, Belafonte claims that eventually it became an advantage.[3] As opposed to Poitier, Belafonte was unwilling to tone down his sexuality in order to advance his acting career. Belafonte agrees that Sidney is a magnificent actor, and he hypnotized audiences with all his performances. However, he insists that Sidney is aware that his success was predicated upon his ability to appear nonthreatening. Performances in movies such as *Lilies of the Field* (1963) and *To Sir, with Love* (1967) mobilized the trajectory of his career; those movies "rocketed him up to new, stratospheric heights of stardom."[4] But Belafonte declined the offers to play the leads in both of those movies because they lacked romance. Even though Poitier's dark skin tone heightened his character's dramatic impact, his success in Hollywood failed to bring him joy. The question remained in Poitier's and Belafonte's minds: where does a black male icon "go with this money and power and adulation from white folks, as a man of race?"[5] Evidently, Poitier and Belafonte felt compelled to ingratiate themselves within the struggle for equality. When two rich black male stars feel physically, socially, and legally limited by America's lack of equality, how could the average impoverished black male be expected to accept second-class citizenry?

Sidney and Harry were as close as brothers. The men were "born within eight days of each other."[6] On their rise to accomplish their dreams as entertainers, they shared similar ambitions of emerging out of grinding poverty. With Poitier's triumphs in Hollywood, and Belafonte's accomplishments as a singer, then as an actor on Broadway and in Hollywood, they were the top two black male entertainers in the world. Poitier and Belafonte were "fiercely competitive, and had ... differences, both political and personal."[7] Poitier was prone to take fewer risks than Belafonte. But Belafonte says he was too angry to hold back his desire for change. Belafonte suggested that they fly to Mississippi to deliver $70,000 to aid the Freedom Summer marches of 1963.[8] They would arrive to encounter a dozen or more bullets from the KKK, but they remained unscathed as they rode in a car to deliver the money.[9] In Greenwood, Mississippi, the Freedom Riders were so happy to see the pair that they began to sing Belafonte's classic "Banana Boat" song, which had become a civil rights anthem because "it was a cry from the heart of poor workers, a cry of weariness mingled with hope."[10] Sidney Poitier and Harry Belafonte risked their careers, families, and reputations for their civil rights convictions and participation; however, it was their dedication and the use of their epic status as black symbols of progress that transformed the dynamic possibilities of black male identity in Hollywood.

Clandestine Allies: Harry Belafonte and the Kennedy Brothers

By the 1960s, blacks in Hollywood yielded a considerable amount of influence despite American apartheid. Perhaps two of the most powerful black symbols of progress were Harry Belafonte and Sidney Poitier. Belafonte's influence on the civil rights movement was so profound that in 24 hours he helped to raise thousands of dollars to free jailed protesters.[11] During Freedom Summer, Belafonte says that many parents were angered by their children's participation in various marches. They resented that their children had been exposed to the violence and the confinement of jail that usually followed.[12] Parents were infuriated with Martin Luther King Jr. and called his decision to include the youth in the movement immoral. Although he wanted his personal contribution to remain a secret, the largest contribution was from Governor Rockefeller in the amount of a $100,000 as a gift to the movement.[13]

Since Attorney General Bobby Kennedy was concerned about furious parents violently filling the streets, he helped free the children sooner.

According to Belafonte, Bobby Kennedy was not sympathetic to the civil rights cause of African Americans; instead, he was shielding his brother, President John Kennedy. The Kennedy brothers wished to contain the sit-ins and bloody arrests; therefore they consulted with black performers to appease the movement. Bobby Kennedy sought out Dick Gregory and activist James Baldwin, the author of *The Fire Next Time* (1963).[14] Baldwin, who was a close friend of Belafonte, contacted Lena Horne and Lorraine Hansberry, the author of the award-winning play *A Raisin in the Sun* (1958) and the screenwriter of the movie starring Poitier, Louis Gossett Jr., and Ruby Dee in 1961.[15] In addition to various entertainers, members from CORE (Congress of Racial Equality) and SNCC (Student Nonviolent Coordinating Committee) and other influential members of the African American community attended this meeting.[16] Belafonte claims Bobby Kennedy wanted the equal rights activists to know how much the government had done for the black community. Furthermore, he was concerned that black Americans were growing more attracted to the messages of militants such as Malcolm X. Despite Bobby's intentions and concerns, he was not trusted by many in the movement. The movement was aware of "Bobby's role as a twenty-seven-year-old legal counsel to Senator Joe McCarthy in his rabid persecution of suspected communist spies and sympathizers."[17] Even though Belafonte and Bobby frequently disagreed and were suspicious of each other's motives, they spoke on the phone regularly.[18] In any case, Belafonte was the closest connection the Kennedy brothers had in the movement. Meanwhile, Martin Luther King Jr. was able to convey the needs of the movement to Bobby Kennedy and John Kennedy via Belafonte, without compromising their official positions. With significant impact, Belafonte used his influence in the world of entertainment to economically and socially further the movement. Finally, Belafonte utilized his powerful position as a performer to influence policy change.

The Civil Rights Movement: The 1963 March on Washington

A pinnacle moment of the civil rights movement was the March on Washington in 1963. According to Henry Louis Gates Jr., the civil rights struggle continues because of "the yawning gap between its revolutionary ideals and its laws."[19] Since the beginning of the black experience in America, their treatment has been marred by disparate circumstances. Gates recollects how the former slave and abolitionist Frederick Douglass urged blacks to fight for equal treatment.[20] African Americans have struggled for fair representation "by launching newspapers, penning slave narratives, building churches and schools, and fighting for their country in every one of its wars even when that country was unwilling to recognize them as citizens, or even as men."[21] Perhaps one of the more fascinating elements of the struggle is the coalescing of blacks and whites who worked together to end discrimination. The march symbolized a progressive force in American society. Gates states that the 1963 March on Washington was a "game-changing" event because they were successful at "galvanizing men and women, young and old, black and white, to teach the world the power of nonviolent protest by demanding justice inside court and legislative chambers."[22] More importantly, blacks and whites gathered "in the streets—from tree limbs, from lampposts, in church basements and atop bridges, and hotel balconies" despites risks to their own personal and families' well-being.[23]

As most American citizens know, Martin Luther King Jr. paid the ultimate price with his life. King stressed that America had benefited from the uncompensated toil of African Americans. Gates adds that American ingenuity results from "fusing European cultural forms with African cultural forms to create a truly American culture, exportable to the world—from the spirituals to the blues, from ragtime to jazz, from rhythm and blues and soul to hip-hop."[24] In essence, Martin Luther King Jr.'s "I Have a Dream" speech acted as America's conscience. The speech reminded the nation of its debt to African Americans for their contributions and the promises America bestows to all citizens. At the prompting of Mahalia Jackson, King "improvised the dream passage."[25] King's dream drew inspiration from "the Bible and 'My Country, 'Tis of Thee,' on the Emancipation Proclamation and the Constitution"; "King, like Jefferson and Lincoln before him, projected an ideal vision of an exceptional nation."[26] King successfully expressed the American Dream in a manner that "defined the best of the nation as surely as Jefferson did in Philadelphia in 1776 or Lincoln did at Gettysburg in 1863."[27] Eloquently, King was able to link historically iconic events with America's promise to its citizens, while at the same time referencing history that all Americans could culturally access. King's dream was a collective hope for the nation that included racial harmony between blacks and whites.

Witnessing the evocation of the dream were numerous celebrities such as Bob Dylan, Charlton Heston, and Marlon Brando,[28] just a few of the celebrities who represented the racially integrated atmosphere of the March on Washington. Harry Belafonte, a close friend and confidante of Martin Luther King Jr., articulates the magnitude of the "I Have a Dream" speech. Belafonte refers to African Americans when he says that "many of us went off to that war and didn't have the right to vote.

Many of us went off to war and didn't have the right to participate in the American Dream. We didn't really think about this thing as a dream until Dr. King articulated it."[29] According to Belafonte, Broadway closed its doors out of respect for the historical event. Huge "delegations of artists and celebrities" arrived "from New York and from Boston and other places. It was not just in the world of cinema and theater. We had a lot of musical artists and record artists."[30] When one considers the history of blacklisting in Hollywood, heightened by memories of McCarthyism and Hoover's FBI blacklist, it is amazing that famous actors such as Harry Belafonte and Charlton Heston were at the helm of the march headed to the Lincoln Memorial.[31] In the second row were also A-list actors—James Garner, Diahann Carroll, and Paul Newman. And marching in the third row, were Anthony Franciosa and Marlon Brando. Belafonte was instrumental in the aesthetic presence of celebrities and noncelebrities uniting for a common cause.[32]

Belafonte insisted that a diverse group of entertainers demonstrate their solidarity with the movement by leading the march for equality. When Belafonte discussed the strategy with his fellow artists, he suggested that the celebrities associate themselves within "the heart of the people gathered at the event, the more we are seen and identified with the everyday citizen, the more we are all linking arms together, not just celebrity to celebrity but a truck driver, a dentist or a housewife, and we're all linking arms together, the more powerful that imagery becomes."[33] Due to the united efforts of many forces, "there was not one act of violence."[34] At the end, there were plenty of tears when the immense crowd sang "We Shall Overcome" as all the arms linked. Belafonte says that "you went through that crowd and you couldn't find any type missing, any gender, any race, any religion. It was America at its most transformative moment."[35] Although Lena Horne did not lead the march like her fellow thespians Belafonte, Poitier, and Carroll, she wore a blue and yellow NAACP hat at the event.[36] As a lifelong member of the organization, Horne also spoke, performed, and listened that day. Not to mention, there were many other black and white entertainers who attended or joined the stage for American progress.

Sidney Poitier: A Black Symbol of Progress

Like Canada Lee, Poitier's upbringing is a direct link to his black pride and desire to shape his image as a black male in America. Sidney was the youngest of seven children; he "was born three months premature while his Bahamian parents were in Miami to sell tomatoes."[37] Since his parents were concerned that he may not live, "his dad purchased a tiny casket, while his mother consulted a palm reader."[38] The palm reader said to Poitier's mother: " 'Don't worry about your son. He will survive,' Poitier recalled. 'And these were her words, she said: 'He will walk with kings.' And it came true: 'Everything she said, including walking with kings, yeah.' "[39] In a manner of speaking, Poitier's performances were regal. According to the *New York Times*, "Sidney Poitier was to Hollywood what Jackie Robinson was to major league baseball: simply put, the man who broke the color barrier."[40] In addition to acting, Poitier has occupied many roles, such as director and producer.

He succeeded in shifting "the racial perceptions long held by both motion picture audiences and executives, rising to superstar status in an industry forever dominated on both sides of the camera by whites."[41] Strikingly "handsome and athletic, Poitier made his Broadway debut in 1946 in an all-black production of *Lysistrata*."[42] Four years later, he would make his film debut in *No Way Out* (1950).[43] As Poitier's popularity intensified with Americans of all racial backgrounds, this "solidified Poitier's standing as a key figure in the burgeoning civil rights movement."[44] Thus his early films prompted both black and white audiences to adore his magnetic performances, while viewing him as a cinematic symbol of racial and social progress. Although Poitier was less involved in the civil rights movement than Belafonte, he refused to play roles that denigrated his character or the images of black people. In Poitier's first lead role, he plays an African American doctor in an urban community in the film *No Way Out* (1950).[45] Since he was a young man, he took this responsibility to his artistic forebears seriously. Therefore, he plainly says in his bestselling autobiography, *The Measure of a Man*, he was not willing to disassociate himself from black actors he admired.[46] Even though his costar Canada Lee was on the blacklist, Poitier was not deterred from playing the young priest in *Cry, the Beloved Country*.[47] Consequently, by the time Poitier was 23, he played major roles in Hollywood films.[48] Even at that early juncture, he was aware that his burgeoning career was not representative of the average black performer. Poitier says "This many accidents and lucky breaks just didn't happen in the movie business, or anywhere else. They didn't even happen in the movies themselves."[49] There were only a handful of black plays in the 1950s, and Poitier objected to the fact that black actors had to compete for a limited number of roles. Back then, "forty-odd plays on Broadway, but none having to do with *our* culture, *our* community, *our* lives."[50] For Poitier, the lack of black representation on the American Broadway stage was a source of frustration. Because Poitier did not accept racial limitations placed on his opportunity to succeed, he decided to act in the movie *Blackboard Jungle* (1955).[51] This movie centers on a low-income interracial high school of a few Hispanic and some African American students among mostly whites. Since it was filmed the same year as *Brown v. Board of Education* (1954), the message about "self-perception, courage, and the abuse of power," coupled with a rock-and-roll soundtrack, was an electrifying mix.[52]

As Poitier was preparing to work on that film, he was pressured to sign a document disavowing his association with Paul Robeson and Canada Lee.[53] Even though the studio labeled Robeson and Lee "questionable characters," Poitier was angered by the studio's request and willing to walk away from the picture. Poitier admired and respected Robeson and Lee because they were men of courage and integrity. In a culture that refused to acknowledge his personhood and forced him to travel the "Jim Crow car in all trains below the Mason-Dixon line," he was appalled by the request.[54] Even as a burgeoning star, he was barred entry into various establishments.[55] According to Poitier, segregation in the South and in various parts of the North was a "constant reminder that the law of this land once declared" blacks "to be three-fifths of a human being, and that only one hundred years earlier the Chief Justice of the U.S. Supreme Court declared black people" as inferior and unworthy of rights.[56] For Sidney, denying Robeson and Lee was equivalent to denying his black identity because they fought for racial justice. The same dignity Poitier displayed in his films, he exhibited behind the scenes; he refused to allow them to take his soul. Poitier realized that his refusal to denigrate Robeson's name caused "the FBI to keep an eye on" him.[57] Even as Poitier promoted the film *Blackboard Jungle*, he was reminded that his skin color denied him equal rights under the law.[58] After completing a publicity circuit by speaking to "black newspapers and black radio," he decided to eat in an upscale restaurant "where all the waiters were black; the maître d' himself, dressed in a tuxedo, was [also] black."[59] The young maître d' recognized him from a movie, but denied Poitier entry unless he agreed to sit behind a screen.[60] In a regretful tone, the black maître d' apologized by explaining that this was the practice and the law in the South. Livid by the absurdity that he accept the dehumanizing treatment legislated under Jim Crow, he never accommodated it and walked out of the restaurant.

To Sidney, the nation should have foreseen the "approaching civil rights storm kicking up dust on the horizon, coming, perhaps, to seek out the young, quiet preacher of the gospel, destined to lead the way across the difficult and painful years ahead."[61] Eventually, African

Americans would watch Poitier break boundaries on the big screen. Meanwhile, Poitier was reading "newspapers, from the radio, from the newsreels in the movie houses, and from poems and sermons, teachers— men of vision" who spoke to him and spoke for him as a black man in America.[62] As African American people watched Harry and Sidney for lead- ership in a segregated society, Sidney was inspired by the humanity of his predecessors Paul Robeson, A. Philip Randolph, Adam Clayton Powell Jr., Walter White, and Langston Hughes. He was further inspired by contempo- raries, such as William Garfield Greaves, Harry Belafonte, William Marshall, and other black pioneers that Sidney would consider as his friends. For a black man in the 1950s and 1960s, black identity encroaches upon one's personal, social, economic, and legal well-being. As proof of Sidney's devotion to the civil rights cause, he never shied away from the issue of race in his movies. With grace, he swelled the hearts and minds of people that denied the selfhood and self-autonomy of blacks on-screen and off. Sidney had accomplished what America had never seen before—a black leading man. Admittedly, Poitier knows that he "was in the midst of a revolutionary process with this institution" he "was so at odds with."[63] Nevertheless, Sidney was less concerned with his career and more concerned with the fact that the average black person was dealing with "unfairness in jobs ... in living space, in the manner in which black Americans were received."[64] While Sidney was committed to playing transformative black male roles on-screen, he was not immune to criticism from the black community.

In 1958, Poitier starred in *The Defiant Ones*, which caused major con- troversy.[65] Yet the film earned him the first Oscar nomination for a black male actor in the cinema.[66] The film was directed by Stanley Kramer and was written by "some very intense and committed progressives."[67] Poitier played opposite Tony Curtis in this groundbreaking film. The plot centers on "two fugitives from a chain gang, one white and one black, literally bound together ... Each misunderstood the other, but they also misun- derstood their own individual limitations; so they scapegoated each other."[68] Overall, Kramer conveyed the message that all people are the same; distinctions are, for the most part, cosmetic. The movie failed to really "define what class was, what race was."[69] In the end, the two men "wound up on that railroad trestle, one guy holding the other guy, struggling to survive, hanging on, but singing a song, a song of hope."[70] Various members of the black community dismissed the simplistic notion that all of society's ills are caused by racial differences. Sidney's friends within the Hollywood community objected to the black charac- ter's sacrifice in the end.[71] The tension is high and this is their last chance to escape.[72] When Sidney is on the train, he is unable to clasp Curtis's hand. Subsequently, Sidney tumbled off the train too, following after his comrade. To some of Sidney's friends in Hollywood, he "should have stayed on the train and said, 'Screw that guy.' "[73] Let Curtis's character suffer his individual fate. But for the writers and directors, their intention was to emphasize the selflessness of the transformed characters. Looking back, Sidney agrees with the director's message of tolerance. As Curtis lies injured in Sidney's arms, he jokes while expressing comfort in his belief that he and his black friend are very much the same. For audiences, this message certainly resonated.

Perhaps the greatness in the film is Tony and Sidney's contribution to the forthcoming black and white comrade movies of the 1980s. Furthermore, *The Defiant Ones* creates a friendship between one black and white man "that takes root down at the deepest level of commonality—down where all of us were molded out of the same clay."[74] Successfully, Sidney and Tony conveyed a partnership that defied the social conventions of their era. Their friendship transcended race before the peak of the civil rights movement. Furthermore, Sidney manifested a comfortable black male image that was safe and benign. Americans both white and black were beginning to accept another perspective of black manhood. Even if that trust did not extend beyond the movie screens, Sidney caused America to trust and fall in love with a black male actor for the first time in cinematic history.

When Sidney played in *Porgy and Bess* (1959) and *Raisin in the Sun* (1961), he became "the premier black actor of his generation."[75] *Porgy and Bess* starred Dorothy Dandridge, Sammy Davis Jr., Pearl Bailey, and Diahann Carroll.[76] In a review for the *New York Times*, Bosley Crowther states that *Lilies of the Field* was a turning point in Hollywood.[77] Poitier earned the first Academy Award for an African American actor for his role in the film. Poitier brilliantly plays a character named Homer Smith, an aimless ex-GI who accepts a job at a southwestern farm occupied by five German nuns. Mother Superior dreams of a chapel on their land. Once Mother Superior meets the personable Homer, she believes that he has been sent from the heavens to aid in her dream. Initially, Homer refuses the nuns' request, but eventually he decides to build the chapel. The townspeople are so impressed with his work that he receives their adoration. Also, Homer is able to avoid an arrest for a previous crime. By committing himself to a selfless act for God, Homer achieves freedom and spiritual renewal. In essence, Poitier plays a black male who is capable of redemption and transformation.

Prior to Sidney's interracial romance in *Guess Who's Coming to Dinner* (1967), he had another relationship with a blind white woman named Selina (Elizabeth Hartman) in *A Patch of Blue* (1965). The movie marked another first for Sidney because he was the first black actor to kiss a white woman on film.[78] Since Sidney is an able-bodied individual, he is protective of "her and teaches her basic life skills."[79] Consequently, the couple falls in love despite her prejudiced comments that she learned from her abusive, prostitute mother. Selina does not realize that her boyfriend is black until a white mob chases Gordon and "shouts that a 'nigger' is walking in the park with a white girl."[80] Poitier plays the black knight in shining armor by liberating Selina from her mother, a cruel woman who keeps her blind daughter "locked up in their tenement apartment."[81] In the end, Selina accepts Gordon even though he is a black man, but their relationship stalls when he sends her to a school for the blind. Therefore the movie suggests that racism is a personal issue and "has nothing to do with economic and power relations."[82] On a progressive note, "in contrast to the film's sordid white characters, Gordon, a newspaper reporter, and his brother, a medical intern, are educated, cultured, well-off, productive members of society."[83] The politics of respectability is the underlying message; if a black individual wishes not to experience racism, they must model perfect citizenship and succeed in American society. Of course, this message is one that many critics opposed. As usual, Poitier was expected to symbolize the exceptional black male in order for audiences to embrace his humanity.

By the time Poitier finished *A Patch of Blue*, he was frustrated by the absence of black sexuality in his roles. Poitier believed that since the "white screenwriters, producers, and studio execs were in control," they were obliterating his sexuality because of established Hollywood tradition instead of a deliberate intent to minimize his humanity.[84] However, many critics would disagree with Poitier's assumption of unintentional racism. Since the implementation of the Hays Moral Code, Hollywood was always conscious of some audience members' moral objections to interracial relationships. To pacify Jim Crow racism in the South, the "eight-second kissing scene between Gordon (Poitier) and Selina (Hartman) was cut from Southern prints."[85] Even in the late 1960s, Hollywood was not willing to sacrifice profits or negative criticism in an effort to fully realize the dynamic humanity of African American males on film.

In 1967, *In the Heat of the Night* won the Oscar for Best Picture.[86] Although Sidney was nominated for a best actor Academy Award, he lost the award to his costar Rod Steiger.[87] Furthermore, the movie won four Academy Awards including best adapted screenplay. This classic movie is "set in a small Mississippi town where an unusual murder has been committed."[88] Despite Sheriff Bill Gillespie's (Rod Steiger) racial prejudices, he's an effective officer for law enforcement. Initially, Gillespie is suspicious of Virgil Tibbs, played by Sidney Poitier. Therefore, when Sidney comes to town, Steiger sees the "well-dressed northern African-American ... [and] instinctively puts him under arrest as a murder suspect."[89] Due to the success of the movie, based on a book written by John Ball, there were two sequels starring Sidney. Eventually, the two men are able to put aside their distrust for one another, which leads to solving the crime. As further evidence of the movie's success, Carroll O'Connor (Gillespie) and Howard Rollins (Tibbs) starred in the hit television version of *In the Heat of the Night* (1998–1995).[90] During the same year as *In the Heat of the Night*, Poitier "appeared in Kramer's *Guess Who's Coming to Dinner* as the black fiancé of a white woman."[91] As result of his success in *To Sir with Love*, *In the Heat of the Night*, and *Guess Who's Coming to Dinner*, in 1968 Sidney was the first black actor "to become the number one box office star in the country (1968)."[92] Yet his economic success and popularity did not mean that people did not criticize the types of roles he played.

Ironically, even though Poitier was a trailblazer, he was criticized for playing black characters that were "whitewashed" in order to gain acceptance by white audiences.[93] Oftentimes, Sidney played the good black male, which seemed idealized and unrealistic to some audience members. Perhaps his role as a doctor in movies such as *Guess Who's Coming to Dinner* could be perceived as a kind of liberal wish fulfillment. Nevertheless, Poitier was an authentic Hollywood pioneer because he presented black males in a positive and professional light. When *Guess Who's Coming to Dinner* was seen by audiences in 1967, "interracial marriage was still illegal in 17 states."[94] Thus Poitier's role was still a remarkable advance. Also, in 1963, when Anne Bancroft presented Poitier with the best actor award for *Lilies of the Field*, she offended some people when she gave him a kiss on the cheek. This further exemplifies that America was not ready to accept a black male fully expressing his humanity. Indisputably, Poitier's accomplished performances opened the doors. However, his Oscar win did not tear down the barriers of discrimination. Although Sidney depicted a more complex and well-rounded black male character, Hollywood would wait "38 years before another African-American," Denzel Washington, would win the honor "with a best-actor award ... for his turn as a bad cop in 2001's *Training Day*."[95]

All things considered, by 2013 Poitier had performed in "more than 50 movies."[96] Poitier made his career choices not based on being the first, but more on the image of his characters. He refused to play characters that he perceived as immoral or cruel. Typically, Poitier played characters who were "dignified, proud, and ethical."[97] For instance, when Rod Steiger's character slaps Virgil Tibbs, Poitier insisted that the script be changed. Poitier had it written into his contract that "'if he slaps me, I'm going to slap him back. You will put on paper that the studio agrees that the film will be shown nowhere in the world, with me standing there taking the slap from the man.'"[98] In one of the great moments of the film, Sidney knew that black audiences would have been offended if he had not slapped Steiger back. Sidney's lack of submission in this scene symbolized racial equality because he defended himself at this pivotal moment. Nevertheless, Sidney did not enter the film " 'business to be symbolized as someone else's vision of me.' "[99] Poitier says that he refused to accept any role " 'that reflects negatively on my father, my mother and my values.' "[100] In other words, Poitier used his power in the industry to shape his own image and he would not become the industry's vision of a typical black male.

Belafonte shared similar concerns with his on-screen image as Poitier. Yet his Hollywood image was not as significant to him as America's racial progress as a culture. Despite Belafonte's on-screen chemistry with Dorothy Dandridge in three films—*Bright Road* (1953), *Carmen Jones* (1954), and *Island in the Sun* (1957)—during the 1960s Belafonte remained devoted to the civil rights movement.[101] In the 1960s, he primarily focused on achieving in the music industry and television. Subsequently, in the 1970s, Belafonte and Poitier would team up in at least two movies: *Buck and the Preacher* (1972), and *Uptown Saturday Night* (1974).[102] As the producer and director of *Uptown Saturday Night* and its sequels *Let's Do It Again* (1975) and *A Piece of the Action* (1977), Sidney "enjoyed a new ride of economic power in Hollywood."[103] In essence, Poitier and Belafonte were safe and acceptable images for Hollywood in the 1950s and 1960s. But behind the scenes, their efforts in the civil rights movement helped usher in the entertainment and cultural opportunities that would follow in the next decade. In the era of the 1970s, blaxploitation films, black male sexuality, self-empowerment, and vigilance became prominent and undeniable, yet remained controversial themes. Shaking up not only black and white audiences, blaxploitation films shifted the institutional practices that barred full representation of black males within every facet of Hollywood. Although racism remained, black male artists in Hollywood were determined to thrive anyway. Without the social progress ushered in by the civil rights movement and Poitier's and Belafonte's transformative images, America would not have embraced the strong black male actors of the blaxploitation era.

CHAPTER 7

1970s

Blaxploitation: Preachers, Pimps, Pushers, and Players

Blaxploitation films are revolutionary yet represent a controversial segment of cinematic history. This genre of films deviates from the strong yet benign black male images of Sidney Poitier and Harry Belafonte's era, into an age where black male characters are outspoken and sexually aggressive. Moreover, blaxploitation films feature urban settings and elevate preachers, pimps, pushers, and players, despite their exploitation of black people and defiance of white authority and white criminal figures. Oftentimes, the quality of these films varies depending on whether they were low-budget or bigger-budget productions. According to James Monaco, author of *How to Read Film: Movies, Media, and Beyond*, "the most important innovation in the U.S. in the 1970s was the Black film, a wide category that included a great deal of cheap material ('Blaxploitation' in *Variety*'s parlance) but also a number of films of lasting value."[1] Not unlike the heyday of the black film in the 1920s, the 1970s is a peak era for all-black casts and black themes. Despite the broad appeal of these urban-targeted films, they failed to maintain their prominence into the 1980s. By the conclusion of the 1970s, black film was almost gone "from the Hollywood scene, but it was to rise again with renewed energy in the 1990s."[2] Nevertheless, the 1970s blaxploitation era represents one answer to the disgruntled Black Power movement of the 1960s.

With the emerging popularity of Sidney Poitier and Harry Belafonte in the 1950s, American audiences saw black characters in a dignified manner. Thus their influence contributes toward the movement featuring blacks in "nonstereotypical roles in American film" in the late 1960s.[3] As evidence of the alienation, hypervisibility, and racism, the Black Power movement pointed toward the racist characterizations promoted by Hollywood throughout the history of film and television. As Monaco eloquently states, "The media faithfully reflected the values of society. But they also exaggerated the real situation."[4] Fortunately, the Black Power movement breached the barrier that pictured blacks singularly in servile roles or in roles where "race was a significant element."[5] Nevertheless, the black images of Poitier and Belafonte symbolized the exception to the monolithic roles in 1960s Hollywood.

But is the blaxploitation era an uplifting reflection of African American advancement or a degrading distortion of popular culture desires? Filmmaker Isaac Julien of *BaadAsssss Cinema* (2000) blames "Blaxploitation's decline by the mid-1970s" on black activists.[6] As a result of "the pressure the NAACP put on Hollywood and the studios' fear of black backlash against their bigger-budget productions," Hollywood lost interest in black films.[7] Various organizations like the National Urban League, the Southern Christian Leadership Conference, and the NAACP viewed the prevalent stereotypes glorified by blaxploitation films as a danger to black communities. According to Fred Williamson, black organizations actually created the term blaxploitation to "discredit these films"; in reality, blaxploitation offered African Americans "the kinds of heroes they needed at the time."[8] Nevertheless, the blaxploitation era promoted economic, political, and social black power coupled with glorification of black beauty, masculinity, and sexuality in an unapologetic manner. The fashion, the cars, the hair, the attitude were symbols of an era that celebrated pioneering black directors, producers, writers, and actors as they played heroes and lowlife emblems representative of black culture. But the musical scores of jazz, funk, and soul elevated everyday preachers, pimps, pushers, and players to urban heroes as they rhythmically strutted through the gritty streets. These black men proudly dominated the metropolis with vengance against those who degraded them, their families, or their communities. Along the way, blaxploitation heroes were picturesque in their beauty, swagger, masculinity, and objectification of the black and white women who worshiped them. Various directors such as Melvin Van Peebles, Ossie Davis, Gordon Parks Sr. and his son Gordon Parks Jr., Michael Schultz, and Sidney Poitier (see chapter 6) made films that explored class differentiation and racial rebellion against white social norms alienating black identity. At the helm of this blaxploitation era of black male dominance are the following actors: *Cotton Comes to Harlem*'s Calvin Lockhart, *Super Fly*'s Ron O'Neal, *The Mack*'s Max Julien, *Black Caesar*'s Fred Williamson, *Blacula*'s William Marshall, *Black Belt Jones*'s Jim Kelly, and *Three the Hard Way*'s Jim Brown.

Blaxploitation Pioneers of Filmmaking: Melvin Van Peebles, Ossie Davis, and Gordon Parks Sr.

When Melvin Van Peebles decided to become a filmmaker, he produced his first movie, the *Story of a Three-Day Pass* (1967) in France; as result, Hollywood took notice and offered Van Peebles a contract. However, Van Peebles's second film, *Watermelon Man* (1969), is considered a "fairly weak comedy."[9] Perhaps the most significant film of the 1970s was Van Peebles's third film. Monaco asserts that "the independently produced *Sweet Sweetback's Baadasssss Song* (1971) is still the purest Black film, in terms of esthetics, that has yet been made—a shriek of pain that is also an object lesson in Black survival in America."[10] According to Roger Ebert, Van Peebles's *Sweetback* is a "landmark in the birth of African-American cinema."[11] Ebert considers this innovative film to be gritty, the story of a man who was born in a whorehouse and loses his virginity at the age of 12.

As a survivor of the city, he attacks two racist cops and eludes capture, which was a revolutionary concept at the time. Audiences were thrilled that the heroic Sweetback "got away with it" and they "were intrigued by ad lines like 'Rated X by an All-White Jury.' "[12] Sweetback engages in a "series of chase sequences and hot sexual adventures," which makes him "the most extravagantly sexual hero audiences ever saw."[13] Josiah Howard proclaims in *Blaxploitation Cinema: The Essential Guide* that *Sweetback* with "its avant-garde presentation of black male anger and sexuality, set a new standard in the representation of African-American males in mainstream American cinema."[14] As previously stated, black audiences were weary of the mild-mannered and sanitized onscreen black male images portrayed by actors such as Poitier and Belafonte. Howard claims that *Sweetback* symbolized an era of militancy because of "the Black Panther Party's across-the-board endorsement; *Sweet Sweetback's Baadasssss Song* was made required viewing for all Panther members."[15] The movie closes with a message: "A BAADASSSSS NIGGER IS COMING BACK TO COLLECT SOME DUES"; and black audiences and some young whites appreciated how Sweetback "met violence with violence and triumphed over the corrupt white establishment."[16] According to Ebert, despite the revolutionary aspects of *Sweetback*, it is not an exploitation film; however, *Variety* magazine credits *Sweetback* for creating "blaxploitation." This pioneering genre "gave us Pam Grier, Shaft, Superfly [*sic*] and a generation of black filmmakers who moved into the mainstream."[17] Van Peebles spent $150,000 on his fly-by-night movie and managed to make an astounding profit; *Sweetback*'s success at the box office proved to Hollywood that movies made by, for, and about African Americans could make money.

Howard states that the movie cost $450,000 to make and by the close of the year profited 12 million.[18]

In Mario Van Peebles's documentary *Baadasssss!* (2005), he presents his "fictionalized eyewitness account ... [of] how and why his father, Melvin Van Peebles, made *Sweet Sweetback's Baadasssss Song*.[19] The docudrama demonstrates Mario's respect for his father's "desperation, deception and cunning" efforts at guerrilla filmmaking even though, at the age of 13, Mario "was pressed into service by his father to play Sweetback as a boy."[20] At the time, Melvin's girlfriend, Sandra, played by Nia Long, disapproved of this decision. Despite objections to his directorial and production choices, "Melvin was a force of nature, a cigar-chewing renaissance man who got his own way. Only sheer willpower forced the production ahead, despite cash and personnel emergencies."[21] Since Melvin could not afford to pay his actors union wages, he was forced to disguise the movie as a porno film. Melvin transformed industry standards by employing a demographically and representative team; he formed a "crew that included at least 50 percent minorities (in an industry where most crews were all-white), he trained some of them on the job."[22] By featuring the struggles and triumphs of his father, Mario demonstrates his respect, despite the remnants of resentment resonating within *Baadasssss!*

Clearly, Mario disapproves of his father's strong-willed, single-minded treatment of people with whom he worked closely. Throughout the production, Melvin is "bouncing checks, telling lies, roughing up a crew member who wants to quit."[23] Perhaps one of the most interesting revolutionary techniques is the unknowing participation of the fire department. Melvin blows up a car, waits for the Los Angeles Fire Department to arrive, and begins shooting free footage of the firefighters. Famously, Bill Cosby, who is played by T. K. Carter, bails out the *Sweetback* film with $50,000. Ebert admires how Mario combines firsthand experience on the set of *Sweetback* and autobiographical elements to create an objective docudrama. With all things considered, Melvin is seen "as brave and gifted and determined, but also as a hustler who gets his movie made"; in fact, using guerrilla tactics Melvin "steps on toes, hurts feelings, expects sacrifices" and "doesn't hesitate to use his own son in a scene that no professional child actor would have been allowed to touch."[24] In many ways, the *Sweetback* production techniques are not unlike typical independent films; as noted by Ebert, members of the production are oftentimes "bludgeoned into hard work at low pay in the service of the director's ego."[25] All things considered, Mario captures the essence of family in *Baadasssss!* Although the film was "historically a film of great importance," it is also "just another low-rent, fly-by-night production."[26] In essence, Mario captures how Melvin represents American ingenuity and African American iconography in his film *Baadasssss!*

After conquering Hollywood, Melvin Van Peebles turned his attention to the stage. During the 1970s, Melvin played "a major role in the development of the Black musical theater (*Ain't Supposed to Die a Natural Death, Don't Play Us Cheap*), which remained a strong and profitable component of the Broadway repertoire."[27] As a result, Van Peebles managed to garner 11 Tony Award nominations for his plays.[28] While living in New York, Melvin made an unexpected turn toward the economic sector. Melvin became the only black day trader on Wall Street.[29] In the late 1980s, prior to reentering the film industry to work with his son, Mario, Melvin authors a book entitled *Bold Money: A New Way to Play the Options Market* (1986).[30] During the 1990s, Melvin was a major force in assisting Mario as they courted "distributors for *New Jack City* (1991)"; clearly, this was an intelligent and strategic move since Melvin is deemed the founder of a new era of black film.[31] Nevertheless, Melvin led an amazing life. Before becoming a filmmaker, he earned a French Legion of Honor award for valor as a U.S. Air Force officer.[32] Ironically, Melvin occupied the position of an honored military officer, an outlier in the entertainment field, and then as an economic insider on Wall Street. Melvin Peebles led a life along the margins pushing back against the establishment. Undoubtedly, this diversity within his own persona and life experience empowered him to depict multifaceted and complex black male characters for audiences.

For the classic movie *Cotton Comes to Harlem*, the actor and author Ossie Davis debuted as the director and cowriter of this screenplay with Arnold Perl.[33] The movie is based on the novel by black novelist Chester Himes. The huge and talented African American cast includes the well-known actors Raymond St. Jacques (Coffin Ed Johnson), Calvin Lockhart (Rev. Deke O'Malley), and Redd Foxx (Uncle Bud). Even with this amazing cast, the movie fails to feature black culture in a nuanced way. The fast-paced action composed of "shootouts, chases, murders and wisecracks say little about the Black Experience."[34] Vincent Canby writes in the *New York Times* that Davis churned out a ghetto comedy-melodrama that is lukewarm and witless. The plot is centered on the $87,000 concealed "in a bale of cotton and with the detectives' efforts to unmask the bogus preacher (Calvin Lockhart) who conceived the back-to-Africa plan as one way of getting himself back to someplace like Las Vegas."[35] Redd Foxx's character is utilized in a satirical manner to criticize the society that gave them birth and various other stereotypes. Reminiscent of Oscar Micheaux in the 1920s and 1930s, he produced African American movies for

African American theaters based on white film stereotypes. Consequently, Canby expresses disappointment with this flimsy plot. Even though the preacher, played by Lockhart, cons his own people, most audience members sympathize with the movie's villain, played with lovely, stylish cool. At the time, intermeshing "comedy, action, and drama, and colorfully telling the story of a diverse group of African Americans living and working in Harlem, USA ... seemed novel and forward-thinking."[36] Now, the movie appears trite with its repetitive dialogue and profuse use of stereotypes to move the action forward. Nevertheless, according to Howard, Ossie Davis successfully proved that black movies with a black cast could make a profit.

Another significant force of the 1970s is Gordon Parks Sr. and his photojournalist background. Prior to transforming black Hollywood, Parks Sr. was a "widely respected photographer for *Life* magazine and an author when he decided to break the race barrier in film" with the autobiographical film *The Learning Tree* (1968).[37] Once Parks Sr. signed a contract with Warner Brothers for the film adaptation of his book, he held the distinction as the first African American male to direct a major American movie. The film was a paradox of the African American experience. In one instance, it was a nostalgic remembrance of a time when "the picture's hero, Newt, can do cartwheels in a field of flowers or steal apples from a vineyard with his buddies. But it is also an age polluted by violence and racism. A creek where Newt swims suddenly turns red from the blood of a black man senselessly shot by a bigoted white sheriff."[38] Newt is a young black male, yet he is not tormented by his skin color. *The Learning Tree* transcends racial boundaries because Newt's coming of age is like other young men regardless of "color or place or time. Yet he is not colorless. Nor indistinct."[39] As society heads toward the 1970s, *The Learning Tree* was "a visually stunning essay on his Kansas childhood, but too static for audiences accustomed to regularly timed stimulation."[40]

Aware of the audience's desire for fast paced-action, Parks Sr.'s second film, *Shaft* (1971), was a commercial success.[41] In the early 1970s, *Shaft* became the prototype of "the Black Action genre that was commercially so popular in" that era.[42] The popularity of *Sweetback's Baadasssss Song* and *Shaft* exemplifies the public's willingness to accept sexually assertive black males in film.[43] To the studio's surprise, the economic success of *Shaft* "singlehandedly saved MGM from financial ruin."[44] Due in part to Richard Roundtree's role as the hero, the audiences rushed to the theaters to see *Shaft*. Roundtree plays the "tough, renegade black detective, John Shaft," who is not afraid to confront any man "who crosses his path, and is a whiz with the ladies."[45] The movie is based on a book by a white author named Ernest Tidyman. Originally, MGM planned for the well-known white actors Charlton Heston or Steve McQueen to play John Shaft, yet the profits of *Sweetback* and *Cotton* caused the studios to reconsider a black actor as the lead; thus they hurriedly rewrote the dialogue.[46] Formerly, Roundtree was "an African-American print model and theatre actor. Articulate, intelligent and suave."[47] To relate to white male viewers, Roundtree's sophistication aided the studios efforts to file down John Shaft's rough edges. Consequently, Donald Bogle claims, *Shaft* is a typical detective story enlivened by a black sensibility. Audiences loved John Shaft because he was "mellow but assertive and unintimidated by whites"; moreover, he smoothly traveled through the "hot mean streets dressed in his cool leather."[48] For black audiences, the image of Shaft was familiar, but such an authentic and relatable black man had never appeared on screen.

When Isaac Hayes's " 'Theme from Shaft' won the 1971 Academy Award as Best Song," his accomplishment rendered Hayes the first African American male to win "the Oscar in this category."[49] The theme song from *Shaft* also won a Grammy award; furthermore, Hollywood was not able to resist capitalizing from the *Shaft* craze: "There were Shaft suits, belts, coats, beach towels, sweatshirts, aftershave and cologne."[50] Two sequels followed the original: *Shaft's Big Score* (1972), which was directed by Parks Sr., but he did not direct the third film of the trilogy entitled *Shaft in Africa* (1973).[51] After achieving a significant level of success with similar ventures, Parks Sr. revisited "a more personal subject with *Leadbelly* (1976)"; the movie is based on "a biography of the Blues singer and a major film in the short history of the new Black cinema."[52] Parks Sr.'s ability to direct commercial films such as *Shaft* and character driven films such as *Leadbelly* demonstrates the talent and diversity of black filmmakers in the 1970s.

Blaxploitation's Typical Archetypes and Themes: Baadasssss, "the Man," the Horror Film, the Kung-Fu Movie, and the Western

According to Mikel J. Koven, author of *Blaxploitation Films*, there are various genres within this controversial cinematic era. In the early 1970s, there are the films such as *Sweet Sweetback's Baadasssss Song* that show black folks bravely "sticking it to the Man"; consequently, Koven claims that the word "baadasssss" is synonymous with blaxploitation. Baadasssss-ness is a "rebellious spirit in African-American thinking." And keep in mind that a baadasssss is not gender specific—an individual does not have to be a "tough guy" or man to warrant the label.[53] To deserve the title of baadasssss, an individual is basically an "outlaw" or someone who operates "outside of, the law"; in other words, they thrive in a tenuous space "between the law, between illegality and vice on the one side and harmless decadence and pleasure-seeking on the other."[54] Baadasssss characters are never "the law; they cannot be the Man, or his representatives; and while some of the later blaxploitation heroes, including Shaft, may have a certain baadasssss attitude," they are actually a part of the establishment and act as authority figures.[55] Thus people who operate within the system or as agents of the system cannot be "real baadassssses."[56] Movies such as *Super Fly* (1972), *The Hammer* (1972), *The Final Comedown* (1972), *Super Fly TNT* (1973), *The Mack* (1973), *Black Caesar* (1973), *Bucktown* (1973), *Hell Up in Harlem* (1973), *Coffy* (1973), *Foxy Brown* (1974), *The Black Six* (1974), *Willy Dynamite* (1974), *Black Fist* (1975), *Mandingo* (1975), *Black Gestapo* (1975), and *Dolemite* (1975) feature real baadassssses as protagonists.[57]

Koven classifies another subgenre within blaxploitation as "the Man"; black people become "the Man" once they transcend from civilians to representatives of the establishment.[58] As previously mentioned, baadasssss prototypes confront the corrupt and brutal police who harass blacks and the racist infrastructure of America. Oftentimes, black films exhibit rebellion and display "black power and emancipation" as means to disrupt the establishment.[59] However, within "the Man" subgenre, blacks fight to transform the system by working within the establishment.[60] The following films best represent these type of movies: *Cotton Comes to Harlem* (1970), *Shaft* (1971), *Shaft's Big Score* (1972), *Across 110th Street* (1972), *Slaughter* (1972), *That Man Bolt* (1973), *Shaft in Africa* (1973), *Slaughter's Big Rip-Off* (1973), *Black Belt Jones* (1974), *Cleopatra Jones* (1974), and *Detroit 9000* (1975).[61]

In addition to the baadassssses and "the Man" archetypes, there are cop thrillers, spy movies, horror films, kung-fu movies, and westerns, which are often classified as subgenres within the blaxploitation era.[62] According to Koven, horror films, kung-fu movies, and westerns have been "blaxed" to some degree during this era. In other words, the aforementioned subgenres contain the traditional elements of horror, kung-fu, and westerns. Yet, like the cop thrillers or spy movies, they are transplanted to an urban setting, with black characters and black themes. However, the archetypal characters, baadassssses and "the Man," operate within these blaxed subgenres because of their shared goals. What baadasssss and "the Man" films have in common is the antihero rebellion against society. Therefore, Koven claims, blaxploitation films signify an American film movement in the first half of the 1970s. Films during this era of "blaxed" subgenre films are *Blacula* (1972), *Scream Blacula*

Scream (1973), *Enter the Dragon* (1973), *Ganja & Hess* (1973), *Blackenstein, the Black Frankenstein* (1973), *Sugar Hill* (1974), *Take a Hard Ride* (1975), *Adios Amigo* (1976), *Black Samurai* (1977), and *The Tattoo Connection* (1978).[63]

The Leading Men of Blaxploitation: Sexual, Rebellious, Militant, and Dangerous

For many audiences, Gordon Parks Jr.'s *Super Fly*, starring Ron O'Neal, symbolizes the archetype of black manhood of the 1970s. O'Neal was a muscular actor with handsome features, but he unwaveringly presented masculinity as a chic drug pusher. *Super Fly* is considered the premier and "landmark film from this period"; the movie successfully "amplified the modes of representation and took both language and clothing to the extreme."[64] Theater actor Ron O'Neal (Priest) played the lead performer in *Super Fly*. Even though the movie was featured in only two theaters in New York City, due to a "word of mouth campaign ... *Super Fly* grossed more than $1 million."[65] The production cost of the movie was $500,000, yet two months after the premiere *Super Fly* made $11 million. According to *Variety* magazine, *Super Fly* knocked *Godfather* out of the top-grossing spot, thereby earning the distinction of "the highest grossing film in America—black or white."[66] Although the audience rooted for *Super Fly*, he was no good guy like John Shaft. The flamboyant Priest is an "ostentatiously dressed (and coifed) Harlem dope dealer planning to outsmart the mob."[67] Bogle describes Priest as "an urban prima ballerina in long, sweeping coats and large wide-brimmed hats ... a romanticized version of the Harlem pimp."[68] The screenplay was authored "by a black former advertising copywriter and was accompanied by a hit soundtrack album by soul artist Curtis Mayfield."[69] During the 1970s, most albums contained only one hit, yet the *Super Fly* soundtrack had three hit singles: "'Super Fly', 'Freddie's Dead' and 'Pusherman' were all" favored by consumers.

Notwithstanding the profitability of *Super Fly*, the movie was considered violent and pornographic by some and "filled with negative and/or derogatory images and themes."[70] African American audiences were enraged "by the glorification of its hero, a Harlem cocaine dealer."[71] During the wake of controversy, reminiscent of the Hays Moral Code era, the National Catholic Office condemned the film. In the words of Josiah Howard, Catholic officials' disapproval failed to compare to the "noisy black picketers who lined the streets outside of theatres carrying signs."[72] The societal outrage over *Super Fly* transitioned "from aggravating to dangerous" when "several employees of American International Pictures (producers of some of the more low-end black films) reported that their cars had been firebombed."[73] More public dissension occurred when the NAACP "combined the words 'black' and 'exploitation' and came up with 'blaxploitation,' a sensationalist phrase that forever categorized any and all black cast films released during the 1970s."[74] Various African American performers of blaxploitation films felt compelled to preserve the audiences' right to view action-packed films featuring black cast.[75] It should be noted that Pam Grier, the era's only female blaxploitation star, and Gordon Parks Jr. defended their participation in the genre; Grier reminded her critics that blaxploitation had value for its action elements and Parks Jr. stated that blaxploitation provided entertainment : " 'Fast cars and fancy clothes, well, that's the American Dream—everyone's American Dream.' "[76] For many audiences, *The Mack* also exemplifies the American Dream that Parks Jr. refers to in his defense of the genre.

The Mack glorified the era of the pimp, his sphere of influence within the community, and the women he oversaw in his urban stable–figuratively speaking, of course. Max Julien plays a pimp that "battles corrupt cops and the Mafia on his way to the top of the hooker trade."[77] The pimp's mother and his best friend are killed by the crooked cops. In response, Julien's character vows vengeance when "he and his politicized brother kill the cops and the pimp leaves penniless for Alabama." As a result of the candid urban plot, *The Mack* became "a huge box office success."[78] Despite the conflicting images of black manhood and the objectification of black and white women, *The Mack* is "one of the most highly respected films of the 70s Black cinema."[79]

Carol Speed who plays Lulu in *The Mack* offers her reflections on the movie and the blaxploitation era itself in *What It Is ... What It Was!*[80] According to Speed, *The Mack* symbolizes the 1970s: "It represents a slice of American life"; after all, African Americans were living in their own microcosm of a segregated world.[81] The 1970s was a period of transition between Dr. King's dream and the Black Power rhetoric of the Black Panthers. Then, there was the impact of Woodstock and the flower children. Women and blacks were seeking liberation and "the Latino community [was] striving for political position."[82] The 1970s embodied freedom and everyone was engaged in self-expression. Since the movie was filmed in Oakland, various people such as Black Panther founder Huey Newton and singers Bobby Womack and Sly Stone would come to the club-like movie set to hang out. Newton invited everyone from the set to his penthouse on Lake Merritt in Oakland and sent limousines to get them. As Newton reminded everyone to incorporate "Black

Power" into the film, he acted as the social conscience behind the scenes of *The Mack*. Then, there were "the powerful personas of Richard Pryor, Max Julien, Annazette Chase, Harvey Bernhard, and Michael Campos [who] were all part of the whole mixture that created the power of this film."[83] Although Speed was never under the illusion that *The Mack* represented all of America, there was an unexpected backlash against the cast members, the film, and the genre. To Speed's dismay, there were many African American people who were embarrassed by the black images portrayed in *The Mack*. Speed analogizes the blaxploitation era with the blues era; she claims that if it was not for "the Europeans who took an interest in it, the blues would've been destroyed because Black people were more moving away from it."[84] Ironically, Speed laments, it lessens the achievements of those who pioneered the blaxploitation era when "your own people spit on you like that."[85] Sadly, many African Americans failed to realize that getting work as a black actor in Hollywood was limited. Many low-budget black actors aspired to be like Cicely Tyson in *Sounder* or Sidney Poitier.[86] However, the opportunity was almost nonexistent. There was a glass ceiling that hovered over blacks in Hollywood.

The Mack was the first film to make as much impact *Guess Who's Coming to Dinner* with Sidney Poitier, Spencer Tracy, and Katharine Hepburn. Various actors from *The Mack* were in *Newsweek* and *Time* magazines and this hurled the NAACP into shock. Speed offers an alternative view to the negative criticisms of various black organizations. *The Mack* cast "were not elected officials"; they did not represent an organization, social cause, or "any type of movement."[87] Speed and the cast members were trying to feed themselves and work through their craft. On this point, some critics may differ with Speed. Based on many personal accounts, the attacks by the NAACP worked in concert to end an era of prosperity in the new black cinema of the 1970s. But on the other hand, *The Mack* was an organization of performers and black representatives of the Hollywood regime. Young people looked up to actors like Julien, Pryor, and Speed like they were role models; hence, symbols of appointed black leadership. The blaxploitation era was emblematic of a social cause or movement declaring that blacks would no longer accept subservient roles in life or in the film industry. Thus blacks wanted agency over their economic, political, and social destinies in America. African Americans were demanding representation in every aspect of American citizenry, which included active participation, visibility, and agency in Hollywood. In a country that elevates Hollywood icons to the level of European royalty, the blaxploitation images had power to shape and shift perceptions of blacks in mainstream America. Although black performers felt powerless to a certain extent over their own economic agency, they wielded aesthetic power in terms of whites' perceptions of black America and African Americans' perceptions of themselves. Although Speed argues that art should not bear the burden of addressing the social issues of "Black people or Brown people or Red people or White people," she must remember that the people who patronized the movies were also trying to survive and thrive in America.[88] Movies like *The Mack* offered an alternative to former movies that encouraged black submission and passivity despite white racism. To many blacks, *The Mack* was the wrong answer for a fractured community in transition from the civil rights movement. Sadly, instead of suggesting more positive role models, various organizations such as CORE, NAACP, and SCLC succeeded at "destroying and not replacing."[89] Once the blaxploitation era ended, the black male image became scarce in Hollywood.

Even though many blaxploitation performers were proud of their roles and contribution to black cinema, they became aware of racial discrimination in their field. Many African American actors were shocked when they discovered that they were not making the same money and not offered the same choices as white performers.[90] Remember, the blaxploitation era saved many studios from descending into bankruptcy. With that being said, many actors still did not receive their worth despite their contribution to the film industry. Nevertheless, Speed hopes that history will perceive the blaxploitation era through different and more positive lens. Prior to the blaxploitation era, blacks had only "Stepin Fetchit, Dorothy Dandridge aboard a slave ship, and *Anna La Lucasia* with Eartha Kitt and Sammy Davis, Jr."[91] But with the blaxploitation era, audiences were offered sexual, rebellious, militant, and dangerous black males who lacked the passivity and submissive demeanor of most black male actors in the 1950s and 1960s.

In terms of black male images, here is an argument that clarifies the importance of cinematic heroism in *The Mack*. For 1970s audiences, Max Julien elevated an urban image of the pimp to cultish status. Julien's charismatic performance transformed the pimp from a low-life representation of urban culture into a transformative figure. In essence, the pimp becomes a conscious thinker once he contemplates his role within America's power structure and seeks to alter his personal circumstances. Julien's character rejects playing the black victim, which is so popular in American cinema. Instead, he embraces retribution as a mantra of his black manhood. By raising the pimp to iconic status, the everyday or common urban person realizes their innate power to rise above their circumstances. Ultimately, the elevation of the pimp, as an urban folk hero, resonates with many black and some white audiences. The black pimp is not prey, but a perpetrator; he is a dazzling survivor of America's racist infrastructure that forced him to seek refuge as a pimp in the first place.

In terms of black gangsters, Fred Williamson had a similar impact on black heroism as Max Julien. Williamson played the lead in the movie the *Black Caesar*. The plot of the film centers on a shoe-shine boy who becomes a "top mafia kingpin"; in other words, *Black Caesar* is "the story of a Harlem youth's rise and fall in New York City's crime world."[92] Howard insists that *Black Caesar* is "one of Blaxploitation's most carefully constructed and consistently engaging entries."[93] Williamson is the quintessential personification of the gangster as Tommy Gibbs. The legendary Williamson is "tall, dark, handsome, charismatic and, most of all, believable, he is perfectly cast and seems to be exactly the type of overly confident, egocentric man who would be able to succeed in the cutthroat underground world of organized crime."[94] The fast-paced narrative is heightened by the performances of Gloria Hendry who plays Helen, Tommy's turncoat ex-girlfriend, and Julius W. Harris who plays Mr. Gibbs, Tommy's remorseful father. One of the most famous scenes occurs when "Gibbs brutalizes corrupt cop McKinney by making him rub shoe shine polish on his face and sing 'Mammy!' "[95] This scene makes a mockery of blackface performers who ridiculously mimic black culture and profit from its mockery. Originally, the lead character was intended to be a star vehicle for Sammy Davis Jr., but evidently Fred Williamson proved to be a much better choice. According to Howard, *Black Caesar* was filmed in 18 days for only $300,000; but the legendary movie made $2 million, which spawned a sequel, *Hell Up in Harlem*. Lastly, typical of blaxploitation movies' phenomenal soundtracks, such as James Brown's for *Black Caesar*, the music heightened the moviegoers' interest and delight in the film.

Blacula is also a major landmark in terms of blaxploitation horror films and black male representation.[96] The movie starred William Marshall (Mamuwalde/Blacula), Vonetta McGee (Luva/Tina), Denise Nicholas (Michelle), and Elisha Cook Jr. (Sam).[97] The story's plot centers on the curse placed upon Prince Mamuwalde by Count Dracula.[98] Marshall's Blacula is forced to "live for eternity as a vampire when the prince's mission to stop the slave trade runs into a snag in Transylvania."[99] Then the movie leaps 200 years ahead. Mamuwalde's coffin is bought by two gay interior designers from Los Angeles. After the Prince awakes from his coffin people begin to die; therefore the police suspect that a vampire is in the metropolis.

Mamuwalde falls in love with McGee's character; she resembles his former wife, Luva, who was killed by Dracula. As expected, Tina succumbs to Blacula's charms. Koven asserts that *Blacula* is distinguished from other blaxploitation films because of its theme. Mamuwalde is not an evil character; white aristocracy (Dracula) placed a curse on him. Thus *Blacula* is a legacy of slave history. Although Mamuwalde kills to satisfy his hunger and his need to survive, the film treats him "as more of a tragic figure than a monster, and it is the white hegemony that sees him as a de facto monster."[100] Thus the Blacula character is a metaphor for the urban monster that is a product of his social circumstances, not his innate nature. Despite winning Best Horror Film in 1972 from the Academy of Horror Films and Science Fiction Films, Koven claims that "*Blacula* is more interesting to talk about then to actually watch."[101] Koven credits the "pretty funky" credit opener to the "great score by Gene Page, the arranger of most of Barry White's hits."[102] As usual, the soundtrack is a necessary and purposeful promotional tool when featuring a blaxploitation film.

A film that falls in the kung-fu subgenre category is *Black Belt Jones* starring Jim Kelly. Unlike the characters played by Julien and Williamson, Kelly is a positive role model for audiences. In other words, he is an attainable image for inner-city youth who live in violent and drug-infested urban areas. Playing alongside Kelly (Black Belt Jones) is Gloria Hendry (Sidney).[103] A black federal agent is compelled to get involved in the story once "the mob puts pressure on an African-American karate school to close down."[104] Howard suggests that the high-kicking fight sequences make the movie worthy of viewing. Kelly was a "middleweight martial arts champion" who wore an "outsize afro, pork chop sideburns and platform shoes"; he "is as colourful and one-dimensional as any super hero could ever be."[105] In a blaxploitation manner, Kelly's "flat line delivery and intonation work in his favor" by adding to the "cartoonish and otherworldly" persona he presents as Black Belt Jones.[106] Hendry as Sidney Byrd is a former *Playboy* bunny who became an actress. In her role as Jones's girlfriend, she is as provocative as she is lethal. Koven notes that one of the important themes in the film centers on an antidrug message. Even though the film acknowledges the urban realities in black life, there is a conflict between black militants who seek to rid the streets of African Americans involved in the drug trade and "African-American profiteers [drug dealers] who, although not controlling the local drugs traffic, are certainly key points in its circulation."[107] Then the message resonates that karate school provides a hip place to hang out with buddies and get "physical exercise, mental and physical discipline, and self-respect."[108] The other alternative for youth is Ted Lange's (Pinky) pool hall, which is a negative influence on the community. Consequently, martial arts becomes a socially cool refuge or alternative to the violence in the streets.

Mandingo is another blaxploitation film of a more serious note. The movie successfully inverts the commonly held views of slavery. Epic films such as *The Birth of a Nation, Gone with the Wind,* and *Uncle Tom's Cabin* present slavery as a benign institution that benefited owners and slaves alike. *Mandingo* is distinguished by its subversion of "Hollywood's popular presentation of contented slaves and fair-minded masters."[109] In this Paramount-produced film, "the daughter of a Southern plantation owner takes a prized fighting slave as a lover. This violent, big budget movie was less than the sum of its parts. However, it was successful enough to have spawned a sequel, *Drum*."[110] The *Mandingo* cast features James Mason (Warren Maxwell), Susan George (Blanche), Perry King (Hammond Maxwell), and Brenda Sykes (Ellen).[111] The movie refused to shy away from sexual relations between black male slaves and white women, and their counterparts, white slave owners and black female slaves. For instance, the "white plantation heir Hammond Maxwell (Perry King) enjoys a fringe benefit—Ellen (Brenda Sykes), a young black slave girl."[112] Howard states that Perry King shines as the "handsome, compassionate and curiously shy son Hammond," yet he suffers from having a permanently injured leg because "he fell off a horse" as a youth.[113] Unfortunately for Hammond, he must navigate "the duplicitous roles that fair-minded whites had to play in the turn of the century, racist South."[114] Sykes is remarkable in her role as the "soft, sincere, sane and sober ... beautiful black woman."[115] Meanwhile, champion prize fighter Ken Norton plays the hard-fighting Mandingo. Norton is noteworthy in his role as the high-ranking Mandingo, in terms of African slave hierarchy. He is well suited to this role because he is "certainly a tall dark and handsome man with an undeniably well maintained (and, as it turns out, highly desirable) physique."[116] Koven eloquently states that *Mandingo* effectively exposes slavery as "brutal, exploitative, dirty, degrading, hypocritical and totally dehumanizing to everyone, black and white."[117] According to Koven, the most overt antislavery message occurs when the only literate slave, Ji-Tu Cumbuka (Cicero), speaks directly to the camera from his cell: "Through literacy comes equality, and then true freedom."[118] Even though *Mandingo* offers a message about literacy, equality, and freedom, the graphic imagery overshadows the positive messages of the film.

Meanwhile, Gordon Parks Jr. depicts black empowerment and virility in *Three the Hard Way* (1974). Due to the success of Fred Williamson, Jim Kelly, and the former football player Jim Brown, Parks Jr. features the money-making trio in his action film.[119] Howard describes the plot by stating that "when a wealthy neo-Nazi develops a serum that will kill all blacks, three powerful African-American men combine forces to foil the plot."[120] Williamson plays Jagger Daniels, a "Chicago Businessman"; Kelly plays Mr. Keyes, a "karate expert" and friend of Lait; and Brown plays "Jimmy Lait, a Los Angeles–based record promoter."[121] The movie promises plenty of action, violence and scenic locations, such as "(at least thirty cars are destroyed), several deftly choreographed fight sequences, and splendid Chicago, New York City, Los Angeles and Washington D.C. locations."[122] The trio of Williamson, Kelly, and Brown "are macho, cool, larger than life super-heroes" who work so well together that the next year they star in the "Italian made Blaxploitation western" *Take a Hard Ride* (1975).[123]

During the blaxploitation era, one of the most significant and controversial elements remains the sexual relationships between black men and white women. In the past, Jim Crow and the Hays Moral Code barred even the insinuation of sexual relations between black males and white women. Remember, Poitier made headlines with his 1967 movie about an interracial relationship in *Guess Who's Coming to Dinner*. But the black-white interaction between Poitier and his mate contains much restraint. When these mixed-race relationships are depicted in the 1970s, the sex tends to be explicit and emphasizes the sexual prowess of the black male and submissiveness of the white female. Koven reminds his readers that "miscegenation is the intermixing of races, usually referring specifically to the sexual mixing of black and white people."[124] Koven states that this "recurring theme" is common where the "the black heroes have white girlfriends, or at least sleep with white women (*Shaft*, *Slaughter* and Priest in *Superfly* [sic] all do)."[125] Even the black pimps tend to "have white prostitutes, who they parade as a sign of status."[126] Particularly with Goldie in *The Mack*, the message is not only can the black male dominate "a stable of beautiful women, they also control beautiful white women" with little or no resistance.[127] Nevertheless, there were people in America who were not ready for this level of black sexual bravado. Koven cites *The Black Six* (1974) as one film that violates the miscegenation code and the resulting death that occurred.

With that said, there were films during this era that are not focused on the typical blaxploitation archetypes of preachers, pimps, pushers, and players. There were movies that focused on loving relationships between black males and black females, such as Billy Dee Williams in *Lady Sings the Blues* (1972) and *Mahogany* (1975) with Diana Ross.[128] Furthermore, there are movies such as Schultz's *Car Wash* (1976), starring Antonio

Vargas as a gay male, Bill Duke as a black militant, and Richard Pryor as a televangelist preacher who acts like a pimp; thus the movie encompasses a multitude of diverse depictions of working-class black men.[129] Although Pryor is a preacher in this film, he is a minor character and not the major impetus of the action. Finally, there is Schultz's *Cooley High* (1975) starring Glynn Thurman opposite Cynthia Davis. This drama is about "a group of seniors attending a Chicago high school [as] they learn about life and love in the streets"[130]—a plot that is the basis for many films that feature black youth and black love in urban movies today. There are many subgenres of the blaxploitation era; however, the blaxploitation era is distinguished by black-themed films, all-black casts, black directors, and oftentimes black screenwriters. But once white studios grew tired of the intense backlash and audiences began to lose interest, only two black movie stars emerged in the 1980s: Richard Pryor and Eddie Murphy.

CHAPTER 8

_____ 1980s _____
Black Comedians Rule: In the Age of Eddie Murphy and Richard Pryor

During the 1970s, the success of the blaxploitation era led "Hollywood producers and agents, directors and studio chiefs" to declare that racial biases were fading in the movie industry.[1] By the mid-1980s, that false prophecy failed to manifest into authentic change for people of color. Increasingly, the growing movie audience ranged between the ages of 14 and 25. Without a doubt, the humorous _Trading Places_ (1983) with _Saturday Night Live_ alumnus Dan Aykroyd attracted young audiences. Following the success of the 1930s-style farce, "Paramount Pictures proceeded to sign the 23-year-old to a $25 million contract for six pictures."[2] For that reason any star, black or white, who could deliver comedic action yielded a huge profit for the studios. _Beverly Hills Cop_ starring Eddie Murphy grossed more than $140 million before the close of 1985; therefore the success of _Beverly Hills Cop_ was not hindered by any racial biases of the audience.[3] For Murphy's career, this was a turning point and a Hollywood milestone for black male performers. In 1982, prior to Murphy's record-breaking success with a different studio, Richard Pryor acquired a "$40 million, four-picture deal from Columbia Pictures."[4] For Pryor's and Murphy's upcoming cinematic performances, they sought more control because they realized their economic value to the industry. Consequently, they produced the films in which they starred. In essence, they chose to acquire agency over their own images and perceptions in Hollywood. If African Americans seek star status and autonomy in Hollywood, actors such as Murphy and Pryor must continue to make money for the studios.

Even though Pryor's and Murphy's comedic stardom was a landmark achievement, Murphy was still concerned about opportunity for other African Americans. The actor who performs in front of the camera is only one of the components for making a well-received film. Allen Johnson writes in *Black Camera*'s "A Year in Review" that the need for black presence extends to blacks playing a role in "production, screen writing, directing and acting."[5] Thus Murphy realized that his on-camera triumphs symbolized racial progress, but there were other phases of the moviemaking process that lacked black representation. Consequently, when he was as an Academy Award presenter in 1988, he stressed the necessity of widening the prospects for black inclusion. Johnson writes that there were some improvements in terms of black roles. Hollywood shed the servant roles of the Stepin Fetchit and Hattie McDaniel days and replaced those stale stereotypes with blacks playing criminals and various villain types. Although movies such as *Shaft* shifted the monolithic view of blacks as villainous characters, they failed to alter the image of African Americans in Hollywood. Now, there were benign black characters who served the purpose of supporting and assisting the white hero. Yet the roles were often minor, static, and lacked artistic range. In actuality, nothing in Hollywood had changed. Black roles in all phases of the movie industry were scarce and when black roles were offered they lacked significant talent range. Nevertheless, there were black filmmakers who were determined to feature blacks in every aspect of the entertainment field. Independent films such as Spike Lee's *She's Gotta Have It* (1986) and Robert Townsend's *Hollywood Shuffle* (1987) demonstrated African Americans' interest in attaining a "fair share of the motion picture pie."[6] Although black filmmakers sought to make money in Hollywood, they were willing to depict blacks in a fully realized manner. Yet commercial films were content to rely on the same monolithic and negative depictions from the past.

However, clearly black filmmakers were influenced by the new black cinema of the 1970s. Oftentimes, they featured character types, themes, or even stars from that era for satirical and/or homage purposes. The comedic Keenen Ivory Wayans channeled the blaxploitation era with his "parody of the black adventure films" in *I'm Gonna Git You Sucka*, a small film that Wayans wrote, directed, and coproduced that starred Jim Brown, Bernie Casey, and Isaac Hayes.[7] Although *Hollywood Shuffle* and *I'm Gonna Git You Sucka* are two of the films that emphasized the lack of involvement by blacks in the film industry, Johnson argues that the "comic buffoon" remained the most prevalent role for blacks in Hollywood. For instance, Johnson cites a well-known box-office bomb of Pryor's to emphasize his point. As a result of the cinematic failure of *Moving*, Pryor's talents were squandered by playing that role. Thus *Moving* signified an impending downturn in Pryor's movie career. Meanwhile, Murphy failed in the role of social commentator when he starred as an African prince in *Coming to America* (1988). Critics were also disappointed by Murphy's reliance on black stereotypes to ensure laughter and profitability. Both Pryor and Murphy subsided into buffoonery in the midst of their black ingenuity. During the 1980s, independent films by the critically acclaimed Lee, Townsend, and Wayans demonstrated an evolution of black images in Hollywood. But in terms of dominant African American actors of the 1980s era, Pryor and Murphy reigned supreme in their representations of black progress and regression in terms of big studio productions.

Comic-Strip Caricatures: Black Comedic Actors

Although Hollywood paid Pryor and Murphy well for their performances, oftentimes the studios pigeonholed them by offering typical roles. Therefore lesser known black comedic actors with far less influence were also bound by Hollywood stereotypes. Unabashedly, the studios believed they were providing a surefire template for audience satisfaction. There are critics who claim that, unlike American audiences, international audiences were willing to accept multifaceted black representations. Since various opportunities for black filmmakers have increased, Albert Johnson writes in "Moods Indigo: A Long View" that African American men and women are accepted as authentic representations for international audiences.[8] Nevertheless, the American cinema encompasses the most positive and negative black screen images "of contemporary American culture and its black sub-culture."[9] By the 1980s, Hollywood recognized the work of black filmmakers due to the filmmaking accomplishments of Ossie Davis, Michael Schultz, Sidney Poitier, Gordon Parks Sr., and Gordon Parks Jr. in the 1970s. Nevertheless, Johnson hopes that the race of the director will not matter in terms of more diverse images. Thus, despite the increase of black filmmakers, roles for black males have not evolved on a mass commercial scale. For instance, once Richard Pryor appeared on the cover of *Time* and Eddie Murphy appeared on the cover of *Newsweek*, there seemed to be "a quest for novelty, a new 'hipness' that linked the perceptiveness of the aesthete and the sophisticate with the streetwise humor of the common man."[10] To some, the popularity of Pryor and Murphy signified comedic performances as a pathway to impactful film work; however, Johnson says that by the early 1990s, comedy had not led to serious work on film. Johnson argues that black images on screen "are still off-balance, treating only a limited range of experience and ignoring the lives of a vast part of America's black citizens."[11] In other words, the success of Pryor and Murphy, among other comedic film actors, had not transformed the perceptions of African American representations. Furthermore, the majority of films starring blacks failed to include the multiplicity of the black experience in America.

Even though Pryor and Murphy exemplified "dramatic talent (particularly with Pryor's work in *Blue Collar*)," they symbolized "an odd mixture rebel-against-society, the black man outrageously confronting social restrictions, and the vaudeville comic brought up to date."[12] In other words, there is a dichotomy of black rebel and vaudeville comic present in Pryor's and Murphy's performances. Neither comedian represented the submissive and downtrodden servile image of Stepin Fetchit. Furthermore, both Pryor and Murphy intermeshed "vulgar language mixed with social criticism" of American society.[13] Albert Johnson credits the white comedian Lenny Bruce, who was influenced by Redd Foxx, as the forerunner of uncouth presentation intertwined with a critique of society. When Bruce said the word "nigger" on stage, he shocked black audiences; however, without hesitation, he chastised American middle-class values. Furthermore, Johnson credits Redd Foxx and Nipsey Russell for reverting back to Bruce's language and incorporating attitudes of the black street hustler. Foxx and Russell are two prototypes that captured Pryor's attention; therefore he modeled his stand-up after them.

Toward the end of the 1980s, Pryor retained the same language but the rage and frustration subsided. Initially, his stand-up signified a genuine African American experience for black and white audiences. Oftentimes, blacks understood the double-edged humor of the stereotypical jokes. Unfortunately, in the film versions of his comic routines, Pryor began to "build a stereotyped image too easily imitated as a stylistic attitude by blacks—particularly black youth—and too easily misinterpreted by the public."[14] Unfortunately, young blacks embraced Pryor's stereotypes as actualizations of their own identity. Then, white audiences interpreted Pryor as the prototype of the black male living in America. Ironically, Pryor's comedic persona failed to resemble his own individuality as an African American. Johnson believes that Pryor's comedic performances reveal an artist who has created a persona far different from himself. According to Johnson, *Silver Streak*, *Stir Crazy*, *Critical Condition*, and *Jo Jo Dancer, Your Life Is Calling* signify "those external aspects of the black comic hero, flippant and hilariously distraught."[15] Meanwhile, *Blue Collar* and *Some Sort of Hero* represent "Pryor's tense antagonisms toward American society's corruptions and conservatism into the realm of high drama and social criticism, on an interracial level."[16] Thus Pryor's roles in the aforementioned films were not for the purpose of buffoonery. Instead, his comedic presence emphasized a sincere social message for America's conscience.

Like Pryor, Eddie Murphy's performances oftentimes descended into tomfoolery for an immediate laugh. Yet Murphy's comedic persona masks a more privileged upbringing than most audiences assume. In opposition to Americans' typical perception of Murphy, he is originally from the suburbs, not the ghetto; specifically, born in 1962, he had a middle-class upbringing on Long Island.[17] As a performer, he offers comedy as a weapon for entertainment and social comment. For instance, in the successful box-office buddy flick *48 Hours* (1988), Murphy is a street-smart criminal compelled to work with a "big Nordic plainclothes detective" (Nick Nolte) to solve a crime.[18] After a violent skirmish between the two, they come to form a connection and attain mutual respect for each other. Albert Johnson asserts that it is a manifestation of wish fulfillment for black audiences and total fantasy for white audiences. During the famous bar scene in *48 Hours*, the smart-aleck bravado manages to strike fear into the "redneck" drinking in an urban-cowboy-themed bar. The same method of employing Murphy's humor as the "wisecracking young black man are the source of humor in *Beverly Hills Cop, I & II.*"[19] Johnson deems Murphy's performance as "outrageous beyond the borders of belief despite the one-dimensional behavior of comic and villainous characters."[20] But in reality, most audience members do not watch comedies for believability. Nevertheless, Johnson views the bar scene as an example of how black humor has been reduced to television-like comic-strip roles—in other words, no different from the comedy featured on Saturday kiddie shows. Yet of course, there is no foul language on those children's shows. Basically, intellectual satire is often cast aside in the films of Pryor and Murphy in their attempts to garner an easy laugh.

When people think of famous comedians of the 1980s, Bill Cosby, Richard Pryor, and Eddie Murphy are in similar company. Arguably, Cosby is "the most influential comedian of the period," but he "never had equal success in film."[21] Johnson claims that Cosby's comedy in films is lacking a certain element of depth; for instance, when Cosby played in movies such as *California Suite* (1978) and *Leonard: Part Six* (1987), his comedy was embarrassing for various audiences.[22] Despite the popularity of Cosby, his films lack intellectual satire because they seek funniness in the "Black middle-class suburban experiences."[23] Moreover, his talents were focused more on television and live performances. During the 1980s and the early 1990s, the primary issue with the "outstanding black comedians best known throughout the world" is that their black images raised their personal fortunes, while increasing the monetary wealth of their film producers.[24] Basically, a plethora of blacks in the movie industry did not directly benefit from the elevated black images in Cosby's, Pryor's, and Murphy's films. What is absent from the universal laughter aroused by their films is the indigenous nature of timeless black American ways. Perhaps some people may differ, but Johnson argues that the "core of black American humor is the street humor of fashion, language, and behavior" that was championed by Bert Williams.[25] Not since Dick Gregory and Godfrey Cambridge of the 1960s has America seen such authentic black humor. However, this comparison may be unfair; both Pryor and Murphy offer raw and authentic street humor in terms of their filmed stage performances. But with regard to movies, with Pryor's servant-like comedic role, his performance in the *Toy* is akin to Stepin Fetchit. For instance, Pryor is hired by a wealthy father who offers him as a "playmate-guardian" to a "spoiled white child" as Pryor "brings happiness and self-discovery to himself."[26] Meanwhile, Hollywood profits from these narrow-ranged performances that lack "humanistic awareness."[27] Pryor's high-profile presence lacks depth because the premise of the film lacks substance. Other than commercial audiences, the direct beneficiaries of such a monolithic depiction are Pryor, the studio, and the marketers. To ensure that audiences occupy seats in theaters, it becomes a formulaic matter to place Pryor and Murphy in comic-strip caricature types of roles that thrill American audiences.

Before Eddie Murphy ... There Was Richard Pryor

Although there are many negative critiques that can be made of Pryor's movie roles, Crystal L. Keels's article entitled "The Richard Pryor Film Retrospective" highlights the many groundbreaking achievements of Pryor.[28] Keels opens her article with the words "before Chris Tucker, Eddie Murphy, and Robin Williams, there was Richard Pryor" who was not only an actor, but a "comedian, writer, actor, and director."[29] Pryor is considered "one of the most significant American artists of the last half-century." Moreover, by acting in over 40 films, he is distinguished from other performers; he has a multitude of "Grammy winning-albums, and legendary live comedy performances."[30] Thus he has influenced American popular culture with his persona in a major way. Pryor won an Emmy award for his writing. Furthermore, Pryor cowrote *Blazing Saddles* (1974) with Mel Brooks.

Although Pryor cowrote the script for *Blazing Saddles*, he still missed an opportunity to create a varied black character for audiences. Pryor's role, according to Donald Bogle, was a New Age coon: "a coon with a double consciousness."[31] In terms of the genre, the movie is considered a wildly energetic spoof on westerns. Originally, Pryor planned to star as the black sheriff played by Cleavon Little; in order to overcome and thrive, the sheriff must feign the position "of a *dumb black nigger*."[32] Obviously, Bogle does not share the same praise for Pryor's work as Keels does for Pryor's *Blazing Saddles*. In 1998, Pryor achieved another milestone: as "the first recipient of the Mark Twain Prize for Humor," he "is perhaps best known for his scathing, irreverent, insightful, and hilarious critique and commentary on all aspects of the human condition. Race relations, sexuality, drug usage, politics, and spirituality are some of the subjects Pryor takes on his performances."[33] Pryor directed himself in his fourth live concert film titled *Richard Pryor Here and Now* (1983). Keels claims the documentary reveals his classic biting humor, onstage sizzle, and sheer artistry. Pryor boldly speaks about "Hollywood and the creation of illusions, slavery, divorce, America's foreign relations" to name a few of his wide-ranging topics; furthermore, he speaks about his addiction to heroin and "the tragic social conditions" that led to his struggle.[34] Evidently, when Pryor invited the audiences to reflect on his personal adversities, he revealed his full humanity as an African American male and performer.

In Pryor's acting performances, he operated with a varying level of accomplishment. Pryor was rewarded with critical praise for his strong performance in *Lady Sings the Blues* (1972). Billy Dee Williams and Diana Ross star as the lead characters in a dramatization of the Billie Holiday story.[35] Pryor ignites the screen with his "hepped-up and high-spirited" performance as the Piano Man.[36] After Pryor's 1967 debut "as pallbearer detective in *The Busy Body*, a gangster comedy starring Sid Caesar," he starred in *Silver Streak* (1976) with Gene Wilder.[37] Many critics claim that Pryor's role acting alongside Wilder transformed him into a premier mainstream star. Perhaps America's "huck-finn fixation" explains the appeal to mass audiences.[38] Bogle claims that when Pryor coaches Wilder on how to be black, Pryor is actually instructing Wilder on how to liberate himself from the strictures of society's rules and regulations. This movie signifies how 1970s black-white buddy films visualized an alleviation of tension between the races. During a scene where Pryor and Wilder are attempting to elude federal authorities, Wilder dons blackface by putting shoe polish on his white face.[39] Notwithstanding the innovative elements within this film, Wilder's reliance on blackface for a laugh is a sign of regression. Though Keels claims the scene offers "insightful commentary on racial differences," she is erroneous when she asserts that this is the first interracial buddy film.[40]

As previously stated in chapter 5, Sidney Poitier and Tony Curtis play escaped convicts in the 1958 *Defiant Ones*. Historically, they offer the first semblance of comradery between a black male and a white male. Nonetheless, Keels states that after the commercial magnitude of *Silver Streak*, many people considered Pryor the hugest black star in film history. Wilder and Pryor would attempt to emulate the box-office success with four more films; however, they failed to garner the profit of the $30 million made by *Silver Streak*. With regard to box-office profits, Bogle offers a different number for the Pryor-Wilder flicks. *Silver Streak* and *Stir Crazy* (1980) grossed in the amount of $200 million.[41] The success of both films caused America to proclaim them as "the first successful interracial comedy team."[42]

According to Keels, many people consider Pryor's role in *Blue Collar* (1978) to be his best performance.[43] Pryor costars in the film with Harvey Keitel and Yaphet Kotto; the three men play Detroit auto assembly line workers. As the men try to change their stark circumstances, they realize their ineffectiveness within a corporate structure as they encounter the unethical unionized labor system. Even though Bogle praises Pryor's performance in this film, he laments over the attempt to "domesticate" Pryor and "transform him into an acceptable, middle-class fellow" who desires nothing more than a good life.[44] Perhaps Bogle interprets the domestication of Pryor as an attempt to attribute a simplified version of white desires onto a black character.

In another hit film, *Bustin' Loose* (1981), coproduced by Pryor, he plays "a con man who drives a group of eight homeless orphans and their prim, fussy teacher (Cicely Tyson) from Philadelphia to Seattle."[45] Bogle refers to *Bustin' Loose* as "congenial," but he still criticizes the movie for seeking to subdue Pryor's "uncontrollable spirits, those nasty urges, those foul imaginings in order to make one believe he's just like us, an ordinary, kind of wild but basically humble guy."[46] Even though Pryor may have suppressed his wild spirit in movies, his intensity and passion remained high in his live performances.

In *Richard Pryor Live on Sunset Strip* (1982), Pryor speaks about "his infamous suicide attempt and a trip to Africa that would forever" transform his perception of African Americans.[47] Then Pryor publicly shined a spotlight on his personal life by starring in the semiautobiographical *Jo Jo Dancer, Your Life Is Calling* (1986). Pryor writes, produces, directs, and stars in the film featuring Jo Jo Dancer's survival from "drug dependency problems ... the most hideous of accidents, self-inflicted burns from a suicide attempt after a days-long bout of substance abuse."[48] As a commitment to racial equality, he assembled a predominantly black cast and crew. With this film, the audiences witnessed Pryor's attempts to shed his personal demons. Unfortunately, when Pryor was diagnosed with multiple sclerosis in 1986, his personal life was struck with an additional tragedy. Despite early trials and tribulations, Pryor never ceased to inspire audiences with his professional and personal survival stories that would have thwarted a lesser talent.

After all, Pryor overcame his humble beginnings: he was raised in a "mid-western brothel by his grandmother to his Hollywood super star status with mansions in Los Angeles and Hawaii."[49] In spite of blatant racism, Pryor managed to succeed in the highly polarized Hollywood film industry. Furthermore, his professional performances were constant manifestations of his early pain as a child. Somehow, Pryor managed to rein in a "ferocious struggle with personal demons ... [and] pushed the parameters of black performance."[50] By pushing the artistic boundaries as a black male performer, a more evolved portrait of the black male image becomes more acceptable to the public. Even though Pryor offers some buffoonery in his comedic roles, his dramatic parts and live performances remain nuanced. Lastly, his willingness to take the helm as the lead actor, writer, director, and producer of his own film representations demonstrates the desire for self-autonomy and desire to reconstruct black images. Consequently, Pryor's accomplishments in the 1970s and the 1980s enabled America to equally embrace another famous black comedian, Murphy, in the 1980s.

The Preeminence of Eddie Murphy: *Trading Places, Coming to America,* and *Harlem Nights*

In 1983, Murphy starred in the box-office hit *Trading Places* directed by John Landis.[51] Set in Philadelphia, Murphy plays a street hustler who trades lives with the preppy stockbroker (Dan Aykroyd). Their lives are dramatically altered when two billionaire brothers played by Ralph Bellamy and Don Ameche wage a debt. Murphy is bestowed with an $80,000 job and a mansion; meanwhile, Aykroyd is accused of being "a thief and drug dealer" and forced out of his former upscale lifestyle. Consistent with 1980s themes, due to the developing friendship between Murphy and Aykroyd, the movie promotes interracial bonding between a black and white male.[52] Ultimately, Murphy plays the role of a "highfalutin supporting player—the rowdy coon—there for gritty laughs."[53] Per usual, Bogle disapproves of this superfluous misuse of a black comic's talents for supporting roles. Toward the end of the decade, *Coming to America* offers Murphy the opportunity to rise from supporting player to the primary comic figure in his films.

With *Coming to America*, Murphy widens the scope of cultural critique to include class. At this time, American cinema reinforces the erroneous belief that blacks are generally impoverished. Although Murphy relies on these racial assumptions for laughs, he pokes fun at wealthy Africans and middle-class African Americans for additional social critique. In "'Uplift the Race!': *Coming to America, Do the Right Thing*, and the Poetics and Politics of 'Othering,' " published in the journal *Cultural Critique*, Tejumola Olaniyan discusses class and race. Olaniyan explores how class position does not negate the influence of race in American society.[54] Even Murphy acknowledges, in a less complex manner than Olaniyan, that "class position has little or no effect on racial subjectification."[55] The problems associated with black identity are not obliterated because a black person occupies a higher rung on the socioeconomic ladder. For Murphy, this was his first film dedicated to "pleasing the black mass movie audience, rather than the white one."[56] In an interview with Spike Lee, Murphy expresses frustration over the reviews of *Coming to America*. Instead of opting for the typical views of Africa centered on "poverty, decay, death, and devastation," Murphy opposes those images by featuring Africans as prosperous and living in immense luxury.[57] *Coming to America* features Murphy portraying the African Prince Akeem; he heads to America in order to rebel against an arranged marriage.[58] At the beginning of the film, the "African prince from Zamunda travels to the United States in search of a bride."[59] Murphy heads to America with his male servant Semmi (Arsenio Hall) and ends up choosing his employer's (John Amos) daughter (Shari Headley) for marriage; meanwhile, James Earl Jones plays Murphy's father as the bombastic Zamundan King and Madge Sinclair plays Murphy's mother as the beautiful Zamundan Queen.[60]

The predominating themes of *Coming to America* center on affluence, notoriety, and "aristocratic heterosexual romance," and other primary themes focus on "the exotic Other, locale, and perspective."[61] For that reason, Olaniyan urges the audience not to view the African locale as racial progress in Hollywood. The image of Akeem's opulent kingdom deep in the African jungle does not negate Hollywood's familiar depiction of "the threatening Other, usually the African."[62] Olaniyan insists that even though *Coming to America* stars Murphy, a major black star, the movie exemplifies the commonly held view that blacks are somehow different than the norm. Thus the point of view displaying the long shot of the "elephants and zebras" is not of an African or African American male but of an American Hollywood cliché.[63] Olaniyan refers to the Western gaze in *Coming to America* as "the classical anthropological gaze par excellence."[64] As evidence of Olaniyan's cinematic concerns, he emphasizes the "narcissistic view" of happiness defined by Western standards, not African; for instance, the movie begins by showing Prince Akeem surrounded by splendor and an endless flock of servants ready to satisfy his every need. There are musicians and women who bathe naked in the pool with Akeem. Nevertheless, Akeem's primary complaint about his arranged wife to be is that "she is not assertive"; he lacks concern for her strict upbringing that has molded her to serve her husband and marry into royalty.

People of Zamunda are featured as prisoners of uncivilized traditions such as arranged marriages; thus Prince Akeem is left with few options but to leave his home for the freedom of living in America.[65] As a result, the Zamunda African culture is featured in a "one-dimensional frame."[66] By extension, the African male played by an African American fails to transcend many Americans' narrow perceptions of Africa, Africans, and blacks living in America. In other words, the concept of Africa and even those ancestrally related is fixed. American culture is often unable to elevate beyond the preconceived notion of the Western gazer. Furthermore, the female in *Coming to America* is presented as the native and the subjugated other based on the "unabashed celebration of a patriarchal and aristocratic gaze."[67] Based on Olaniyan's interpretation of the African male, the African American male, and the dominance of the Western gaze, one may understand the negative criticisms of *Coming to America* despite its mass success with the audience.

After *Coming to America*, Murphy stars in another black-themed film with a mostly black cast. *Harlem Nights* (1989) is a movie that features three generations of comedians: Richard Pryor, Eddie Murphy, and Redd Foxx.[68] Johnson credits Murphy for the box-office success of the film. In an effort to "update his image and connect to the black audience," Murphy transforms into multiple roles as the writer, director, and executive producer of *Harlem Nights*.[69] Yet there are critics who believe that this film devalued black images even further by its release.

Albert Johnson surmises that Murphy created the "most offensive portrait of black American modes and manners since *Check and Double Check* (1930)—which features Amos 'n' Andy in blackface."[70] Prior to Murphy's profitable movie career, he was best known for his irreverent imitations and boyish unpredictability on the television show *Saturday Night Live*. By the time Murphy performs on stage in his film documentary *Raw* (1987) and acts in *Harlem Nights*, his face is consumed with self-satisfaction. Johnson considers Murphy's decision to act as master-director, writer, producer, and performer to be a disastrous move. The popular movie *Harlem Nights* is filmed in the tradition of classic gangster films. The nightclub that is the main locale in this film is a place "where blacks and whites drink, dance, and gamble in evening dress; where Duke Ellington's music is heard; where gangsters hold conferences in well-appointed offices, and machine gun fire sounds in the night."[71] Regardless of Murphy's intent to present three generations of humor, he lacks the bitter wit of Pryor and earthy uproar of Foxx. However, white critics provide African American filmmakers with a certain measure of encouragement. Nevertheless, the negative criticisms of black audiences is generally disregarded. For those reasons, even if a movie portrays African Americans in a negative light, if the movie is profitable, Hollywood continues to make films that make a mockery of blacks and black culture.

Black images are damaged when white audiences interpret fantastical elements as realistic representations of black society. These films may unconsciously relay underlying racial bitterness that can transform social commentary into bigoted messages. Popular entertainment has now manifested new stereotypes that are as malignant "as the racist magazine illustrations of Octavus Roy Cohen."[72] Johnson blames the influence of the 1970s on the miseducation of Murphy; since he grew up during the era of blaxploitation films, Murphy witnessed the "end of censorship" and "witless escapades of black superheroes and a café-au-lait temptresses which enriched their producers."[73] According to Johnson, the femme fatales in *Harlem Nights*, Della Reese, Lela Rochon, and Jasmine Guy, lack the dignity of the women who performed in 1970s blaxploitation films, such as *Coffey*, *Sheba Baby*, and *Cleopatra Jones*.[74] In a scene that many audience members found humorous, Murphy has a street fight with Reese's character. The Murphy-Reese fight transforms the black female image into a thug "for whom violence is a major passion." Lela Rochon plays the "madam's prize prostitute"; thus "she and the equally attractive Jasmine Guy are extensions of the oversexed black siren."[75] Johnson attributes Rochon's and Guy's sultry performances to the days of Nina Mae McKinney and Lena Horne in *Cabin in the Sky*. When Bogle refers to the female characters played by Reese, Rochon, and Guy as emerging "from the imagination of a vindictive misogynist," he is even less complimentary than Johnson.[76] Ultimately, most of the humor in the film depends on racial "epithets and vulgar retorts"; however, Johnson notes that Arsenio Hall's humorous performance as "a crybaby gangster seeking to avenge his brother" renders real hilarity to the film.[77] With that said, *Harlem Nights* fails to enhance the gangster film genre with nuanced perspectives. Instead, Murphy offers trite and narrow depictions of black male-black female relations that substantiate previously held stereotypes.

Richard Pryor and Eddie Murphy managed to dominate the movies in the 1980s with their comedic styles.[78] In the early 1980s, Pryor's stardom held dominion, and by the mid- and late 1980s, Murphy's career surged forth with a blazing rise. Unlike Murphy's predecessor, Pryor is one of the few successful comedians of the period who did not star on *Saturday Night Live*.[79] However, cinematic productions such as *Moving* made people wonder about Pryor's movie choices.[80] According to Bogle, Pryor was faced with an artistic struggle that even "fascinating American stars such as a Brando" encountered; therefore, as Pryor acted in films that failed to equal his talent, members of the audience could not fathom why "he selected such trash."[81] Bogle laments over the physical decline of Pryor—toward the late 1980s, Pryor "looked thin, haggard, enervated," yet audiences continued to hope that he would "reclaim his throne."[82] Ultimately, Pryor connected with audiences because they saw a part of themselves, their "faults and failings . . . insecurities and doubts" in him; nevertheless, Bogle insists that Pryor "remained one of the few great stars, black or white, of the era."[83] Unfortunately, in 2005 Pryor died of a heart attack at the age of 65, but he never regained his movie status from the 1970s and 1980s.[84]

Contrary to Pryor, from the beginning of Murphy's film career, he had a large white following. Bogle claims that Murphy's nonthreatening demeanor was appealing because his behavior did not interfere with white viewers' feelings of superiority. But although Murphy's films failed to take "stands" on issues including race, Bogle says "Murphy himself, through his unbridled confidence, presented a black man, quick-witted and sharp tongued, undaunted and unconquerable."[85] Even now, Murphy has continued to attain lead star-status roles during the 2010s. Yet Dorothy Pomerantz declared in the title of a 2012 article for *Forbes* magazine that "Eddie Murphy Tops Our List of the Most Overpaid Actors in Hollywood."[86] Murphy landed at the top of the list because "for every $1 Murphy was paid for his last three films, they returned an average of $2.30 at the box office."[87] Pomerantz listed *Tower Heist* (2011) as one of Murphy's box-office failures; the cost of *Tower Heist* was $75 million, but the movie profited only $153 million. Prior to *Tower Heist*, Murphy starred in three other box-office disappointments: *Meet Dave* (2008), *Imagine That* (2009), and *A Thousand Words*

(2012). Even though the aforementioned films failed to inspire a high return at the box office, Murphy received critical accolades with the movie *Dreamgirls* (2006). Famously, Murphy left the Academy Awards when his supporting role in *Dreamgirls* failed to win an Oscar in 2007.[88] Then, in 2011, Murphy snubbed the Academy Awards again when he accepted the hosting position and then changed his mind when Brett Ratner, director of *Tower Heist*, decided not to produce the Oscars. In terms of movie offers, industry insiders declared that his career would suffer as a result of snubbing the Oscars. But their predictions were erroneous. Murphy's decision to reprise his role as Axel Foley in the fourth installment of the *Beverly Hills Cop* movies, *Beverly Hills Cop IV*, in 2016 made headlines.[89] Apparently, audiences still love seeing Murphy on the big screen. Consequently, then and now, Hollywood studios are willing to pay major dollars to feature him in their films. Even back in the 1980s, 1990s, and 2000s, Murphy's movie career remained on the upside regardless of positive or negative criticism. In the same manner that Murphy's films captured the 1980s youths, the gangsta film of the 1990s would also captivate the younger audiences' imagination by transforming rap artists into movie stars.

CHAPTER 9

1990s
Gangsta Rappers Transcend Music: Ice Cube, Ice-T, DMX, Nas, and 2Pac

With the advent of gangsta rap, America witnessed how a generation of teenagers embraced this new hip musical form. Most definitely, this popular musical craze and the rappers who humanized the streets captured the attention of Hollywood. Unapologetically, rap artists spun narratives of urban lives and the pitfalls of 'hood life. As black filmmakers depicted street life from their own perspective, directors such as John Singleton, Mario Van Peebles, Ernest Dickerson, and Hype Williams envisioned an opportunity to make money while telling their version of urban truth. Thus there was a new wave of interest in black stories, the black rappers who starred in the films, and the black directors who shined a light on inner-city life. Kenneth Chan writes in "The Construction of Black Male Identity in Black Action Films of the Nineties" that there are "alternating waves of prolific production and sudden dearth."[1] In other words, there are decades like the 1920s and 1970s where there is a large production of black films starring black actors that are produced by black filmmakers. Then there are decades like 1930s, 1950s, 1960s, and 1980s, where there are only token black performers and rarely celebrated black filmmakers or films. According to Chan, during the 1970s Melvin Van Peebles's *Sweet Baadasssss Song* (1971) marked a black and white artistic explosion of blaxploitation films.[2] During the early 1980s, black films were almost nonexistent. Although Richard Pryor and Eddie Murphy are major stars in the 1980s, generally they are the primary face of color in those flicks. Then the cinematic achievements of both Spike Lee and Robert Townsend caused a resurging interest in black films. In the 1990s, Lee and Townsend are responsible for the booming interest in black cinema. Yet the accomplishments of Lee and Townsend are not the focus of this chapter; instead, Lee along with Tyler Perry are featured in the next chapter on the 2000s. This chapter will focus on rap musicians, such as Ice Cube, Ice-T, DMX, Nas, and 2Pac, who reinvented their image by transitioning into films in the 1990s.

Rap Music and Gangsta Films: The Commodification of Black Rage and Black Youth Culture

Due in part to the creation of rap music, new black cinema in the 1980s continues into the 1990s.[3] As a result, rap music is emblematic of the black youth cultural movement that is rooted in urban America. Quickly, producers realized that the popularity of rap music resulted in monetary gain: "Rap musicians created the conditions under which an art that describes black rage from a black point of view is commodified in order to raise black consciousness and to uplift black music producers in the economic sphere"[4]—meaning, black rage is transmuted into art in the hands of rap musicians. As a result, rap music becomes a profitable method of making money from black frustration. Thus lawbreakers feel a kinship toward hip-hop music because they feel a semblance of justification for their anger and struggles within the community. Rap artists such as Ice Cube and Ice-T are featured in films for the purpose of starring as criminals; meanwhile, these movies play rap music to embody various themes and to reinforce identification with the audience. The most significant connection bears on the fact that "rap music and the new black films picture black men and women trapped by systems; their performative acts enable them to reinvent themselves."[5] In essence, audiences feel cathartic satisfaction by watching people like themselves improve their lives on film and/or with music. The merging of rap artists and black cinema was bound to resonate with youth urban culture. Thus when directors feature credible rap musicians, they appropriate street credibility and they exemplify relatability for young black audiences.

Simultaneously, these films recognized the appeal that hip-hop holds for white audiences. Thus 'hood films are constructed to have a built-in crossover appeal.[6] However, high interest in black urban films and their directors does not mean "that black filmmakers have been able to entirely overcome decades of racism and the inequitable distribution of power and resources."[7] As stated in chapter 7, during the 1970s Hollywood realized that young white males were their primary ticket holders. Thus black action and crime films had an opportunity to flourish in this environment. In the 1990s, white-dominated Hollywood was inspired to present black stories because a large number of their movie ticket sales were attributable to black audiences; therefore movie studios made a concerted effort to appeal to

African American audiences. Basically, profit was the motive for creating more black urban stories by black filmmakers. Thus major movie studios began to produce black action films "directed by African Americans, set in black communities."[8] Films that were focused on black male gangsters living in the ghetto became popular due to the following films: John Singleton's *Boyz N the Hood* (1991), Mario Van Peebles's *New Jack City* (1991), Ernest Dickerson's *Juice* (1992), Bill Duke's *Deep Cover* (1992), and Matty Rich's *Straight out of Brooklyn* (1991).[9]

Popular 'hood films have an intriguing mix "of trendy rap music, rap singers turned actors, and volatile filmic action to the political and social issues that concern African Americans, thereby increasing both their entertainment and political aesthetic value."[10] In terms of the black male characterizations, Chan points out the following: generally, "new black action films feature characters that oppose, flourish, or are assimilated in the political and social climate of poverty, crime, drugs, and violence, ... emplaced within the spatial confines of the inner-city projects or the ghetto."[11] Due to the capitalistic interests of the Hollywood power structure, filmmakers yield to stereotypical constructions of black characters. In other words, there is a level of authenticity in terms of the socioeconomic hardships. Yet for the most part, the black male image fails to evolve along with the narratives that depict their struggles. With the exception of their videos, most of the rap artists who starred in these gangsta films lacked acting experience. However, their charisma on film resonated with audiences despite their oftentimes bad-boy images on film. Consequently, the powerful acting performances by Ice Cube, Ice-T, DMX, Nas, and 2Pac broaden their universal appeal as multifaceted and transformative hip-hop artists; yet their movies still substantiate Hollywood's negative image of blacks as criminals who are willing perpetrators of violence against members of their own community.

Gangsta Films: The Sudden Rise and Fall of the Glorified Black Criminal

Much to the dismay of parents, gangsta films focused primarily on the negative aspects of the black culture. These movies reinforced the idea that blacks generally live in drug- and gang-infested areas. Furthermore, inner-city youth and parents are held captive in a cycle of poverty by black criminal thugs who enjoy profiting from urban decay. Moreover, as a cinematic motif, the black criminal was feared because he had power over his 'hood and everyone living in it. Meanwhile, as black filmmakers and black performers profited from the profligation of black culture, the black male image took a critical plunge in the eyes of the public. Bakari Kitwana explains the fascination, purpose, and effect of black gangster films in his book entitled *The Hip Hop Generation*. Kitwana writes in one of his provocatively entitled chapters, "Young, Don't Give a Fuck, and Black: Black Gangster Films," that the movies produced "between 1991 and 2001 that depicted gun-toting, ruthless, violent, predatory Blacks killing other Blacks (dubbed 'hood films by industry insiders) have been the most effective medium for defining and disseminating the new Black youth culture."[12] In other words, for a period of 10 years, the movie industry described and distributed "Black youth culture" to the masses. With voracious ambition, Americans of all races consumed black youth culture. Therefore 'hood movies became a popular method of infusing black youth culture into mainstream American culture. Hood films flourished in an environment that viewed criminalization as the answer to any "social problem disproportionately involving Black youth."[13] Previous generations of blacks were barred from various areas of public space due to the Jim Crow era of segregation. But the hip-hop generation gained access to white spaces via rap music and the cinema. Thus, during the post–civil rights era, black youth had the opportunity to share their stories with every ethnic group because they were "gaining more significant visibility and leverage than ever before."[14] Needless to say, the 'hood films served a tertiary purpose of informing and entertaining while defining an emerging hip-hop lifestyle.

Arguably speaking, Kitwana asserts that movies such as *The Godfather*, *The Untouchables*, *Scarface*, or *Goodfellas* were not produced to explain different ethnic or immigration experiences. Yet in the case of gangsta films, advertisements and film reviewers promoted these stories by expressing "what it means to be young and Black in America at the dawn of the millennium."[15] In essence, these movies gained ethos or credibility by defining their authenticity for their intended audience. African Americans strongly participated in this attempt to authenticate 'hood films as an accurate depiction of street culture. Under the guidance of young black directors, "the star power of popular rappers turned actors (such as Ice Cube, Ice-T, MC Eiht, Tupac, Nas)" and their "hip-hop soundtracks [were used] to ensure their success."[16] Filmmakers defended their films by claiming that the movies were rooted in youth hip-hop culture. Kitwana states that some "films precisely hit the mark. At other times, they mythologized rather than illuminated the new Black youth culture."[17] Kitwana disparages these films for their distortion of what it means to be young and black in America. Gangsta flicks bear the responsibility of malignantly defining and distributing misinformation via young African

Americans themselves through African American popular culture. Ultimately, these films capitalized from purposeful glamorization and misinterpretation of the black experience, resulting in a stereotypical definition of young blacks, particularly young black males. Kitwana cites this era as unfortunately having "done more to exacerbate the new crises in African American life rather than solve them."[18] In the past, with the exception of the blaxploitation era, whites primarily benefited from black images in Hollywood. But in the case of the gangsta film era, white studios and white producers were not the only ones who commodified black images. Based on Kitwana's interpretations, with the advent of the 'hood films, black directors, black artists, and black actors had an opportunity to profit from their own urban stories. Consequently, the complexity of the black male image is further frustrated in Hollywood. Now, African American culture must accept some responsibility for the malignant black image disseminated via the black gangsta film.

John Singleton's *Boyz N the Hood* Featuring Ice Cube

For the purpose of broadening black narratives in America, black films, including *Boyz N the Hood*, unconsciously perpetuated the glamorization of the black criminal thug. On the other hand, black youth culture became a profitable commodity in black and white spaces. Thus blacks consciously sought not to be excised from the economic loop filling the pockets of white producers and media. As America transitioned from the late 1980s into the 1990s, the "media and corporations rediscovered blackness as a commodity."[19] At this time, blacks became more visible to the masses because of "the heightened commercialization of rap music as well as the mainstream visibility of black fashion models, entertainers, and athletes."[20] As an independent filmmaker, Spike Lee is one director who cashed in on this new profitability of black faces on the big screen. Popular black images ranged from "clown-like to buppie [black urban professionals]" in movies such as *A Rage in Harlem* and *Harlem Nights* to *House Party* and *Strictly Business*, to name a few.[21]

By the early 1990s, the movie that resonated most with the hip-hop generation was John Singleton's *Boyz N the Hood*. Kitwana credits Singleton's directorial debut with jump-starting that gangsta flick trend. *Boyz N the Hood* is a coming-of-age story that features the main characters' lives "from their 1984 childhood to their 1991 teenage high school years."[22] This movie is significant because it is used to define the new black youth culture. *Boyz* was the first movie to feature the interrelated and dire consequences for urban black males living in America: prison, illegal drugs, early death, and gun violence generally caused by another young black male. This film profoundly focused on "the young Black male under siege by new economic realities" that led to a cycle of negative outcomes.[23] In other words, *Boyz* demonstrates how urban survival perpetuates tragic circumstances and lifestyles within the black community.

Despite this enlightening perspective, Kitwana mentions that *Boyz* fails to examine young black women who are uniquely affected in the 'hood. For instance, the movie generally glosses over teenage pregnancy and single parenting, which may hinder a young woman's possibilities. In these new 'hood films, nobody, including society or parents, is doing anything to bring about meaningful social change. Unfortunately, community solutions are not thrust forward in the narrative. Each character is consumed by his or her own individual problems. Yet there is no deep introspection into the systematic and institutional factors that affect each character negatively as an individual. Singleton opts to hint only at the primary cause for this ongoing cycle of tragedy: "unemployment, inadequate education, and urban economic neglect."[24] Perhaps he could have focused on how characters are caught in a cycle of poverty and violence due to the absence of decent jobs and good education systems. Instead, Singleton focuses his narrative on the following themes: "the underground economy and the drug war" such as "the crack cocaine explosion."[25] As a result of the drug war and crack, the black criminal thug is elevated as a hero and his story is placed on a mantle. Nevertheless, with the black criminal thug's success comes grave harm and restrictions to the community. Crack cocaine's contribution to urban decay results in "policing (the recurring helicopters overhead), police brutality, and exposure to horrific events at a very young age (dead bodies, random gunfire, victims of crime, and much more)."[26] However, urban teenagers must confront more than the average suburban teenager. Therefore Singleton presents his characters' complex and human struggles with urban realism. In the midst of a violent environment, the teenagers in the film are dealing with everyday "coming-of-age issues as other American teens, regardless of race or class, urban or suburban."[27] The characters in the film are entering adulthood; therefore they are concerned with SAT scores, romance, sexual experiences, AIDS, sports, rivalries, and gangs. To add to the weight of the troubling teenage years, urban youth must also cope with traditional and nontraditional household structures.

Kitwana claims that one of the most unique elements of the film is the juxtaposition of single-parent and two-parent homes. Both family structures are exposed to the dangerous lifestyles of the 'hood. Furious Styles (Laurence Fishburne) and his son Tre (Cuba Gooding Jr.) represent how the black middle class lives in close proximity to the black poor. Even though Tre is middle-class, he encounters the same drama as his lower-class peers; due to the guidance of his father, he comes close to succumbing to the dangers experienced in the 'hood. Although Tre is playfully teased by Doughboy (Ice Cube) and Monster (Baldwin C. Sykes) for being intelligent, "for having his father in his life, and for being a little more on the straight and narrow," he is envied and revered for these distinctions.[28] With that said, Singleton demonstrates that even a young black criminal thug, such as Doughboy, desires guidance, mentorship, or leadership from a father, father figure, or mentor.

According to Kitwana, the most significant message of the film is centered on the mounting sense of pessimism in African American youth culture. Despite the massive achievements of the civil rights movement, in terms of demographics there has been very little progress for the majority of black youths. The hip-hop generation witnessed "the largest economic expansion in our country's history, even though Black youth are more visible than ever and have become icons of American popular culture, we still remain demonized in American society."[29] Thus *Boyz N the Hood* reflects the overall skeptical sentiment of young blacks that their parents, like American society, have failed them. By extension, the male characters in the film symbolize the dismal outcome of the failed American Dream. To the parents' defense, even if they do not fit the traditional family mold, *Boyz* features parents who are trying the best they can.

Yet even in the depiction of other characters there is an element of "nihilism in the eyes of Ricky's attackers in *Boyz*, but you also see a different strain of it in Doughboy's worldview."[30] Kitwana does not consider Ice Cube's character to be a rebel without a cause; instead, Doughboy makes choices based on survival. Therefore as a child, in order to retrieve his younger brother's football, he stands up to stronger kids, or to seek "revenge for Ricky's murder—even if it means his own death."[31] Ice Cube's character lives by the street code, but his choices are limited. After all, Doughboy does not have the means to navigate any other way. Thus he is beset in a society where emotional, physical, and economic resources are limited. In essence, Doughboy epitomizes how his household, neighborhood, and society have failed to guide, nurture, and shield him from the perilous world. By this time, Kitwana says, the audience knows that Doughboy does not know where his birth father is and his mother has always favored his brother Ricky (Morris Chestnut) over him. The young urban culture relates to Ice Cube's feelings of estrangement and alienation because he is symbolic of the hip-hop generation. Doughboy is unwelcome in his household, lost in his community, and frustrated by his society. Due to Singleton's understanding that "nihilism is central to, but not interchangeable with, the new Black youth culture," his successors' films are generally inferior to his groundbreaking contribution to the genre.[32]

As a result of the success of *Boyz N the Hood*, Hollywood surged into bandwagon form; they attempted to emulate the success of *Boyz* and reach the black youth market. Kitwana claims that these films were overbroad. They depicted ridiculous violence and resulted in the construction of "the young Black thug genre"; these Hollywood 'hood films became "Black parodies of white gangster flicks."[33] Gangsta films transitioned from realistic portrayals of urban life to reckless, "bloodthirsty, buck willin' [*sic*] violence for violence sake"; for audience members, this pessimistic portrait of black urban America becomes the perception of "the new Black youth culture itself."[34] Needless to say, the nihilistic young black thug image became symbolic for black males living in America. In agreement with Kitwana, *Boyz N the Hood* is a noteworthy film. However, the harm of these 'hood films occurred when American audiences failed to distinguish mythology from authenticity. Furthermore, Hollywood placed profit over the humanistic portrayal of black males in America.

Mario Van Peebles's *New Jack City* Featuring Ice-T

Mario Van Peebles, the director of *New Jack City*, had the advantage of having Melvin Van Peebles as a father. As a matter of opinion, Peebles directed one of the most popular films and villains of the gangsta genre in the character of Nino Brown. Still, there are various similarities between *Boyz N the Hood* and *New Jack City*. Both films illustrate the 'hood decades after the close of the civil rights movement. Moreover, each movie includes the skepticism of failed dreams and unrealized opportunity. Chan discusses how the civil rights movement offered "hope for equal rights and, most of all, equal opportunity for African Americans to advance economically and to step out of the clutches of poverty."[35] Unfortunately, American dreams and opportunity were thwarted due to racism within America's system of capitalism. Consequently, capitalism upholds an economic hierarchy that maintains the wealthy members of the society and oppresses the strivings of the African American underclass to overcome poverty and misery.

According to Chan, movies such as Spike Lee's *Clockers* (1995) expose the frustrations for characters such as Victor (Isaiah Washington) who struggle to maintain a close relationship with their children, but experience the economic and time restrictions caused by working two jobs. The confines within the capitalistic system propel Washington's character toward murder; nonetheless, he receives temporary satisfaction from releasing his frustrations, but now, he has ruined his unblemished record because he has transformed into a criminal. By extension, crime is a form of rebelling while profiting from a system that is closed generally to black males' economic strivings. Chan surmises that young people see drug dealing and crime as an alternative to working a dead-end job that has few intrinsic and extrinsic rewards and reneges on the promises promoted by the theory of capitalism. Thus, Chan claims, American capitalism creates a vacuous space leading to an upsurge of crime and violence via the drug trade existing in African American areas and urban districts. Even though Chan appears to sympathize with the frustrations of black male characters, he labels these complex views "of American capitalism and government in a criminal enterprise" as symptomatic of " 'paranoiac' notions of racial conspiracy."[36] In other words, Chan states that racism plays a part in the inequities of American capitalism, yet he simultaneously dismisses black voices of dissent. In terms of a "racial conspiracy," Chan labels black voices as "paranoiac" once they associate the rampant rate of black crime with the maintenance of American capitalism. Subsequently, he returns to the discussion of black crime as symptomatic of American capitalism. For that reason, he expounds on the notion that the drug trade leads to violence perpetrated by the narcotics dealers deep within black districts.

In the character of Nino Brown and the detectives who hunt him, director Mario Van Peebles channels two archetypal figures of 1970s blaxploitation films: "Baadasssss" and "the Man."[37] Furthermore, he incorporates musicality, drugs, and gangstas into *New Jack City* for the purpose of urban realism. According to Melvin Donalson, author of *Hip Hop in American Cinema, New Jack City* combined the "urban setting, gangsta and action genre elements, a rapper-actor in a major role, and a hip-hop soundtrack"; in actuality, the title of Donalson's book represents the "cross-fertilization occurring between music and movies."[38] Donalson attributes the hybridity of hip-hop and cinema to "journalist-screenwriter Barry Michael Cooper"; during the 1980s, Cooper labeled "songwriter-producer Teddy" Riley's melodic "sound as 'new jack swing.' "[39] Ultimately, Cooper created a term to define a "musical movement with its own specialized language."[40] Subsequently, following his "assessment of Teddy Riley's contribution to hip hop, Barry Michael Cooper went on to co-write the screenplay for *New Jack City*."[41] Detective Stone (Mario Van Peebles) is the mastermind behind the fall of drug kingpin Nino Brown (Wesley Snipes), and Stone forms a team of " 'new jack' undercover officers, who blend street experience, hip-hop knowledge, and a respect for the law."[42] The primary force is Scotty Appleton (Ice-T) who must operate within a "den of thugs who exploit the black neighborhood with their drugs" and intentionally murder their enemies.[43]

Undoubtedly, Ice-T is an ironic choice to play a cop. Although many public officials, law enforcement entities, and various members of the public have trouble separating the rap lyrics from the rap artist, Ice-T's title song "Cop Killer," from his album *Body Count*, failed to damage his audience appeal.[44] At the time, various law enforcement agencies of Texas demanded a boycott of Time Warner, at least 60 congressmen condemned the song, and Vice President Dan Quayle and President George Bush were disgusted by "Cop Killer."[45] Nevertheless, this media attention heightened Hollywood's interest in featuring Ice-T as a cop in this role. Ice-T proved that rap image persona and musical performance are not necessarily the same. Representing the "interracial face of hip hop, the new jack squad includes a white Detective Peretti (Judd Nelson) and the Asian Detective Park (Russell Wong)."[46] As part of his strategy to take down Nino Brown's empire, Appleton places Pookie (Chris Rock), a recovering crack addict, into the inner workings of Nino Brown's drug empire. Thus Van Peebles represents the victims of drug addiction in the characterization of Pookie. Donalson asserts that Rock's character signifies how drugs turn black males into hustlers, thieves, and indifferent losers. Although Rock's character tries to resist the lure of drugs, he subsequently falls back into addiction and is killed when his identity is discovered. Ice-T's character is also personally affected by the urban epidemic fueled by the presence of crack cocaine. Appleton's mother was murdered by a crack head; therefore he is inspired to use his badge to avenge her memory and render support to the African American community. Due to Appleton's personal motivations, the rapper of "Cop Killer" appeared believable in this movie. Undoubtedly, most black male audience members empathize with the desire to avenge one's own mother regardless of whether the means is legal or illegal. Additionally, the crossover appeal is heightened because most white males can relate to the desire to avenge their mother's death as well. Although Donalson's explanations of Van Peebles's, Ice-T's, and Rock's characters are intriguing, Chan offers an even more intricate analysis of black male identity. In the midst of American capitalism, Nino Brown is one of the more fascinating depictions of the black criminal thug and the society who made him flourish.

Amid this complex "relationship between capitalism and the narcotics trade," *New Jack City*'s Nino Brown is the Hollywood prototype of a malignant black male character.[47] Even though the character supports the perceived evidence of negative black males, Nino signifies a deterring aspect of the capitalistic system. Instead of opposing capitalism, Nino functions within the underbelly of the system and then rises to riches. Essentially, Chan refers to Nino as an intriguing parody of the ultimate capitalist. Mario Van Peebles utilizes Nino's character to critique the American capitalist and criminal justice system that is supposed to support not denigrate citizens. There are two pivotal scenes wherein Nino becomes the negative voice of capitalism: the New Year's Eve party and the final court scene. In two paralleling scenes, he inspires his crew "to purse the 'new American dream' in the 'entrepreneurial spirit.' "[48] Then, at the final court scene, Nino criticizes the prosecuting attorney for being born into privilege; meanwhile, Nino was forced to employ his "American work ethic to rise above his circumstances and succeed in a capitalistic world."[49] Consequently, Nino refuses to be a victim of the system. Instead, he will exploit the negative consequences of capitalism to his economic advantage. However, the movie reveals destructive aspects of capitalism without fully indicting the system. As an alternative, the malignancy of the capitalistic system is thrust upon the "monolithically evil character" of Nino; thus the construction of Nino Brown effectively exonerates capitalism and places the "blame on the evil nature of Nino as an individual."[50] The audience views a person, in the manifestation of Nino Brown, whose life demonstrates the absence of positive value; therefore he "deserves to die at the hands of the old man who takes justice into his own hands at the" conclusion of the movie.[51] As a result, Van Peebles appeases the interests and preconceived notions of the white audience—meaning, black-on-black crime is blamed for the demise of the black community. As opposed to blaming the economic forces of American capitalism, the black male is blamed for his own self-destruction and economic demise.

Chan is uncertain of whether Van Peebles "consciously or unconsciously" avoids probing "the real evil of racist capitalism," which is "its links to the drug trade"; instead, Van Peebles chooses to support the belief that "notions of individual morality and personal psychopathology" are the inherent defects in the American system of capitalism.[52] In other words, the problems in the 'hood are not attributed to failed governmental policies, dysfunctional business enterprises, or limited opportunity. *New Jack City* places the blame on bad black males, such as Nino, for the systematic urban economic and moral decay. Since the justice system has failed the black community in the past, the burden of curbing the Nino type of criminal element is placed upon a good black male in the midst of vigilante justice. In this case, Nino is mortally silenced by a community member's bullet, not by the justice system that is sworn to protect its citizens. Chan emphasizes that there is "an intense frustration within the African

American community" caused by the "oppression of the capitalistic system and the violence and crime arising from the drug trade."[53] Based on this "filmic construction of the black male identity," the black male is left with only a few choices: "an obvious distrust of the white dominant political establishment, and the unfortunate phenomenon of autodestruction and racial self-hatred."[54] Based on the 'hood narrative structure, the black male ends up blaming whites for his plight or he succumbs to self-destruction because he hates himself. Additionally, he resents his community in its complacency and holds it socially culpable for his predicament. Consequently, black males, according to Hollywood's construction, are in a monolithic and perpetual state of anger due to their disdain for a particular philosophy, entity, or society that limits their potential and represses their progress.

Tupac Shakur: The Man, His Music, and His Movie *Juice*

Another complex yet negative black male is Tupac's famous character in *Juice*. This movie was a major vehicle in 2Pac aka Tupac Shakur's transformation from hip-hop phenomenon to movie star. Melvin Donalson discusses this transition in his chapter entitled "Tupac Shakur: Hip-Hop Icon and Screen Idol" in *Hip Hop in American Cinema*. With regard to hip-hop, there is profound "debate which MC was the most outstanding in style, content, and image."[55] Varying answers can be attributed to the listener's age, geographical location, and stylistic preference. But according to Donalson, most people would concur with the viewpoint that the rapper Tupac Shakur "excelled in life and death, in both the music and movie fields."[56] By 2007, there were already "six books and numerous articles written about him, as well as documentaries exploring his life."[57] Thus Tupac distinguished himself from other rappers because he dominated gangsta rap, while simultaneously playing roles in mainstream Hollywood cinematic productions. Although Tupac's music career was brief, Tupac was a gargantuan figure. Once he appeared in movies and was murdered, he became a legend. Films such as *Juice* and *Poetic Justice* (1993) received critical acclaim and featured Tupac in "convincing roles that suggested his potential significance as an actor."[58] Tupac intentionally utilized his rap bad-boy image as a transition into major Hollywood roles. For Tupac, acting was an artistic escape from real life. Furthermore, he sought to demonstrate that young black males' talents are boundless and without limits. Nonetheless, Donalson claims, the same qualities that endeared him to younger audiences incensed the old-school crowd. By the time Tupac appeared in *Juice*, he was already a major star who "demonstrated the contradictions often associated with someone in the spotlight who attempts to be many things to many people at the same time"; but these contradictions wore on his public image and exposed "extremes in behavior and decision making."[59] In essence, Tupac's complexity as a human being surpassed the boundaries and labels that society used to constrict his image. But once one learns of his humble beginnings, the confining contradictions become more comprehendible.

Even Tupac's entry into the world was marked by turmoil and controversy. Around the time his mother, Afeni Shakur, was acquitted of "conspiracy charges to set explosions in New York City department stores," the single mother gave birth to him in New York City in June 1971.[60] Inspired by her Black Panther Party membership, Afeni bestowed the name of Tupac Amaru on her son; Tupac Amaru means "shining serpent" and Shakur means "thankful to God." For Tupac's high school years, Afeni decided to move to Marin City, California, in 1988 after surviving "a phase of drug dependency, an abusive boyfriend, and poor living conditions in Baltimore."[61] Once Tupac was in California, he would have a chance to explore his musical talents. Tupac performed as Shock-G, the leader of the musical group Digital Underground. Tupac's first movie performance was in a dark comedy called *Nothing but Trouble* (1991), and the group Digital Underground appeared as themselves before a fanatical judge (Dan Aykroyd) who forces them to play music in his traffic court.[62] Then Aykroyd joins in by playing on an organ. Eventually, Tupac sought the solo stage and reinvented his image beyond the persona of his former group Digital Underground.

With Tupac's debut solo album *2Pacalypse Now* (1991), he carefully constructed an outlaw image. However, Tupac's artistic outlaw image intersected with his real-life escapades. From 1991 to 1994, he had a series of volatile encounters: arrests, police brutality, public brawls, a fight in a studio lot, a fight with filmmakers Albert and Allen Hughes; "in Atlanta he was arrested for shooting two off-duty white policeman; and in New York, he was accused of rape."[63] To those who contemplated the social, moral, and cultural value of gangsta rap, Donalson claims that reality and fiction merged in the persona of Tupac. For many people, Tupac epitomized "the thug image of the nihilistic, felonious male who sought life only through selfish excesses."[64] Adding layers to Tupac's multifarious image, he referred to himself as a thug; however, he didn't mean "thug" in terms of criminalized behavior. Tupac glorified the term "thug" in the sense of an alienated individual, placed on the sidelines of life, but who rises above his circumstances.

In *Juice*, Tupac plays Bishop who aspires to become a gangsta. Although *Juice* is "less glossy" than *Boyz N the Hood*, it is heralded as one of the "masterpieces of black realism as *film noir*."[65] Perhaps Tupac's complex background brought a level of realism to the character. Tupac was able to excavate "experiences and memories from years of interacting on the streets of New York."[66] Due to his impressive personality and talent, when he walked into the room the director Ernest Dickerson said there was no need for Tupac to audition for the part. The timing of this movie was perfect for Tupac. *Boyz N the Hood* and *New Jack City* were profitable, but both movies were criticized "for linking screen violence and violence in the theaters."[67] Compounding the negative critiques, the Los Angeles Police Department attacked Paramount Studios for their exploitation of gun violence in their print advertisements and movie trailer campaigns for *Juice*. One promotional poster positions Tupac's Bishop in the foreground of the other three main characters holding a handgun; in response to political and social pressure, Paramount airbrushed the gun out of future posters. In their defense, Paramount advertised to audiences what they could expect and what they wanted to see once they arrived to see the movie.

Juice is set in Harlem and focuses on an average day of "four adolescent black males" as they "hoodwink their parents, ditch school, and take to the streets to hang together and pursue their brand of fun."[68] The movie highlights the clothing and shoes typical of the hip-hop generation and the music and the language of the foursome as they debate "numerous topics, including the acquisition of 'juice' or power and street respect."[69] Donalson quickly points out that the young men are distinctly different from each other despite their common street origins: Raheem (Khalil Kain) is the thoughtful leader, mediator of the group, and teenage dad who has a conflictual relationship with his baby's mother. Then there is Steel (Jermaine Hopkins) whom Donalson describes as "the chubby follower"; Q is played by Omar Epps and he wants to be a "famous hip-hop deejay"; and lastly, Bishop is "the angry and volatile one, seeks 'juice' as a way of forming an identity."[70] In other words, Bishop's self-concept and self-worth revolve around the respect and fear he receives from residents of the 'hood. But the desire for self-autonomy and economic opportunity manifests itself in a negative manner. As the audience continues to watch, their childish antics evolve into more felonious behavior.

In an effort to gain street credibility, Bishop convinces the group to engage in criminal activity, and once Raheem acquires a gun, they use "Q's competition at a deejay battle as a cover" to rob a corner store.[71] Deviating from the plan, Bishop kills the owner for no reason, kills his childhood friend Raheem, and attends his funeral while pretending to be in mourning. Subsequently, Bishop entices Steel to meet him with the bad intentions of murdering him. Although Bishop believes he has succeeded, Steel does not succumb to his wounds. Since Bishop believes that he has killed Steel, he begins to destroy Q's life by framing him for three shootings. Now, Bishop has gained the height of power that he has sought all along. In the resolution of the film, the scene revolves around the confrontation between Bishop and Q. According to Donalson, Tupac as Bishop is "credible and effective," yet intentionally, or as a possible oversight, Bishop's problematic childhood is not explored, but "the character's stormy and explosive nature is tangible."[72] Perhaps due to an insecure home life, Bishop obsesses over a life of crime, hoping to fill his emotional void and empty soul. Bishop is seduced by the image of James Cagney in old gangster films; therefore he "worships the self-destructive hoodlum who chooses a violent lifestyle and death."[73] The street code is the motivating factor that causes Bishop to cross moral lines. Once the fear and control Bishop evokes empower him, the loyalty he feels for his friends fades. Subsequently, the movie ends with one character realizing the vicious cycle of the downward-spiraling lives and gravitates back "toward a black good-life society,"[74] Demonstrating that the pitfalls of 'hood life fail to overcome everyone. In essence, *Juice* signifies "a rite of passage from childhood to adulthood, from chaos to organization, from powerlessness to empowerment."[75] Additionally, *Juice* exemplifies a sense of evolution and agency over one's own destiny despite the violence of the streets. Basically, once the protagonist Q "takes a step toward emancipation of the community from the ghetto," the individual has an opportunity to not only survive but thrive.[76]

Hype Williams's *Belly* Featuring DMX and Nas

Another film, by Hype Williams, offers emancipation from the streets. The director takes advantage of the popularity of 'hood films to infuse his perspective into the gangsta genre. Popular rappers DMX and Nas star in director Hype Williams's feature film *Belly* (1998).[77] Williams is a well-known "veteran music video director" whose scenes are composed of "heavy bass thumping of rap music"; however, "*Belly* deserves credit for telling a story of the black underworld where the protagonists have choices to ponder."[78] Williams's cinematography skills become evident in his "stylized visualizations and rapid shifting among the settings Queens, New York; Manhattan; Omaha, Nebraska; Jamaica; and Atlanta, *Belly* designs a captivating story."[79] By shifting perspectives via DMX's and Nas's characters, the narrative alternates between two first-person points of view. Working in opposition to the theme of nihilism, Williams offers a new perspective for his audiences by suggesting that "survival requires elevation out of the muck and mire of senseless murder and dead-end living."[80] Initially, Tommy "Buns" Bundy (DMX) and Sincere (Nas) share the typical desires of gangsta film heroes: getting money, by any means, as the solution. As Sincere begins to evolve, Buns transitions from "theft to drug dealing"; Buns heads to prison and ends up becoming an undercover FBI "informant within a Black Muslim organization."[81] When Buns cannot bring himself to assassinate the Muslim leader, he converts to Islam. Thus the killer Tommy abandons his merciless roguish lifestyle for enlightenment and decides to transform and redeem himself.[82] In contrast to Tommy, Sincere is affiliated with street people, yet somehow he lacks a street mentality because his level of awareness is beyond some of his peers. Thus Sincere wants to change the trajectory of his life because he knows "the hand young Blacks have been dealt."[83] In other words, Sincere knows that racism and intracultural violence are additional factors that exacerbate poverty and the absence of opportunity in the 'hood.

Another positive element of the movie centers on the loving relationship between Sincere and Tionne (Tionne "T-Boz" Watkins). Audiences view a healthy relationship that is nonaggressive and functioning despite the odds. For years, Sincere and Buns have been "leaders of the same crew of thieves," but Sincere grows weary of the uncertainty within the criminal lifestyle and seeks refuge in solidifying his familial union with T and their child.[84] Once Tommy, Sincere, and Tionne have spiritual revelations, their lives begin to transform and "come full circle (Tommy to accept the spiritual and political teachings of the film's spiritual lead, Reverend Savior, and Sincere and Tionne to follow their dream of getting out of the 'hood and moving to the motherland)."[85] By displaying options for escaping the downward spiral of 'hood living, Williams creates "an alternative definition of the new Black youth culture" and a plausible path out of the chaos.[86] After all, they must navigate a path in a wilderness of "mercurial violence and treachery from all sides, leaving little space for virtue or optimism."[87] Then there are "the most extreme outlaw types" like Tommy "Buns" who are willing to accept spirituality and the "Black traditional message of social responsibility."[88] Thus Williams offers a spiritual component to survive the malignant elements in the 'hood.[89] *Belly* rejects the nihilistic message of preceding "Black gangster films—that our generation lacks self-determination, and personal responsibility is not part of our generation's identity—*Belly* embraces a more redemptive theme."[90] Consequently, Kitwana asserts, *Belly* occupies a space between our parents' generation and our own. Ultimately, the message of *Belly* resonates with its audience: even those who have been tempted, jailed, or soiled by the streets have the opportunity to rise out of their circumstances.

Other Popular Gangsta Films and Their Hip-Hop Stars

Even though this chapter focuses mainly on Ice Cube, Ice-T, DMX, Nas, and 2Pac, it must be noted that there are many hip-hop artists who have contributed to the genre and black cinema. Since the 1980s, movies and even television have offered the opportunity for these stars to reinvent themselves by showing another facet of their talents. Thus all of the following rappers have used movies as vehicles to broaden their appeal and transform their image beyond gangsta rap.

Including Ice Cube, Ice-T, DMX, Nas, and 2Pac, there are a multitude of rappers listed who transformed themselves into actors in both 'hood films and mainstream films during the 1980s and 1990s: Big Daddy Kane in *Posse* (1993) and *The Meteor Man* (1993); Busta Rhymes (Trevor Smith) in *Who's the Man* (1993), *Strapped* (1993), and *Higher Learning* (1995); Coolio in *Dear God* (1996) and *Midnight Mass* (1999); Dr. Dre (Andre Young) in *Coming to America* (1988), *Deep Cover* (1994), and *Natural Born Killers* (1994); The Fat Boys (Darren Robinson, Damon Wimbley, Mark Morales) in *Krush Groove* (1985) and *The Disorderlies* (1987); Heavy D (Dwight Myers) in *Life* (1999) and *The Cider House Rules* (1999); Ice Cube (O'Shea Jackson) in *Trespass* (1992), *Higher Learning* (1994), *Friday* (1995), *The Players Club* (1998), and *Three Kings* (1999); Ice-T (Tracy Marrow) in *Breakin'* (1984), *Breakin' 2: Electric Boogaloo* (1984), *Ricochet* (1991), *Trespass* (1992), and *The Heist* (1999); Kid N' Play (Christopher Reid and Christopher Martin) in the *House Party* series (1990, 1991, 1994) and *Class Act* (1992); LL Cool J (James Todd Smith) in *Deep Blue Sea* (1999), *In Too Deep* (1999), and *Any Given Sunday* (1999); Master P (Percy Miller) in *The Players Club* (1998) and *I Got the Hook Up* (1998); Method Man (Clifford Smith) in *Don't Be a Menace while Drinking Your Juice in the Hood* (1996), *Wu-Tang* (1998), and *Belly* (1998); Mos Def (Dane Terrell Smith) in *Ghosts* (1997); Nas (Nasir Jones) in *In Too Deep* (1999); Redman (Reggie Noble) in *Colorz of Rage* (1999); Run-D.M.C. (Joseph Simmons, Darryl McDaniels, and Jason Mizell) in *Krush Groove* (1985) and *Tougher than Leather* (1988); Silkk Tha Shocker (Vyshonne Miller) in *Hot Boyz* (1999); Will Smith in *Six Degrees of Separation* (1993), *Bad Boys* (1995), *Independence Day* (1996), *Men in Black* (1997), *Enemy of the State* (1998), and *Wild Wild West* (1999); Snoop Dogg (Cordozar Calvin

Broadus) in *Half-Baked* (1998) and *Urban Menace* (1999); Tone Loc (Anthony Smith) in *The Return of Superfly* (1990), *Posse* (1993), *Poetic Justice* (1993), and *Heat* (1995); Treach (Anthony Criss) in *Juice* (1992), *The Meteor Man* (1993), and *Jason's Lyric* (1994); Tupac Shakur in *Poetic Justice* (1993), *Above the Rim* (1994), *Bullet* (1996), *Gridlock'd* (1997), and *Gang Related* (1997).[91]

The aforementioned list does not include all of the most popular rappers and their films. Yet it does include the most well-known rappers in their game-changing performances. By offering another aspect of themselves via cinema, rappers have been able to transcend their success into the mass-cultural realms of American society. Moreover, their transition from rappers to various other realms of moviemaking help to evolve society's monolithic perception of black males in society. By featuring Ice Cube in *Boyz N the Hood*, Ice-T in *New Jack City*, DMX and Nas in *Belly*, and Tupac in *Juice*, Hollywood "takes advantage of audience recognition of the rap performer turned screen performer."[92] Furthermore, their music benefits from this transition. Various marketing strategies are centered on a "sense of realism with the gangsta rap star and the promotion of a soundtrack."[93] Yet the wise entrepreneurial rapper takes advantage of this skepticism to heighten his own visibility despite the realities of the streets. However, the manner in which the cinema depicted the "complexity and paradoxical nature of gangsta rap in the 1990s" was frustrated by these contradictions.[94] Similar to blaxploitation films of the 1970s, music was used to buffer the urban narrative in 1990s gangsta flicks.[95]

The following elements proved to be economically profitable and consumed with crossover and universal appeal: "The poverty, bullet-sprinkled buildings, vacant lots, and violence of those neighborhoods, or 'hoods, functioned well for stories of struggling outlaws, who displayed their own brand of dress, codes of conduct, and vernacular."[96] But black urban characters were not the only ethnic groups that intrigued audiences. Along with the appealing Cuban and Italian characters in films by "directors Brian De Palma (*Scarface*, 1983), Francis Ford Coppola (*The Godfather* series, 1972, 1974, 1990), and Martin Scorsese (*Goodfellas*, 1990)," Americans loved gangsta films.[97] Donalson claims that the symbiotic and interrelated relationship between "existing urban gangs, prison culture, and gangsta genre films created a winning business formula" since many of the 'hood films cost less to fund than "other studio projects."[98] Ultimately, 'hood films feature elements of action genres that overwhelmingly attracted male audience members who enjoyed the "physical confrontations, chases, gun battles, stylized violence, masculinity themes, and revenge themes."[99] After all, the studios are constantly aware of the male audience demographic when producing gangsta films of any ethnic group.

Perhaps hip-hop at the theaters continues to resonate due to what Nelson George says in *Hip Hop America*: "Like flesh, it [hip-hop] keeps regenerating itself and with each new generation becomes more rooted and builds new alliances."[100] Hip-hop is not only a musical or cultural movement; it is also an economic movement. Nelson claims that the thirst for profit heals the rifts between those who embrace hip-hop and those who fear its prominence. In reality, as Jeff Chang expresses in *Can't Stop Won't Stop*, hip-hop resonates with music and movie audiences because "the Hip-Hop Generation brings together time and race, place and polycultural-ism, hot beats and hybridity" and represents the transition from "politics to culture, the process of entropy and reconstruction."[101] In other words, "the hip-hop generation" symbolizes chaos and a restructuring of the American identity by incorporating black male perspectives, trials, and tribulations via gangsta films. According to Chang, hip-hop music and rap artists in the movies resonate with audiences because they signify the communal dreams and nightmares, desires and disappointments of a society that deems itself beyond issues of race, class, and gender. Hip-hop artists embody the American Dream; they represent the reinvention of the black male image through musical and cinematic narratives. Lastly, black rap artists represent the ingenuity of Americanism that profits from the dissemination of black youth culture and black rage as a commodity. In this system of American capitalism, the black male image may be one of the most profitable aspects of American pop culture and cinema. For that reason, despite their profes-sional rivalry, Spike Lee and Tyler Perry use their iconic status to further reconstruct and shape the frayed image of black males in the 2000s.

CHAPTER 10

──── 2000s ────
Black Icons: Control, Agency, and Self-Appropriation: Spike Lee, Tyler Perry, and Will Smith

At the close of the 1990s, audiences sought a wider range of black stories than gangsta films. Spike Lee, Tyler Perry, and Will Smith are three African American artists who produced diverse black narratives. As a result, during the 2000s African American filmmakers continued to make an impact by starring, writing, directing, and/or producing movies that highlighted the black experience. Despite the success of black movies and black filmmakers, producers, such as F. Gary Gray, Tyler Perry, Will Smith, and Tim Story, must still prove that there is an audience for their films.[1] Generally, black filmmakers have two main goals: presenting their personal vision by telling stories for blacks and sharing the African American narrative with future generations. Even though black films often appeal to a wider spectrum of the American audience, there is ultimately a need to include the black perspective of the American experience. According to filmmaker Julie Dash, there is a concerted effort "to demand more balanced images"; in some ways, "people say things have changed. They have changed, but in many ways they have not."[2] In other words, even though movies feature a myriad of black images and possibilities, the past trite images reappear even in black films; however, there are African American filmmakers such as Spike Lee, Tyler Perry, and Will Smith who are demonstrating control, agency, and self-appropriation despite the restrictions of Hollywood's past and present.

Spike Lee: Achievements and Activism

Like many filmmakers, within Lee's revolutionary style he employs stereotypes for the purpose of satire. Consequently, he is interested in relaying more than just humor to the audience. Lee focuses on "featuring

African Americans and African American concerns"; he enjoys sparking a conversation that resonates beyond the African American community.[3] As Aaron Barlow states in *Star Power: The Impact of Branded Celebrity*, "He does not speak for African Americans, but for Spike Lee, an African American" since the issue of race is at the forefront of his mind.[4] Contemporary issues resonate with him as much as they "would have been a century ago during the height of Jim Crow or, even further back, during the Civil War."[5] Lee's commitment to confronting race and celebrating his culture influenced him to name "his production company 40 Acres and a Mule Filmworks after the Civil War era, [due to the] belief among some that freed slaves would receive just that as a means of starting their new lives—a belief that, of course, never panned out."[6] This unrequited promise fuels the ambitious projects of Lee. To further his narrative of African American and American possibilities, he delves into other artistic art forms such as music.

To explore the interactions between cultures, music has a heavy impact in his films.[7] Clearly, Lee links the African American narrative with the melodies performed by blacks. Unabashedly, he has delved into rhythm and blues, jazz, and even hip-hop to further define and explore black identity. For instance, in *Do the Right Thing* (1989), Public Enemy's "Fight the Power" plays as the movie opens. In the video directed by Lee, Public Enemy, the Fruit of Islam, and the famous director march through a New York neighborhood, with many young people following their lead.[8] The demonstration for the video is an effort to pay homage to the 1963 March on Washington. Furthermore, Lee is indicating that along with the religious leaders, the current protests will be led by filmmakers and hip-hop artists. Traditionally, music has been used to protest systems of oppression. However, all music has a way of expressing the multiplicity in American culture.[9] Consequently, music has always played a major part in black productions.

Not only does Lee use his fame as an artist to make movies that include amazing soundtracks, he has profited from his fame by becoming a retailer. When the movie *Malcolm X* was released, the cap and other merchandise promoting the movie caused him to open a second store (Spike's Joint West in Los Angeles).[10] Basically, Lee combined moviemaking, activism, and accessories to enhance his profit and star power. Consequently, he uses his star status "as an off-screen advocate for the value of black culture and, yes, of black lives in a nation that still seems to often devalue them."[11] To further Lee's emphasis that black lives matter, he ventured into black narratives via children's story books. Even though Lee's clothing store closed in 1997, he has "written children's books (with his wife), continuing even there to make social concerns central to his art and his enterprise."[12] Barlow asserts that every entrepreneurial venture by Lee is for the purpose of advocating social progress for the African American community. Consequently, Barlow proclaims, "Lee has established a power over his brand that few manage, a power that he continues to use not simply for self-promotion but for what can be called his own cultural crusade."[13] Thus, even though Lee has entrepreneurial ambitions, he remains socially active.

Lee was so impassioned about the Trayvon Martin case that he was one of the celebrities featured in "*Ebony* 'Trayvon' Covers: The Martins, Spike Lee, Boris Kodjoe, Dwyane Wade and Their Sons for September Issue."[14] To Lee, who directed the classic *Do the Right Thing* about racial tensions that result in death, this *Ebony* cover was a chance to pay homage to a young man whose life and death affected a community and the American culture as a whole. After all, it was the racial incidents of violence that socially and politically motivated Lee to "depict the polarized city of New York under a contemporary lens."[15] Sadly, New York was besieged by racial violence in the 1980s. For instance, there was a Howard Beach incident that occurred when "three black men were beaten by a group of white teens because they mistakenly wandered into an Italian neighborhood."[16] Unfortunately, one of the young black males was killed as he escaped across a nearby freeway. For that matter, Lee's core passion for his people drives him to produce films that feature African Americans in a multifarious manner. By the same token, Lee never abandons his quest to lift the veil of mystery, fear, and animosity associated with black males.

Spike Lee's *Malcolm X*: Heteronormative Black Masculinity

To demonstrate the evolution of Lee, this section will examine black masculinity in *Malcolm X* (1992). Even though Lee directed several classic films, such as *She's Gotta Have It* (1986), *School Daze* (1988), and *Do the Right Thing* (1989) during the 1980s, and *Mo' Better Blues* (1990), *Jungle Fever* (1991), *Crooklyn* (1994), *Clockers* (1995), *Get on the Bus* (1996), *He Got Game* (1998), and *Summer of Sam* (1999) during the 1990s, *Malcolm X* is based on a complex and controversial African American icon. Thus *Malcolm X* is the ideal motion picture film to study black manhood. With that said, Maurice E. Stevens discusses the problematic issues of black masculinity and heteronormative identity in the cinema in his article entitled "Subject to Countermemory: Disavowal and Black Manhood in Spike Lee's *Malcolm X*." Stevens expresses that African American identity involves considering issues of selfhood and historical and communal interpretations of black identity.[17] Various historical events such as "the Atlantic slave trade, plantation experiences, community-supported lynching, Jim Crow laws, systematic social marginalization, and state-sanctioned violence" complicate the discussion.[18] Furthermore, when an individual celebrates his or her black identity in America, there is immediate suspicion and trite feelings directed toward the speaker. Almost instantaneously, when the discussion of black images is initiated by an individual or group, some blacks and whites become defensive. Coupled with the brutality that is present in American history, there are "unspeakable features of living (and dying), of being (and not)," that "are submerged within narratives comprising African-American history and are overlooked or unexamined."[19] Thus there is an attempt to gloss over, ignore, or erase the difficult parts of that African American male identity formation and his subsequent narrative scribing and redefining his existence.

Furthermore, Stevens states that in the American imagination African Americans are dehumanized or dehistoricized. In other words, blackness is interpreted as a biological or cultural product, not a product of historical interpretation. Consequently, African American historiographers, functioning "within a social context that has understood African-Americans as disempowered and as lacking full humanity, have had great difficulty writing African-Americans into an agency-filled story of historical progress."[20] Many of the images associated with black identity or blackness are evidenced by reinforced devaluation, social infirmity, and inhumanity. For those reasons, countermemory is a "form of popular cultural production that provides a space on which the desire for full African-American humanity, full discursive recognition, can be advanced, represented, and ultimately shaped into a viable object of identification."[21] In essence, countermemory empowers the storyteller with a method to subvert former historical production that devalues or debases black culture. Within the space of countermemory, African American humanity may be fully realized, acknowledged, progressed, characterized, and reconstructed into realistic black experience. Movies are one form of cultural production that gives the storyteller tools to reinvent the black narrative within the American landscape. Therefore, Stevens claims, countermemory and the visual component of American identity formation explain why the Hollywood production *Malcolm X* is immensely valuable. Based on the aforementioned elements, *Malcolm X* is "a social force and, subsequently, a political relevance to cultural producers interested in increasing identificatory options for African-Americans."[22] In other words, for writers, directors, producers, and studios interested in evaluating broader perspectives of African American identity, movies such as *Malcolm X* further those intentions.

Effectively, Lee creates a countermemory for African Americans historical trauma while describing and confining "authentic blackness," which is "a prerequisite for nationalist identification."[23] Basically, Lee reconfigures and expands the boundaries that define black identity within a black nationalistic perspective. Early in *Malcolm X*'s production, Lee insisted that the movie be perceived within the lens of "realistic representation of—if not particular black people—particular truths about black experience."[24] Lee depicts the struggle for acknowledgment as an authentically black quest within the African American community and comprehensive recognition as fully realized citizens in America. Furthermore, *Malcolm X* intentionally probes into authentic African American masculinity and femininity to deepen the distinctions within the black experience. Stevens believes that although Lee attributes his screenplay to the book *Autobiography of Malcolm X* the movie must be considered "as a fable of revelation, ascension, and, through the movie, resurrection."[25] Written by Alex Haley and Malcolm X, the 1965 book version sought to depict epic heroism and American exceptionalism.

According to Stevens, *Malcolm X* tells the story of Malcolm Little's transformation from troubled youth to streetwise "hustler" (Detroit Red), to proponent of African American cultural nationalism (Malcolm X), and finally to orthodox political nationalist (El Hajj Malik Al-Shabazz). This is a trajectory of metamorphosis, a narrative of transformation, and a dream of evolution into consciousness. In a series of flashbacks, moviegoers witness the "traumatic moments in Malcolm's early life": an encounter with the Ku Klux Klan, the murder of Malcolm's father being "ruled a suicide"; and Malcolm's mother losing her children because she is "determined unfit" by the government.[26] Throughout the powerful imagery submerged in racial violence and social oppression, Lee expresses "a picture of black power and pride . . . of what it means to be a black man or black woman in the United States."[27] In addition to racial violence, issues of gender threaten black male identity in America.

Based on the aforementioned characterization of Malcolm (Denzel Washington) and his wife, Betty Shabazz (Angela Bassett), masculine, feminine, and racial identity are threatened by homosociality, feminine agency, and interracial ambiguity. Stevens articulates the aforementioned factors as "threats to Lee's strict conception of a gendered (male) black cultural nationalism."[28] As the film opens, a symbolic montage of imagery, such as "an American flag burning away to a red, white, and blue flaming 'X,' intercut with found footage from the Rodney King beating, Lee introduces masculinized themes of state control, popular protests, and nationalism."[29] Consequently, Stevens determines Lee's relentless need "to defend against threats to heteronormative black masculinity" to be disturbing.[30]

In opposition to Stevens's interpretation, one may view Lee's incessant desire as a cultural reproducer to define black male identity as deeply rooted in America's violent assaults against its fluid formation. Basically, Lee attempts to mend the fractured black male identity by explaining its malformation in the face of a violent racialized history. Stevens speaks to this evaluation when he says that Lee continues "his desire to produce political possibility in the present by piecing together an image of black identity from the wreckage of the past."[31] Yet he arrives at a different conclusion than I. Basically, Stevens insists that Lee's *Malcolm X* constructs "black masculinity in response to the institutionalized and systematic targeting of black men constituted as the embodiment of criminality and threat."[32] For those reasons, Stevens argues that "disavowal plays a central role in constituting the structure of countermemory and limits the transformative potential of Lee's *Malcolm X*"[33] In essence, Lee's overemphasis on black masculinity condemns aspects of African American identity that fail to fall neatly within a "heteronormative image of gender (and its performance)."[34] When reconstructing black male identity, Lee should consider a wider lens that is inclusive rather exclusive. Quite frankly, heteronormative masculinity should not be the singular interpretation of black male identity. Nevertheless, what distinguishes Lee from his peers is his keen presentation of black manhood. The director does not fall back on the angry black male critique with no rational, reason, or justification for black rage. Lee features the charismatic Denzel Washington as a multifaceted and fully realized human being with a tragic history, character flaws, and heroic tendencies. Thus audiences are able to relate to Malcolm X in a multidimensional way.

Spike Lee's *Inside Man*: The Mockery of Americanization

With Lee's multifaceted presentation of black males and African American culture, he still directs his reflective lens on American culture. In terms of his films, he is undaunted by negative criticism or public controversy. For that reason, Lee causes Americans to question their assumptions, beliefs, and identity with each of his films. According to "Inside 'Inside Man': Spike Lee and Post 9/11-Entertainment," written by Lori Harrison-Kahan, during Spike's "three decades as a filmmaker" he has earned a "reputation as an in-your-face provocateur."[35] Spike has become legendary for his forward approach when encountering issues of race; thus he is known for directly addressing his audience on the subject matter. For instance, in the movie *Do the Right Thing*, Spike employs a "racial slur montage" to grab the audience's attention. Even though Spike's discourse confronts intense racial epithets and issues, he has made "significant inroads in the landscape of American cinema in the process."[36] Consequently, Spike has created a niche for himself, and he has opened the doors for black filmmakers in Hollywood. Harrison-Kahan reiterates that Spike is not known for his restraint; thus he has been criticized for "sacrificing both art and entertainment for polemics."[37] In other words, Spike's politically charged racial messages can be overwhelming and repetitious for some critics and audiences. Due to Spike's subtle approach, when *Inside Man* (2006) was released, there were a few critics who missed Spike's didactic messages. Some critics truly believed that Spike was no longer driving home a message and instead created a movie for the purposes of entertainment. However, Harrison-Kahan disagrees with those critics, since she compares *Inside Man* to "the entertaining, gritty, New York-based 1970s thrillers such as *Dog Day Afternoon* (Sidney Lumet, 1975) and *Serpico* (Lumet, 1973) to which Lee's film self-consciously alludes."[38] With further introspection, the viewers will discover that Lee did not abandon his politics when he made this box-office hit about a bank robbery.

Harrison-Kahan examines race in *Inside Man* in terms of a post-9/11 world. Subsequent to "the terrorist attacks on the World Trade Center and the Pentagon," Spike approaches politics in a more sophisticated and subtle manner for this film.[39] During the opening of the movie, Spike "sets the stage for an exploration of racial tensions in a multiethnic urban environment."[40] Dalton Russell (Clive Owen) heads a band of bank robbers as they take over the Manhattan Trust Bank. Most of the action takes place "inside of the bank" with the "hostages (both customers and employees) and the robbers."[41] There is standoff between the NYPD, headed by the "white Captain Darius (Willem Dafoe), and two maverick black detectives—Washington's Keith Frazier and sidekick, Bill Mitchell (Chiwetel Ejiofor)" who play the roles of hostage negotiators.[42] There is a triangulated power structure because the NYPD perceive Frazier and Mitchell as incapable of managing the volatile situation. Then, there are the suit-wearing power players that work not for the safety of the hostages, but for their own personal gain. Jodie Foster plays Madeleine White; she acts as the suit-wearing fixer. White works for the "bank's president, Arthur Chase (Christopher Plummer)" and he is primarily concerned with the "carefully guarded secrets of the safe deposit box."[43] In order to gain access to the crime scene, White bribes the New York City mayor. This singularly corrupt act symbolizes the corruption with which problems are solved on a statewide or mass scale. Later, it is discovered that Case's hands are unclean. Instead, Case's "bank was built with 'blood money' he made while collaborating with the Nazis during World War II."[44] Because of the large Jewish population in the United States and the emotional wounds that still exist due to Hitler's reign, Lee knows that he is reaching and striking a chord with his audience. Based on this revelation, in the minds of the viewers the bank robbers transform from "robbers/terrorists into ethically justified, if not completely heroic, characters."[45] Since Lee interweaves the dichotomy of cultural betrayal and the ethnic complexity of wealth building in the United States, these issues speak to America's perceived position in the world. Thus from the inception of the film, there is a statement on class and global politics that can no longer remain hidden or invisible within cultural debates.

Yet Lee still includes cultural and religious clashes within his class critique of America. At the beginning of the movie, an African American investigator, "Keith Frazier (Denzel Washington), and bank employee Vikram Walia (Waris Ahluwalia)" have an intense interaction with one another.[46] The employee Walia is roughed up by the police; he is thought to be "a perpetrator rather than a hostage" and "desperately tries to convince them that he's a Sikh, not an Arab, as they claim."[47] Walia will not stand for the mistreatment by the detectives; therefore he declines to answer "Frazier's questions until his turban, presumably removed in a search for explosives, is returned to him."[48] At this moment, Walia's religious garment transmutes into a veiled weapon in the possession of the officers. Immediately, the Sikh is presumed suspicious by the black investigator who has traded his cultural sensitivity for the opportunity to participate in crime solving as an agent of the state. Thus Walia will receive no sympathy from Frazier. Apparently, Frazier mocks Walia's complaints about the violation of his civil rights. Frazier responds by issuing a wisecrack in reference to "the racial profiling that makes it difficult for black men to hail cabs as well as the large number of Indian and Pakistani immigrants who make their livings as cabdrivers [sic]."[49] By juxtaposing the "interethnic conflict between African Americans and the nation's recent immigrants," Lee makes evident "shifts in racial tensions."[50] Effectively, he is transferring his "indictment of white authorities" onto the competition between minorities as "most targeted outcasts within" American society.[51] Thus, Harrison-Kahan claims, this exchange is evidence of Lee's masked political agenda to critique American culture by addressing the subgroups within.

Spike interweaves "into the film's aesthetics" America's tendency toward hypocrisy in terms "of American imperialism, the fear mongering that produces racial profiling, and the dominance of white cultural capital in a global society."[52] Basically, Lee embeds the issue of racial profiling into this movie about bank robbers and their hostages without directly critiquing white racism. With the opening exchange between Frazier and Walia, Lee "sets the stage for an exploration of racial tensions in a multi-ethnic urban environment."[53] Lee takes advantage of the concept of racial invisibility and cultural assimilation to further explore American identity. Except for Russell, who happens to be white, the audience does not know the identity of the bank robbers.[54] According to Harrison-Kahan, the robbers "emerge from different ethnic locales, even as their outward appearances are identically white."[55] Yet the bank robbers lack any individualized identity because they mask their faces in a uniform manner. Furthermore, they adopt similar nomenclature when referring to one another. They call each other a "variation on the same name: Stevie, Steve-O, Steven, and Steve."[56] At first viewing, this jargon may not seem significant. However, in America, regardless of race, culture, or national origin, it is common to have similar-sounding birth or nick-names. Additionally, in the process of assimilation, individuals shed their cultural identities, such as their names, in order to adopt the language, values, and mannerisms employed in their new home. As the robbers engage in this verbal and visual performance, Spike is emphasizing the masking of race in their "mockery of Americanization."[57] By engaging in this deceitful "orchestrated performance of assimilation," via their similar-sounding names and disguises, the criminals are able to "commit and get away with a crime."[58]

Harrison-Kahan details how the robbers' performance is both a masking of race and a mockery of Americanization. When the hostage takers make their captives wear white masks and black body suits, they mirror their captors.[59] Except for the dark sunglasses worn by the bank robbers and the black eye masks worn by their captives, the criminals and the victims appear identical. The bank robbers employ this method for the purposes of confusing the police.[60] Thus as the bank robbers elude police, the government is visually fooled because of their preconceived notions of who fits the profile of a criminal. This method blurs the line between "hostage and terrorist, innocent and guilty, abused and abuser."[61] Thus Lee is making a veiled commentary on racial profiling. The criminals direct guilt to everyone by causing the hostages to appear as suspects instead of guiltless parties. By implicating the innocent, the guilty may go free because the enemy within is the most sinister of all. In this manner, "Lee is addressing American imperialism abroad and racial profiling on the domestic frontier."[62] Because the police are unable to differentiate "between the guilty and innocent," everybody is taken "into custody."[63] Sadly, this is grave commentary on the American experience. When one group is subjugated to unjust and unequal treatment, everyone bears the brunt of that mass injustice.

Spike incorporates "a powerful visual metaphor" in the rescue portion of the hostages.[64] As the audience views the "black outfits and hoods," the captives are transformed "into an undifferentiated sea of racial others in which darker outward appearance is the only determinant of guilt."[65] Once Lee forces the "abuses of power out of the shadows, the costumes serve as a painful reminder of how easily the threat of terrorism can transform the threatened from victim to villain."[66] In other words, profiling is dependent upon issues of race. There is an assumption that "beneath every turban is an explosive and behind every black skin a criminal intent."[67] But the message of racial profiling is submerged under the true hidden evil lurking within the American capitalistic system. Unfortunately, there are those who secretly profit from the discrimination of the state and the cultural discord on both a domestic and global scale. For those reasons, Lee is a provocateur who seizes the images of Hollywood and reconstructs them into a filmic narrative that more accurately reflects black manhood and the black experience.

The Tyler Perry Effect

To the audience, Tyler Perry films serve as an alternative to the sociopolitical and culturally astute Lee movies. This is not to say that Perry lacks social messages in his films. However, his approach to taking control and agency of the filmmaking process differs immensely from Lee's. In one respect, Perry and Lee have a different approach to marketing and selling their films to the American public, and as a result, Perry has made more money than Lee at the box office. Thus filmmakers, businessmen, and marketers like Tyler Perry provide many artists hope for a progressive future. When the "*Diary of a Mad Black Woman* came out during the second week Will Smith's movie *Hitch* was in theaters," Perry's movie performed better monetarily because Tyler has successfully "created a niche and worked the niche"; and he has been able to open "eyes at the top of the distribution pyramid."[68] Prior to Perry's film success, he initially created his niche audience with play performances that toured the country. Furthermore, Perry follows in the footsteps of Oscar Micheaux and beyond. Like Lee, Perry will write, direct, produce, and even star in his independent films, ensuring he has an active role in every major stage of filmmaking. The mainstream success of Perry's movies has opened the doors for more independent voices;

now, some black filmmakers believe that if they keep producing work, their race or gender will no longer matter in the industry. But keep in mind, Perry's appeal is linked to his comedic timing, which is not the dominant component of Lee's films.

Another distinction between Lee's and Perry's films is the Madea drag motif. For most audiences, Tyler Perry's Madea elicits laughs upon seeing her entry onto the stage or the screen. Yet, Perry is not the first black male to perform in drag onstage. Both Martin Lawrence and Eddie Murphy have performed in drag; nevertheless, they have all become "this black hero or icon."[69] Up until this point, even though Lee has acted in many of his own films, he has not performed in drag. According to Robert Patterson who writes in " 'Woman Thou Art Bound': Critical Spectatorship, Black Masculine Gazes, and Gender Problems in Tyler Perry's Movies" that no matter the "ideological or aesthetic quality of Tyler Perry's films and/or plays" the public's and critic's fascination with Perry, "Madea, and his corpus of works" is undeniable.[70] Regardless of the public's obsession with Perry's movies, as this chapter will explore further and Patterson discusses, there are problematic issues with Perry's presentation of black masculinity and gender roles. Nevertheless, Perry's success and fame is incomparable to everyone except Oprah Winfrey. As an African American cultural producer, he appears to satisfy the desires of the female consumers with his films and plays.

Tyler Perry Puts the Drag in Black Masculinity and Patriarchy

For some audiences, the implementation of drag causes them to probe into the sexuality of the performer. However, some critics focus on the performance rather than the authentic identity of the performer for analysis. Thus Timothy Lyle opts to discuss drag in terms of gender and queer theory. His discourse on drag centers on how Perry utilizes the mask of the zany grandma, Madea, to reassert patriarchal American values. In the article " 'Check with Yo' Man First; Check with Yo' Man,': Tyler Perry Appropriates Drag as a Tool to ReCirculate Patriarchal Ideology," Lyle discusses gender, masculinity, and femininity in Perry's cinematic productions. Generally, the "primary demographic and financial backbone" of Perry's films is women; he acts as the all-wise and knowing adviser to women and he manages this dogmatic role by parading around in drag.[71] Perhaps Perry's drag performance of Madea is the main draw for the female audience. Lyle gives Perry accolades for being "quite possibly the most popular, most visible, and most financially successful African American playwright of the twenty-first century, if not of all time."[72] Consequently, Perry's family-based themes are also drawing people to the theater.

Lyle examines whether "Perry appropriates drag in a politically liberating or constraining manner."[73] In other words, is Perry making a political statement about freedom or is his drag performance restricting the prescribed roles of men and women? Furthermore, Perry co-opts stereotypes to emphasize his traditional views of femininity and masculinity. For instance, in the play *Madea's Family Reunion* (2002) and the film version in 2006, Perry upholds stereotypes about African American women when Madea threatens people with her gun. Simultaneously, Perry "deconstructs, reclaims, and reconstructs the images to offer a different vision."[74] In other words, Perry upholds stereotypes of black women with Madea. Yet via other characters, he deconstructs typical views of African American women. Then, he reappropriates them for the purposes of redefining black images and black gender roles in America. In this classic movie, Madea is confronted with many problems: taking care of her ornery brother, dealing with a rebellious teenage foster child, taking care of her nieces, guiding various other family members, and planning and organizing a family gathering.[75] Just as the title suggests, *Madea's Family Reunion* emphasizes the historical and modern significance of familial connections.

Generally, critics attempt to separate the artist from the text. But Perry's multiple roles in the filmmaking process blur the lines for analysis. However, Perry interjects himself as a mouthpiece for the masculine gender because he performs as an "actor in addition to already being director, producer, and writer."[76] Thus Perry's patriarchal rhetoric as a director is evidenced by the words and actions of the characters. There is more than one way to interpret the character of Madea. On one hand, Perry's drag performance could be considered a sociopolitical statement or as misogynistic rhetoric. Is the mask of drag a veil for a subconscious hatred of women? Lyle probes into that question. Initially, Lyle perceived Perry's use of drag as an act of radical feminism.[77] Later, Lyle contends that Perry treats his female audience in a paternalistic manner. When Perry dresses as Madea and wears makeup in drag, he instructs women how to get out of abusive relationships and learn to respect themselves. Moreover, once women abandon their state of domestic abuse, they must take up with another man who is not abusive. Nevertheless, Lyle claims, the patriarchal message remains the same: women need a man to sustain themselves. In essence, it is "a man (drag or no drag)" who "must come to the rescue, sustaining the prince charming-like fairy tale scripts that are rooted in female passivity and subordination."[78] But in Perry's defense, the media, movies, and even church appeal to women's desire for a fairy tale ending. Thus Perry realizes the female desire for relationship consultation via his films. In a way, Perry's discovery of the black female niche is ingenious. Due to his authoritative tone, women feel as if they can trust Perry. Thus viewing the courage displayed by Madea and other female characters in Perry's films, women are empowered.

With regard to queer theory, how does Perry's use of drag address sexuality? Lyle agrees with other critics who claim that drag performance is not necessarily subversive or queer. In other words, the use of drag in *Madea* is not necessarily progressive or an endorsement of homosexuality. Acts of drag "perpetuate the construction, maintenance, and reiteration of gender norms, upholding hierarchal gender relations and normative power scripts that ultimately privilege the masculine political category."[79] Basically, Perry is upholding traditional gender constrictions and social restraints; therefore he is preserving norms of patriarchy and masculinity with his dogmatic performance of Madea. Lyle says that Madea in drag represents conservative patriarchy and has "oppressive consequences for females (and those males who fall outside the gender binary)."[80] With that said, for females or males who do not prescribe to traditional gender roles, Madea's instruction on family values is inflexible.

As previously mentioned, Perry is not the first black actor to perform in drag. By dressing in drag, Perry joins a long-standing custom of black comedic actors who have performed as "females in popular culture productions": "Martin Lawrence's Big Momma; Eddie Murphy's Mama Klump, Grandma Klump, and Rasputia; and Flip Wilson's earlier Geraldine."[81] But the character of Madea plays into the commonplace stereotype that outspoken black females are big, fat, and ugly. Yet women who are considered good-looking, "sexualized and desired" by males, behave in a "submissive, passive, and obedient" manner.[82] Unlike the aforementioned drag performances, Perry does not include the act of passing as a woman in *Madea*. Nor does he have the male character in drag reassert "his male identity and his heterosexuality."[83] Perry stays in drag as Madea for the entire movie and does not feign any other identity than womanhood.[84]

Still, there are problems with the underlying message of Perry's films. Patterson suggests that people reconsider Hollywood's perpetuation of negative black images. Before deeming Perry's films benign media representations, one must contemplate "the products that Perry disseminates and the audiences that consume them."[85] Like Lyle, Patterson implores the audience to consider Perry's peers in his use of drag: "Flip Wilson in

The Flip Wilson Show (1970–74); Wesley Snipes in *To Wong Foo: Thanks for Everything! Julie Newmar* (1995); Martin Lawrence in the trilogy *Big Momma's House* (2000), *Big Momma's House 2* (2006), and *Big Mommas: Like Father, Like Son* (2011); and Eddie Murphy in *Norbit* (2006)" cross-dress as women for the purpose of profiting by engaging in the "commodification of black female sexuality."[86] Ultimately, Patterson claims that Perry's work is profitable because his cultural productions "rely on the racial, gender, sexual, and class ideologies and discourses that produce these problematic stereotypes."[87] In essence, Perry's films address these disparities in American society, and his audience relates to his thematic concerns in a personal way. Since Hollywood has a history of ignoring black churchgoing women, Perry claims to intentionally appeal to those women.[88] Thus Perry prominently features an underserved group who feels invisible in American society and on-screen. For the average black female, she may see herself or a family member in one or more character types projected onto the big screen. Sometimes these characters are stereotypical for laughs or they may address issues that have not received much treatment until Perry's depictions.

For the purposes of connecting to his primary audience, Perry addresses serious issues in a comical manner. Gender issues are prominent and reveal Perry's effort to target his female audience in many of his films:

> These crises of faith, more often than not, revolve around issues of domestic violence (*I Can Do Bad [All] by Myself* [2007] [sic], *Madea's Family Reunion* [2006], *Diary of a Mad Black Woman* [2005]); sexual abuse, including child molestation (*I Can Do Bad [All] by Myself* [2007] [sic]); and familial dysfunction (*Madea's Family Reunion* [2006], *Daddy's Little Girls* [2007], *I Can Do Bad [All] by Myself* [2009], *Why Did I Get Married?* [2007], *Why Did I Get Married Too?* [2010], and *The Family That Preys* [2008]).[89]

After women view Perry's films, he hopes that they will feel inspired and armed with the tools to leave their troubling situations. Madea is the vehicle of empowerment that will guide women forward. Perry's works repetitively mandate marriage for the purposes of "cultural, political, and economic values."[90] The patriarchal message is clear: marriage resolves all issues for males and females. Furthermore, Perry's films project the message that marriage has the power to solve social ills as well. Thus Perry fails to dismantle black patriarchy because he insists that women conform to heterosexual normative views of marriage. In essence, Patterson believes that Perry's message binds women and sustains them in an oppressive state because of "patriarchal ideologies."[91] Historically, traditional family structures have operated in a manner that oppressed (black) women. Furthermore, this restrictive view of gender roles oppresses those who operate outside the traditional boundaries of femininity and masculinity. With that said, Perry takes control of black images by targeting a segment of the population who feels ignored by and invisible to the movie industry. Finally, even if Perry engages in buffoonery for comedic purposes, he addresses serious issues that appeal to them.

Will Smith: From Philly "Ghetto" Kid to Superhero Status

When audience members think of black filmmakers and production companies, people do not usually think of Will Smith's Overbrook Entertainment. Yet as this chapter progresses, it becomes clear why Smith should be considered a powerhouse of filmmaking along with Lee and Perry. Generally, when people think of Will Smith, they think of an incredible actor who generally plays the star in blockbuster films. Moreover, Smith is considered an archetypal figure of black heroic masculinity. But Smith is more than an actor; he is a cultural producer and image maker. Early in Smith's career, he was not content to allow Hollywood to shape his image, and with Overbrook Entertainment, he and his partners are redefining the way America views black culture and black possibilities in America.

Matt Doeden speaks of Will Smith's roots in *Will Smith: Box Office Superstar*. By the year 1990, Smith had already received success as a rapper, but he managed to get deep in debt.[92] Since Smith's music career was fading, he arrived in Hollywood with the hope of acting despite his lack of cinematic experience. During a chance meeting with Benny Medina, producer for Warner Bros. Records, at *The Arsenio Hall Show* in 1989, the trajectory of Smith's career was altered.[93] Smith's groundbreaking role was starring as the Fresh Prince in the sitcom *Fresh Prince of Bel-Air* (1990–96). In reality, Smith was definitely not a black kid from the ghetto like his comical character Fresh Prince. The rapper turned actor was born into an economically privileged, two-parent household in West Philadelphia, Pennsylvania. Smith's articulate speech and good looks made him appeal to Medina despite his lack of acting experience.[94] On the other hand, Smith's ambitions extended beyond his sitcom character. Not to mention, his acting range would excel beyond his street kid character who entertained audiences for a good laugh.

Smith's first movie demonstrated his determination to make an impact and widen the perspective of African American actors in Hollywood.

Doeden references Tom Green's article entitled "Will Smith's Exponential Leap: 'Six Degrees' Elevates Rapper and TV Star" published in *USA Today* when he discusses Smith's transition into the film industry.[95] Subsequently, Doeden explains that Smith starred in this "drama about an African American con man (Smith) who tricks rich white families out of their money."[96] *Six Degrees of Separation* (1993) received rave reviews from *Entertainment Weekly* and the *Hollywood Reporter*. Perhaps the film appealed to critics because it delved into controversial issues of concern such as racism, homophobia, and class bias. But Smith did not elevate his career without some negative comments from critics. Smith's refusal "to kiss another man" caused the director "to film the scene another way."[97] Basically, Smith was concerned with how his image would change if he engaged in a homosexual kiss. Later, Smith was apologetic, yet people were enraged by his decision not to partake in a sexual scene with another man, accusing him of being homophobic. Early on, Smith demonstrated that he wished to portray heteronormative heroes in his films. Clearly, he was deeply invested in the construction of his own image and how he would be received by audiences.

With *Bad Boys*, costarring Martin Lawrence and Smith as cops in Los Angeles, Smith's career received another boost in 1994.[98] The producers chose Smith for the part because he reminded them of a young Eddie Murphy. Since the producers had a major hit with Murphy in *Beverly Hills Cop*, they believed that the meshing of comedy and action would reap another hit for them. The desire to create another Murphy character type proves that Hollywood is content to recycle the same images for commercial gain. Although *Bad Boys* was a success, Smith was not content to only play a cop who was an action hero. In Smith's next hit, he is an everyday military guy that becomes the savior of humanity in the sci-fi flick and mega summer blockbuster *Independence Day* (1995). Smith played the Air Force pilot Steven Hiller.[99] The story's plot centered on alien invaders. Originally, this role was not intended for an African American actor. Yet this original designation did not deter him; Smith broke barriers when he secured a role that had been written for a white male, not a black male. Smith had achieved global action hero status because he was "fighting aliens and dodging explosions."[100] For that reason, Smith not only made audiences visualize the possibilities of black masculinity differently, but he managed to open the eyes of Hollywood producers who previously limited the possibilities of black actors. In essence, even in a film with many other white actors, Hollywood was beginning to see that audiences would accept a black male as a major action hero.

Due to Smith's mainstream success, playing a superhero in *Hancock* (2008) is believable. Perhaps one of Smith's most intriguing roles occurs as he inhabits the role of the disillusioned lead character. John Hancock is "an alcoholic and reluctant superhero" and his presence is not welcome in Los Angeles.[101] Hancock has brought structural devastation; meanwhile, the cost of repairing his damage to the community has caused the citizens to demand for his exodus. Once Hancock saves the life of Ray Embrey (Jason Bateman), the community begins to envision another side of Hancock. Embrey is a spokesperson who is so grateful "to be alive, Ray pledges to change Hancock's public image and" is successful at this endeavor.[102] Although Smith's cinematic image is positive, Hancock symbolizes the fragmented identity of the black male. Like the superhero Hancock, the black male is perceived, oftentimes, as unjustifiably angry and destructive to the community.

For Smith, the choice of playing the "disillusioned superhero in need of a PR makeover" was box-office gold.[103] The movie profited $66 million during its opening weekend. According to Nielsen EDI, the success of *Hancock* placed Smith above "the ranks of stars with consecutive blockbusters."[104] What makes Smith arguably the greatest African American star and American star is the distinction of having "eight straight movies eclipse $100 million."[105] Smith has discovered a formula that works for him by releasing his movies over the July Fourth holiday. Furthermore, *Hancock* ranked as Smith's 12th number one film. All of the following films debuted at number one thanks to Smith's star power: *Independence Day* (1995), *Men in Black* (1997), *Wild Wild West* (1999), and *Bad Boys II* (2003). Keep in mind that some of these films have not all received rave reviews from critics. For the critics who praise Smith, they credit his diverse performances in various genres such as science fiction, action, drama, romantic comedy, and animation. Few actors have the skill to perform in such a varied array of movies. Not to mention, many actors would refuse to take such risks, fearing the destruction of their well-formulated image.

Will Smith's acting range and wise movie choices have naturally led to his production company Overbrook Entertainment. Evidently, Smith sought even more script control and influence in terms of his characters. Truly the best way for an actor to play the roles he or she seeks is to create and produce them with his or her own production company. Perhaps, it is no coincidence that Smith's public high school and neighborhood were named Overbrook.[106] People skills he developed at Overbrook transcended into future moviemaking appeal. Due to his personality, making the transition from white schools to a school with mainly African

Americans was easy for him. Smith credits his youthful experiences with teaching him how to adapt his humor to the interests of white and black audiences.[107] Most definitely, Smith's ability to cope with diversity by entertaining others has influenced his rap, television, and movie career. Thus, since Smith plays the lead in most Overbrook films, his enigmatic appeal has led to the immense success of his production company.

According to Overbrook Entertainment, they are "committed to offering the highest quality film and television entertainment."[108] The company's goal is to offer diverse films that are "both critically acclaimed and blockbuster feature films."[109] As of 2015, Overbrook films have profited "more than $3.0 billion dollars [*sic*] in worldwide box office receipts and even more in home video sales."[110] Amazingly, Smith and his partners have created a profitable filmmaking company featuring positive stories with African Americans as the lead characters.

Will Smith founded Overbrook Entertainment with his business partner, James Lassiter; they operate the company along with his wife of many years, Jada Pinkett Smith. With the exception of the *Secret Lives of Bees*, as previously mentioned Overbrook's most lucrative films star Smith as the lead character. Overbrook's most profitable movies are: "*Ali* (2000), *Hitch* (2005), *Pursuit of Happyness* (2006), *I Am Legend* (2007), *Hancock* (2008), *Secret Lives of Bees* (2008), and *After Earth* (2013)."[111] Despite the raving report from Overbrook Entertainment, the *Wall Street Journal*, in conjunction with various other sources, refers to *After Earth* as a box-office failure.[112] *After Earth* cost Overbrook Entertainment $150 million to make, but it opened to dismal box-office returns of $27 million on its opening weekend in both the United States and Canada.[113] But with further inspection, another source states that the movie made $243,843,127 worldwide when the foreign profits are factored into the total box-office receipts.[114] Moreover, Smith's real-life son, Jaden, with wife Jada, starred as his progeny in both the *Pursuit of Happyness* and *After Earth*. Not only is Smith revolutionizing black male images, he is reinventing the perception of black fatherhood both on-screen and in real life due to his Overbrook productions featuring his son.

However, unlike the *Pursuit of Happyness*, *After Earth* was not well received by many and savaged by critics. Initially, *After Earth* is credited with being Smith's biggest "flop since 2000's 'The Legend of Bagger Vance.'"[115] Even Spike Lee joined the critics who disapproved of his role as the "mystical golf caddy Bagger Vance."[116] As a matter of fact, the director of *The Legend of Bagger Vance* (2008) is Robert Redford, but Smith plays a supporting role to Matt Damon.[117] Lee was disappointed by the fact that Smith accepted "a role that ignored the plight of African

Americans during the 1930s (the period in which the film was set)."[118] In essence, Lee was appalled that Bagger Vance lives in the "Depression-era Georgia, a time when lynching of blacks in the South was commonplace," yet Bagger is more concerned with his job as a caddy.[119] In actuality, this criticism by Lee has some validity. However, more than likely the caddy's complacency reflects the director's perception of blacks in the 1930s, instead of Smith's attitude about 1930s Georgia.

Although Smith has received both negative and positive criticism along the way, he is utilizing his star power and influencing the perceptions of black images with other well-known, critically acclaimed, or profitable movies produced by Overbrook Entertainment: *Lake View Terrace* (2008) with Samuel L. Jackson and Kerry Washington, *Seven Pounds* (2008) starring Smith, *ATL* (2006) starring "T.I." Harris and Evan Ross with story by Antwone Fisher, and *I Robot* (2004) starring Smith and Bridget Moynahan.[120] Apparently, Will Smith is not content with simply playing a superstar movie actor. His success at producing films for himself and others demonstrates his economic power to shape and reconstruct his own image and the images of others. Thus he is reimagining the possibilities of blackness and disrupting the industry's typical notions of black male performers.

After *The Legend of Bagger Vance*, Smith starred as Muhammad Ali in the boxing movie produced by Overbrook Entertainment. The starring role of *Ali* earned Smith an Academy Award nomination.[121] Obviously, Smith's performance as the Muslim convert, controversial, and champion boxer impressed critics. But despite his win at the Golden Globe awards, he was up against incredible competitors at the Academy Awards: "Sean Penn for *I Am Sam*, Russell Crowe for *A Beautiful Mind*, Tom Wilkinson for *In the Bedroom*, and Denzel Washington for *Training Day*."[122] Ultimately, Washington won the Oscar for his role in *Training Day*, but in the minds of the youth audience, Smith was still a hero; he won for Best Male Performance at the MTV Movie Awards. Also, the African American community awarded him for his performance with a Black Entertainment Television Award. Of course, Smith had competition in terms of action star and superhero status. In 2011, according to an *Entertainment Weekly* headline, "Samuel L. Jackson Is the Highest Grossing Actor of All Time, and by God, He's Worth Every Penny."[123] Superhero roles in the *Star Wars* prequels and "four Marvel-verse blockbusters—*Captain America*, *Thor*, two *Iron Men*—but his Nick Fury is less a character than a walking commercial for *The Avengers*."[124] Nevertheless, Jackson and Smith are two of the few black actors who play superheroes in Hollywood. As a producer, Smith's films have a range of varied topics that appeal to diverse cultures and generations. But as the lead, he generally plays the action hero and reluctant superhero as in *Hancock*. For *Hancock 2*, reportedly Beyoncé will act alongside him.[125] Even if Beyoncé does not star alongside Smith, with his star power he will have his pick of lady leads. Nonetheless, in terms of Smith's Overbrook Entertainment, he will continue to dominate perceptions of African American images if audiences continue to see his films.

With respect to the Lee's and Perry's cinematic rivalry, it is understandable that the directors would differ in terms of their artistic visions. However, both directors have contributed to a wider range of opportunities for black actors. Still, the directors disagree on the manner of projecting black images. Historically, Lee has been known to negatively criticize Perry: "Lee called Tyler Perry's imagery 'troubling,' sparking a rift which caused Perry to fire back in 2011, stating that Lee 'can go straight to hell.' "[126] Nonetheless, Perry attributes their backgrounds to their varying visions. Later, in an interview with Oprah, Lee suggested that their divergent regional upbringings explains their perspectives.[127] But on *Oprah's Next Chapter*, Lee reportedly said "I love Tyler"; furthermore, Lee has been to Perry's house. In other words, Lee values Perry as a person and as a competitor. All things considered, Lee is at home with his position as an instigator; he was born to spark controversy. For Lee's immense fan base and his critics, his provocateur status is necessary to alter or at least widen the perception of the black male in Hollywood. Meanwhile, only time will tell if Spike Lee and Tyler Perry will continue to feature themes that reinforce a strict definition of heteronormative and masculine values. Even though critics disapprove of Lee's and Perry's patriarchal values, both filmmakers depict black manhood with its varied possibilities in America and the world. Lastly, both Lee and Perry have refused to allow Hollywood archetypes to stifle their productions or visions of the African American experience. As cultural producers, Lee's 40 Acres and a Mule Filmworks and Tyler Perry Studios define how audiences interpret the black images and the type of stories visualized on-screen.

CHAPTER 11

_____ 2010s _____

Black Power Hollywood: In the Age of Obama's Hope and Change

During the early 2010s, films featuring African Americans inhabited an unusual paradox: blacks played slaves, servants, presidents, and superheroes. Still, these movies reminded the audience of America's conflictual and racial past or functioned as fantastical escapes. Also, some of the best performances of African Americans occurred during this decade. Moreover, films offered a deeper and more authentic depiction of black humanity: passivity and violent resistance. Movies such as _Django Unchained_ (2012) achieved box-office success and offered the same violence one can expect in _Savages_ (2012) and _A Good Day to Die Hard_ (2013). That is to say, there is a "celebration of violence in both virtual culture and real life [that] now feed each other."[1] In addition to the carnage, there is the excessive use of the derogatory term "nigger" in _Django_. Exhaustive use of the epithet in some circles harnesses some objections from both whites and blacks. Nevertheless, both white and black characters superfluously utter the term, much to the dismay of some critics and audiences.

Tarantino's use of the derogatory term liberates rather than erodes the humanity of black characters. Conversely, he employs the word to emphasize the height of black oppression in American society. Chris Vognar writes in "He Can't Say That, Can He?: Black, White, and Shades of Gray in the Films of Tarantino" that there is textual tension between the language of Tarantino's films and his well-crafted black male characters.[2] Still, Tarantino writes "more complicated and fully developed black characters, than any white film-maker before or since."[3] His love for black lingo and mannerisms is explicitly evident with Samuel L. Jackson in _Pulp Fiction_ and the movie _Jackie Brown_. Frustrating the fantastical slave narrative even further, the most inflammatory character in

Django is Stephen (Samuel L. Jackson), the house slave. Tarantino specializes in textual tension for the purposes of provocation. Vognar believes that "the clash between Stephen and Django is a vivid embodiment of the historically chronicled animosity between house slaves and field slaves."[4] Stephen is the embodiment of the racially passive and subservient stereotype Uncle Tom on steroids or analogous to the cable television hit Uncle Ruckus on *Boondocks*. Yet Django symbolizes the armed resistance that is rarely featured in movies about slaves. Then, in 2013, there were other movies that focused on slavery, such as *Twelve Years a Slave* and *Belle*, which sought to tell the forgotten and untold true stories of narratives on slavery.[5] The aforementioned movies star black British actors, which has revelatory impact on storytelling; meanwhile, *Django Unchained* and *Lincoln* offer extremely different perspectives in terms of race, slavery, liberation, and passive and armed resistance.

The Black British Invasion

An interesting aspect to the African diaspora and black male identity is the recent influx of black British actors to Hollywood. As a result of the racist exclusion, black British actors have sought artistic refuge in the United States. Due to the "lack of diversity in castings on television and film," actors such as of Chiwetel Ejiofor, Idris Elba, and David Oyelowo have left Britain for American television and film opportunities.[6] Notable films starring black Brits are Chiwetel Ejiofor in *American Gangster* (2007) and *12 Years a Slave* (2013); and Idris Elba in *Daddy's Little Girls* (2007), *This Christmas* (2007), and *Mandela: Long Walk to Freedom* (2013). Not only has David Oyelowo starred in *Red Tails* (2012), he also played in *Lincoln* (2012) and *Lee Daniels' The Butler* (2013). Adewale Akinnuoye-Agbaje starred in *Get Rich or Die Tryin'* (2005) and *Pompeii* (2014).[7] British-born actor and comedian Lenny Henry is the son of Jamaican immigrants; he disparaged the Baftas (British Academy of Film & Television Arts) for their lack of black representation.[8] Henry says that "we live in a majority white country, with a majority European literary tradition both in TV and theatre. For European, read 'white' . . . But we still have a long way to go till we reach the dizzy heights of a brochette of major black performers in our homegrown, mainstream theatre, TV and films."[9] Within the context of Henry's criticisms, there is an element of irony. Due to America's willingness to revisit our racial atrocities and the desire to explore divergent perspectives in film, black Brits have discovered fertile ground to express their wide-ranging artistic talents.

Even more so, Henry says there are producers who believe the presence of black actors will reduce the audience to a niche market. Thus British filmmakers believe fewer people will patronize their films. For minorities in Hollywood, Henry believes that "great African-American stars who can command major theatre and film roles in successful international projects are not uncommon: James Earl Jones, Denzel Washington, Halle Berry, Whoopi Goldberg and Jamie Foxx, to name just a few."[10] However, for black British actors they must cope with a "smaller industry ... and many actors of whatever colour have found success in the US that had eluded them here."[11] To emphasize the disparity, Henry closes his comments by listing black Brits who have found success in America: "Chiwetel Ejiofor, Sophie Okonedo, David Harewood, Marianne Jean-Baptiste and Idris Elba."[12] Clearly, when actors of such caliber must abandon their homeland for television and movie success, there are some grave issues. Whereas black British actors are faced with the absence of on-screen black images, many African Americans are still disturbed by the negative black depictions in Hollywood. However, the invisibility and alienation of black representation has caused black Brits to become expatriates to the United States. In essence, the 2000s through the 2010s has been a prolific period for black British actors seeking independent and commercial film work.

Jim Crow Stars Brightly in the Age of Obama

For those interested in movies featuring blacks or black issues, yet their stomachs churned when confronted with the subject of slavery, there were movies that focused on the Jim Crow era: *The Butler* and *The Help*. Both movies featured at least one black British actor, yet each attempted to show blacks as heroic targets of segregation. Audiences were enthralled by black narratives, demonstrating the human capacity to excel, despite racial tensions, separate facilities, and inadequate resources. For young male audiences, the movie industry offered *Red Tails* (2012), *42: The Jackie Robinson Story* (2013), and *Fruitvale Station* (2013) starring Michael B. Jordan (Oscar Grant) and Octavia Spencer (Wanda).[13] George Lucas, director of *the Star Wars* trilogy and prequels, directed *Red Tails*, which is about the World War II Tuskegee Airmen fighter pilots.[14] Black Brit David Oyelowo stars as Joe "Lightning" Little, Terrence Howard plays Colonel A. J. Bullard, and Cuba Gooding Jr. plays Major Emmanuel Stance.[15] Chad Boseman and Harrison Ford star in *42*, which is a biopic about the "Dodgers GM who signed Jackie to the team in 1947, [and] recounts

Jackie's journey from playing in the Negro leagues to ultimately breaking the color barrier in Major League Baseball and winning the inaugural Rookie of the Year honor."[16] Although movies featuring Jim Crow policies were popular, there were also movies that proved the hostile remnants of segregation remain present in postmillennial society.

Fruitvale Station contemplates contemporary racism is an insidious American plague: the gunning down of young black males by cops or overzealous individuals in positions of authority. One critic compares the public outrage of Trayvon Martin's death to the death of Oscar Grant. For *Cinema Journal*, Mark D. Cunningham concludes in "No Getting around the Black" that the Oscar Grant story failed to incite the national upset caused by Trayvon Martin's death.[17] With that said, Cunningham focuses his attention on the tragedy of Oscar Grant and how he "was shot down in the prime of his life on a Bay Area subway platform by an overanxious white officer."[18] For Cunningham, "fictionalized or not," *The Butler* and *Fruitvale Station* are emblematic of the "horrific part of black experience."[19] Meaning that, for blacks, there remain those who aggressively resist their presence or integration into mainstream society. Moreover, presence in a hostile space or justified resistance to maltreatment may lead to brutalization or terrorization of a black body. The lead character in *The Butler*, Cecil Gaines (Forest Whitaker), has to concern himself with his college son traveling with the activist Freedom Riders. Especially in the South, social resistance was often met with ferocious backlash for protesters and citizens. Even though Gaines is far more politically passive than his son, he still exhibits courage as a father and husband. With regard to Cecil's personal well-being and his obligation to his family, he must gather "his own courage to confront a bigoted employer who failed to pay black butlers" the same wage as his white butlers.[20] Thus Gaines's passive resistance or failure to object to Jim Crow policies must not be confused with racial complacency.

During this Age of Obama, is the fascination with black oppression representative of a nostalgic desire for when black males remained in their place? Or, are these historical movies for the purpose of celebrating America's progression beyond racism? To Cunningham, the answer to the aforementioned questions revolves around the myth of a postracial America. The idea of a postracial America is derived from the belief that "after the election of Barack Obama as the nation's first black president," racism is now extinct, nonexistent, and equality has been achieved in American culture.[21] Conversely, some critics view the words "black experience" in terms of the human experience as erasing the "complexities in identity, ethnicity, ethnography, experience, and gender."[22] But Cunningham argues that exposure to the black experience via movies and music does not equivocate compassion. For instance, popular music permits passive participation in the black experience without "having any empathetic and meaningful investment"; consequently, Cunningham argues against the notion of the black experience, in movies such as *Fruitvale Station* and *The Butler*, as "interchangeable with universal, human experiences."[23] Notwithstanding the election of Obama, some may resist the notion, but there are some events, such as slavery and Jim Crow in America, that are exclusive to the black experience. With that said, vestiges of slavery exist even in the Age of Obama.

Tarantino's *Django Unchained*: Blood, Carnage, and the Justification of Violence

Director Tarantino realizes that the Age of Obama is not a postracial era. Thus he created a film that appeals to the suppressed fantasies of those frustrated by contemporary race relations. Yet some critics of Tarantino's *Django Unchained* are troubled by his stilted or inauthentic depictions of slave and black resistance. Therefore historical accuracy is more important than exploring subversive or unique perspectives. According to Glenda R. Carpio, in her article entitled " 'I Like the Way You Die, Boy' " for *Transition* journal, Tarantino's intentions are misunderstood by many viewers because *Django* is not a "historically accurate representation of slavery."[24] With that clarification, *Django* occupies a tenuous space between "both the history of cinema and historical fantasy"; the name of the ex-slave Django derives from "a reference to the titular hero of Sergio Corbucci's 1966 spaghetti Western, himself named after the virtuoso jazz musician Django Reinhardt." [25] For inspiration, Tarantino relied on various aspects of popular culture for his film. Thus Carpio claims *Django* delves into blaxploitation films such as *The Legend of Nigger Charley* (1972) and its sequels, *The Soul of Nigger Charley* (1973) and *Boss Nigger* (1975).

In addition to Tarantino's homage to blaxploitation films, there is "direct and oblique references to Norse mythology, to D. W. Griffith's *The Birth of a Nation* (1915) and the novel that inspired it (Thomas Dixon's 1905 *The Clansman*), to the slave narrative genre, and a host of other cultural artifacts."[26] These literary and cinematic allusions should not come as a surprise. Perhaps these popular culture references opened *Django* to a wider range of cultures and generations. Yet Carpio also considers the violent imagery employed for shock value; there is the scene where "a slave is torn apart by dogs or when two slaves are made to fight each other to death with bare hands."[27] According to Carpio, it is shocking that Tarantino desires "to treat a national wound with pop aesthetics," but Tarantino's willingness to explore controversial topics, such as slavery with a pop culture sensibility, speaks to the tendency of "highbrow forms" to ignore certain topics.[28] Tarantino teeters between the comic and horrific, which prevents the movie from mulling around in a languid space too long.

Within this mythical slave narrative fantasy, Tarantino interweaves a love story between Django and Hildie (Kerry Washington) to emphasize the humanity of black slaves; for that reason, Dick Gregory, a comedian and activist, relishes the "romance and the sheer pleasure of seeing a black man in the role of a bad-ass cowboy."[29] For a person who is between 80 and 90, a love story between two African Americans is basically foreign in American popular culture. To Gregory, Jamie Foxx as "a bad-ass cowboy" and his passionate romance with Washington's character are the reasons "he claims to have seen [Django] a dozen times."[30] Tarantino suspends disbelief in the humanity of slaves by playing an Italian love song by Elisa Toffoli, "Ancora Qui" ("Still Here").[31] Django and his lover Hildie reunite as "a female voice sings of her lover's return after a painful separation, during which she thinks she sees him in the very nature around her."[32] Despite Hildie's status as chattel, by blending Italian culture within a black love story, Tarantino emphasizes the depth of their union. Thus the sophisticated moment temporarily liberates the viewer from the uncivil world of barbaric slavery.

Tarantino refuses to allow this tender moment and civil bliss to last; subsequently, he shifts into the appalling nature of slavery and its ability to distort humanity. Evidently, *Mandingo* (1975) is another blaxploitation film that influenced Tarantino in terms of *Django*. In the 1970s, *Mandingo* derives "mostly from the perspective of the crippled son of a rheumatic master in a plantation that, in its very surroundings, invokes decay."[33] Various scenes speak to the moral and systematic decay of slavery for both owners and slaves, such as the disturbing depiction of the sexual appetites and the commodification of black bodies for owners' pleasure and monetary gain. In one scene the slave trader is compelled to scrutinize "a slave's anus" for hemorrhoids; then there is another instance where a white woman plays with "a slave's genitals to test his prowess; and later another white woman makes this slave pleasure her."[34] The overall emphasis of *Mandingo* is "the cancerous nature of slavery, its capacity to twist every human relationship beyond recognition."[35] More importantly, this movie emphasizes how the institution of slavery robs both the slaver and the enslaved of their humanity and morality. But unlike *Mandingo*, Tarantino is more interested in the racial violence than the sexual interactions between blacks and whites. Despite the fact that "Tarantino quotes from *Mandingo* incisively," he spares the audience from a "focus on sex or, to be more specific, on rape," like the movie he apparently admires.[36] Instead, he focuses on the "violence that slavery inflicted upon the black body as well as the grief, bitter acquiescence, and resistance it demanded from the enslaved."[37] Tarantino resists sex scenes in favor of violence: to demonstrate the severity of Hilde's treatment for trying to escape Candie Land, her slave owner places her in a box. Viewing Hilde as they free her from the "coffin-like iron 'hot box'" causes Django "stunned grief and anger."[38] Even though Tarantino slants slave narratives for fantastical and melodramatic purposes, he still captures the emotional pain felt by slaves and those who loved them. Thus he sets the stage for the impetus of racial violence spawned by Django.

Nonetheless, Tarantino explores the intraracial violence that operates as a result of a slave society. The controversial director borrows from a scene in *Mandingo* when he shows the ferocity of "black on black bare-knuckle combat to the death."[39] The master, Calvin Candie, relishes the "sadistic form of entertainment mixed with" the monetary satisfaction of profiting "at the expense of black people's pain."[40] The viewer is confronted with "long and up-close shots of the" gruesome combat between two men who are treated like savage animals.[41] Violence between blacks is encouraged in order to entertain and fill the pockets of plantation society. Regardless of the blood and cries of pain, the dehumanization of blacks prevents white society from realizing the personal and communal scars of orchestrated black violence. Moreover, the atmosphere of dysfunction is heightened by Candie's fashionable lover, a female servant "dressed in a sexualized but doll-like uniform, a bartender, and finally Django who" refuses to watch by turning away from the barbaric violence.[42] True to Tarantino's fascination with *Mandingo*, there is a "cameo by Franco Nero, the Italian actor who plays the original Django in Corbucci's film."[43] For Tarantino's contemporary classic, Nero plays the part of a Mandingo owner who bets against Candie. Once Nero's slave is killed, he heads over to the bar with his white gloves and speaks with Django. Even though historians claim that Mandingo fights lack historical basis, this scene demonstrates the paradox of slaves as "passive spectators to brutality against the enslaved and [the] compromised... position of would-be heroes."[44] At this point, Django knows he should hold back his disdain for the sanctioned violence. Consequently, Tarantino artfully employs scenes where Django must compromise his integrity to justify impending violence.

To advance audience empathy, Tarantino implements scenes that explain Django's internal and external motivations and justify the relinquishment of his fantastical styled vengeance. In terms of slave resistance, this is where *Mandingo* and *Django* differ, especially since Tarantino is in touch with the mood of his audience. 2Pac's rap song "Untouchable" is intermeshed "with James Brown's 'Payback,' " which is the ultimate song in terms of seeking revenge; both songs are playing as "Django comes out shooting with both hands, wasting bodies left and right."[45] Brilliantly, Tarantino appeals to hip-hop culture and interweaves the desire for retribution from the *Hell Up in Harlem* blaxploitation soundtrack. As a result, the audience is hyped up for violence. Now the time has arrived for Django to tap into his inner hero. From the tight grips of slavery, he has almost liberated Hildie from Candie Land, but now King Schultz, his emancipator, is dead. After all, much to the chagrin of some critics, "Jamie Foxx's Django becomes a hero only after a German-born white man, Christopher Waltz's King Schultz, frees him and enables him."[46] However, there is another way to view the relationship between King Schultz and Django. That is to say, Tarantino thrust forth the evolution of an emancipator turned advisor who dies once Django's skills exceed what Schultz can teach him. The student has now become the master; therefore Schultz's death symbolizes Django's dispossession of even benign white authority. Lastly, this mentor-mentee relationship evolves into comradery between two men, emphasizing that Django does not hate white people. Django simply hates the institution of slavery and those who insist in maintaining and upholding the repugnant practice. Therefore even blacks are subject to Django's retribution if they harm those he loves or interfere with Hildie's or his freedom.

Still, despite the actual violence of slavery, there are those who are dismayed by the volatile aesthetics of *Django*. Further carnage occurs when "Django does blow bodies apart as he shoots, using dead white men as his shield. He must ultimately surrender but not before he makes blood spurt to high heavens in a violence that is so extreme it is hyperbolic."[47] As if Tarantino is a grown man playing with his toys, he tears up people and structures while suspending the audience's disbelief; in a moment of directorial narcissism, Tarantino appears in "a cameo where Django blows him to smithereens with dynamite."[48] This is another historical inaccuracy because dynamite was not invented until after the Civil War; thus the use of dynamite prior to its creation places *Django* in the realm of fantasy. Or perhaps, by presenting a weapon prior to its existence, Tarantino is expanding the possibilities of achieving and maintaining freedom in his fantastical production.

In many ways, Django's violent resistance and survival is fantastical. Thus Tarantino employs outlandish means to bolster Django's superhuman possibilities. Hip-hop solidifies Django "as a 'bad' black man while adding to the mythic aspect of his plight."[49] Tarantino masterfully mixes movie genres and the accompanying music to intensify Django's quest for human dignity. Mimicking the internal conflict within an ex-slave's heart and mind is the "sound of Rick Ross's '100 Black Coffins,' a Western-style rap anthem that opens with the kind of whistles and ominous bells that Ennio Morricone used so exquisitely in the spaghetti Westerns he worked on."[50] Vognar recognizes that paying homage to the indignities of slavery via "a spaghetti Western" appears to diminish "the horrors of slavery."[51] According to Vognar, there is no "major Hollywood movie that takes more pains to show the damage slavery inflicted on the human body."[52] Yet Tarantino emphasizes how black male desires for love and freedom are equal to any white man's.

Django's horse ride signifies the liberated mind, spirit, and body that is free to love and exist outside the confines of bondage. As Django rides on a horse into and "from the circle of hell that is Candie Land," his motive to free his love Hildie consumes his mind.[53] Django's memory weighs on him; he has not forgotten the humiliating episode of "having to beg the Brittle brothers for mercy when he was forced to watch her bleed in impotent rage. He must, in this sense, also avenge his manhood."[54] Even for those critics who disapprove of Tarantino's harsh depiction of violence, the theme of Django's love for Hildie and his overwhelming need to assert his manhood exemplifies motive for engaging in violence. Rick Ross's "100 Black Coffins" is an original song produced for *Django*.[55] By Tarantino's implementation of gangster rap, he is furthering the fantasies of unrestrained black male prowess. Tarantino employs various artistic methods "to enact rituals of redress for the crime of slavery, a crime that in its enormity can never be repaired," yet *Django Unchained* represents "several cultural texts" interweaved into "a richly allusive pop aesthetic that works in the service of a necessary fantasy."[56] In other words, the fantastical elements enable the narrative to move forward and engage the audience in cathartic satisfaction despite slavery's resonating pain.

By incorporating an authoritative black male perspective, *Django* signifies Tarantino's awareness of those who challenge his artistic authority on issues of race and slavery. With those objections in mind, Tarantino intends to push back assumptions about black male identity, while simultaneously challenging presumptions about his own identity as a white male director. Tarantino seeks to challenge, contradict, and question previous texts and narratives on the African American experience.[57] Movies such as "*To Kill a Mockingbird, Glory, Amistad, Lincoln, Mississippi Burning*" reiterate a familiar notion "of right-minded white liberalism; historical legends of the era of civil rights."[58] But Tarantino rejects the notion of black liberation resulting from white benevolent interference. Instead, Django is the arbiter of the full actualization of his humanity. As previously stated, once Django's mentor, Dr. King Schultz, dies, the movie transforms from "white racial mentorship" to a militant's justifiable revenge.[59]

The concept of vengeance toward one's transgressors represents individualized self-possession; for Django, emancipation from slavery means he's "free to stay, and to punish at will those white people who have wronged him in the past, to make his own history in the South rather than in exile."[60] Once Django transforms his black body into a weapon rather than continue his half-existence as an instrument of slavery, he reinvents himself as the symbol of viciousness. Tarantino subverts many post–civil rights films with this rebellious black male narrative in *Django*. From the controversial movie's perspective, Django does not seek inclusion "through integration—not through civil rights, or even 'freedom' "; instead, others like Django assert their humanity "through recognition as men; as killers; as Americans."[61] Perhaps Vognar is right in terms of director Tarantino's character development of Django, that Tarantino writes the most complex and fully-developed black male characters of any of white male director living or dead.[62]

Spielberg's *Lincoln*: The Absence of Blackness in a Movie That Opposes Slavery

When interpreting both Tarantino's *Django Unchained* and Steven Spielberg's *Lincoln*, this chapter seeks not to elevate one director's skills above another. That is, this is not a review of Spielberg's and Tarantino's entire body of work. By highlighting the work of two legendary white male directors, *Black Hollywood* hopes to highlight the disparate treatment of their black subject matter. Both movies were profitable in terms of box-office receipts. For instance, "as of March 21, 2013, the film *Lincoln* has grossed $181.5 million in the United States and garnered twelve Academy Award nominations with victories in Best Achievement in Production Design and Best Actor (for Daniel Day-Lewis)."[63] Furthermore, Day-Lewis received numerous awards such as the "Golden Globe, Screen Actors Guild (SAG) Best Actor, and several film critic organization accolades"; not to mention, "Lincoln received the American Film Institute Best Picture" award.[64] As evidenced by these prestigious honors, many critics would suggest that *Lincoln* was a better picture than *Django Unchained*.

Nevertheless, when examining *Lincoln*, various critics object to missing elements in the film. First is the cinematic absence of African American contribution prior to emancipation. Second, those few African Americans present in *Lincoln* are monolithic representations of real human beings.

Jon Wiener challenges some of the racial and gendered presumptions made in *Lincoln* with his *Nation* article "The Trouble with Spielberg's 'Lincoln.' " Wiener objects to Spielberg's presumption that the abolishment of slavery occurred "because Lincoln and the House of Representatives voted for the Thirteenth Amendment."[65] Wiener states that Eric Foner's book *The Fiery Trial: Lincoln and American Slavery* (2010) is the best book published on the abolishment of slavery. Foner received the Pulitzer Prize, the Bancroft Prize, and the Lincoln Prize. Wiener's chief objection, along with "Foner and many other historians over the last couple of decades," is the omission of "the central role played by the slaves themselves, who are virtually invisible in this movie."[66] Spielberg's version of *Lincoln* reflects the continued omissions of black contribution. Wiener expounds further on this argument by stating, for instance, "Sherman's army was marching through South Carolina, where slaves were seizing plantations. They were dividing up land among themselves. They were seizing their freedom."[67] In essence, blacks were no longer waiting for the government or plantation owners to liberate them.

Yet President Lincoln operated under the presumption that the demise of slavery would occur on the state level. Since slavery was implemented on a state-by-state basis, President Lincoln believed that slavery should be abolished in the same manner. Therefore "Lincoln did not support the Thirteenth Amendment when it was proposed in 1864—by the Women's National Loyal League, led by Susan B. Anthony and Elizabeth Cady Stanton."[68] Despite Spielberg's brilliance as a director, his cinematic account is not historically accurate. The subjects of emancipation are virtually invisible in the movie. Eric Foner corroborates Wiener's commentary with his article in the *New York Times*: "Even as the House debated, Sherman's army was marching into South Carolina, and slaves were sacking plantation homes and seizing land. Slavery died on the ground, not just in the White House and the House of Representatives. That would be a dramatic story for Hollywood."[69] Based on Foner's analysis, as the White House and the House of Representatives continued to fight in a power struggle, *Lincoln* solidifies that Hollywood is not ready for an accurate portrayal of blacks seizing power for themselves. If Spielberg had included passive and violent resistance by blacks, *Lincoln* would have been quite a different movie.

In Kate Masur's *New York Times* article entitled "In Spielberg's 'Lincoln,' Passive Black Characters," she discusses the absence of slaves in a movie about the emancipation of blacks. As a historian, Masur objects to Spielberg's "liberties with the historical record. As in *Schindler's List* and *Saving Private Ryan*, his purpose is more to entertain and inspire than to educate."[70] According to Masur, during the war fugitive slaves "transformed Washington's streets, markets and neighborhoods."[71] Masur suggests that if there had been more extensive portrayal of African Americans, "they might have shown Lincoln interacting with black passers-by in the District of Columbia."[72] According to African American oral tradition, Lincoln was emotionally transfixed by his visit to "at least one of the capital's government-run 'contraband camps,' where many of the fugitives lived"; inundated by "singing and prayer," the visit had a significant impact upon him.[73] Masur claims that "one of the president's assistants, William O. Stoddard, remembered Lincoln stopping to shake hands with a black woman he encountered on the street near the White House."[74] Not only does *Lincoln* fail to include the president's emotional interactions with blacks, the movie does not incorporate black female contribution to liberation despite her connection to the White House.

Due to the servant Elizabeth Keckley's activism, the White House became a symbol of black progress long before President Obama inhabited the residence. Masur claims that even the White House was a symbol of emancipation, despite the ongoing bloody Civil War that had socially and politically divided the country:

> In fact, the capital was also home to an organized and highly politicized community of free African-Americans, in which the White House servants Elizabeth Keckley and William Slade were leaders. Keckley, who published a memoir in 1868, organized other black women to raise money and donations of clothing and food for the fugitives who'd sought refuge in Washington. Slade was a leader in the Social, Civil and Statistical Association, a black organization that tried to advance arguments for freedom and civil rights by collecting data on black economic and social successes.[75]

To be quite honest, Keckley (Gloria Reuben) and Slade (Stephen Henderson) play a diminished and archetypal role in the film; Keckley is always "sitting with the first lady, Mary Todd Lincoln (played by Sally Field), in the balcony of the House of Representatives, silently serving as a moral beacon for any legislator who looks her way."[76] As a matter of fact, she appears as the loyal, silent, and submissive black servant who is content with her status. Then there is the generic representation of Slade "as an avuncular butler, a black servant out of central casting, who watches in prescient sorrow as his beloved boss departs for the theater on a fateful April evening."[77] Thus Slade is marginalized in a tale of black liberation that he assisted in propelling forward. The cinematic production of *Lincoln* fails to portray Keckley and Slade as the historically and political active players they were in real life. Instead, they become stock characters whose only ambition is to serve their masters. Consequently, Keckley and Slade are alienated and made invisible in the movie *Lincoln*. For an American audience that often depends on historical movies for their entertainment and an agonizing dose of Civil War history, this black minimization and exclusion is significantly flawed.

Based on Wiener's and Masur's commentary, *Lincoln* erroneously appropriates whites as the main arbiters of black people's destiny during the Civil War. In Spielberg's award-winning dramatization, whites are solely credited with the emancipation and salvation of blacks. Even within the context of a clandestine interracial relationship, *Lincoln* reemphasizes white prowess in liberating blacks. Whereas in *The Birth of a Nation*, Griffith depicts the relationship between Thaddeus Stevens (Tommy Lee Jones) and his mulatto housekeeper in a "notoriously racist" manner, Spielberg navigates their interaction in a different manner. When Stevens heads to bed with his mulatto lover (S. Epatha Merkerson), he hands her an official copy of the Thirteenth Amendment. This scene further reiterates the film's intention to feature "emancipation as a gift from white people to black people, not as a social transformation in which African-Americans themselves played a role."[78] Nevertheless, Masur credits Spielberg for omitting the toxic "stereotypes of subservient African-Americans for which movies like *Gone With the Wind* have become notorious, it reinforces, even if inadvertently, the outdated assumption that white men are the primary movers of history and the main sources of social progress."[79] Simultaneously, Masur dismisses Lincoln's message of white male dominance. Singularly, the white male Congress is given credit for their ability to come together on perhaps one of most significant ideals of American identity: freedom. By omitting the very subject of slavery, the movie fails to acknowledge the humanity and contributions of blacks who were instrumental in their own abolition movement and in the formation of the American story.

Director Steve McQueen's Black British Invasion: The Reimagining of Southern Slavery

With Steve McQueen's interpretation of enslaved blacks, he offers a more representative aspect of the black experience. Not only are blacks highly visible, but they are the primary leads in a hauntingly true portrayal of black liberation. Jasmine Nichole Cobb acknowledges the concern for historical accuracy in "Directed by Himself: Steve McQueen's *12 Years a Slave*" for the journal *American Literary History*. Cobb claims that "despite the long and varied history of slavery representations on US screens, scholars and viewers alike continue to ask questions about historical veracity in these cultural productions."[80] During the early 1900s, films such as *Gone with the Wind* and *The Birth of a Nation* emphasize white supremacy instead of historical accuracy. During the 1970s, the blaxploitation films reflected the black political activism of the 1960s. Thus there are elements of embellishment in favor of black heroism. *Drum* (1976) and *Mandingo* subvert the sentimental portrayals of slavery, but their representations of the ideal oppressor are monolithic and lack the complexity for scholars to authentically examine their depictions. Even the classic ABC mini-series *Roots: The Saga of an American Family* (1976), based on Alex Haley's novel, was criticized for what he referred to as "faction," both fact and fiction. The record-breaking series featured "the enslaved African, Kunta Kinte and his progeny, from eighteenth-century capture and enslavement through the death of Lincoln and the end of the Civil War."[81] Cobb even discusses the veracity of Tarantino's epic slave narrative. With respect to *Django Unchained*, Tarantino promoted his film as "a spaghetti Western about a formerly enslaved title character turned bounty hunter, as more empowering and realistic than Haley's saga."[82] Cobb includes Spielberg in her negative critique of "immense distortions of easily accessible truths about slavery."[83] Cobb refers to *Amistad* and *Lincoln* to emphasize her point about artistic liberties, and she makes reference to Masur's criticisms of Spielberg.[84] As stated earlier, *Lincoln* emphasizes white male hegemony as the singular influence in terms of social progress.

Keeping in mind the past criticisms of monolithic depictions of the enslaved, Cobb intends to analyze McQueen's movie in terms of historical accuracy. Cobb attempts to place *12 Years* within a restrictive context of "objective, empirical, realistic, [and] verifiable as a concern for screen representations of slavery."[85] When imagining "new possibilities derived from slavery as a concluded event," she emphasizes the limitations of contemporary society.[86] The release of *12 Years* marks the first time a movie adapted "its portrayal of US slavery on a slave narrative"; "*12 Years* collapses the distance presumed between" the historical truth of slavery and its cultural reproduction onscreen.[87] Within Cobb's analysis, she compares the slave narrative to the filmic treatment of slavery. As a bolster to the credibility of the film, McQueen based his cinematic adaptation on Solomon

Northup's slave narrative. Furthermore, Henry Louis Gates Jr. served in the capacity of a historical consultant to ensure accuracy: "Gates is renowned as an African-American studies scholar, with publications on nineteenth-century African-American literature, and as a television host for PBS programs on race, enhancing the credibility of *12 Years* as a well-researched film offering."[88] During the process of reimagining slavery, "McQueen's *12 Years* demands a willful commitment to the fetishization of black visibility and suffering as essential elements of transatlantic slavery."[89] However, when film and television director Gordon Parks Sr. approached the slave narrative in PBS's *American Playhouse*, the television adaption *Solomon Northup's Odyssey* (1985) featured an "attractive slate of actors" who seemed complacent about slavery.[90] Then, Parks corrupts the picture by altering one of the most poignant scenes of the book: Patsey's beating. McQueen's attention to accuracy surpasses Parks's intention to sanitize slavery for a television audience; "the entire plantation must observe the beating before viewing Patsey's bloody back as the aftermath—Parks entirely revises to show Northup pretending to beat Patsey inside a woodshed until Mrs. Epps is satisfied and retreats to the big house."[91] Deviation from essential truth, such as in the aforementioned instance, removes the compromising positions of those enslaved. Moreover, by distorting the reality, Parks Sr. alleviates the viewer from the guilt associated with the perverted institution of slavery: orchestrated intraracial violence and the slaver's pressure on a black male to abuse rather than protect a black female.

Another excruciating and brutal scene centers on the distinction between a free black man and an enslaved black man. Valerie Smith confronts these opposing ideals in her essay for *American Literary History* entitled "Black Life in the Balance: *12 Years a Slave*." In a scene where "a malicious white journeyman carpenter named John Tibeats (played by Paul Dano) criticizes the quality of Northup's work on an outbuilding on his master's plantation," Northup's inability to accept his enslaved station in life causes him to nearly lose his life.[92] After Tibeats criticizes his work again, the carpenter "flies into a rage when Northup defends his work."[93] Tibeats does not care that Northup is following previous orders as issued to him; Northup has dared to talk back to a white man. When Tibeats tries to whip him, Northup refuses to acquiesce to his rightful punishment under the laws of slavery; "unable to feign subservience any longer, he asserts his own superior physical strength, mercilessly whipping the white man."[94] However, this act of aggressive resistance is met with an attempt by Tibeats to end Northup's life. Together with "his two henchmen," the embarrassed carpenter "restrain[s] Northup, bind[s] his hands, and prepare[s] to lynch him making a public example of him by hanging him in a central location between the slave quarters and the main house."[95] The overseer "prevents the lynching," yet does not stop him from "hanging for hours until his master, Ford (Benedict Cumberbatch), orders that he be cut down."[96] The graphic imagery of this scene holds Northup "literally suspended in the balance between life and death."[97] Smith feels that McQueen makes "this visually arresting scene—an excruciatingly long set piece—we witness Northup's fellow slaves go about their duties; only one is willing to risk her own safety and offer him any comfort."[98] If it were not for his strength at sustaining "the slightest contact between his toes and the ground," Northup would be unable to "keep himself from suffocating."[99] For the unobservant eye, this scene may not resonate as a battle of wills that tests Northup's masculinity and by extension his humanity. As a result of Solomon's enslaved condition, he is relieved of the right to assert his manhood even in the midst of oppression. But for the scholar Valerie Smith, this scene signifies the difference in status between a free black male and an enslaved black male during the pre–Civil War era.

In terms of freedom, "the very qualities that Northup valued in himself as a freedman—his intelligence and resourcefulness—imperil him as a slave."[100] As a freedman, his demeanor, his skills, his assets, and his capability to afford his family a middle-class life fill him with pride; however, once Northup is enslaved "his name and his claim to all of these attributes" are stolen from him.[101] The aforementioned scene with the bigoted carpenter exemplifies that Northup must conform to his noncitizen status in order to stay alive. Further, Smith offers the commonly held belief that slavery interferes with the community bonds that function to enhance humanity's existence. Except for the slave who brings Northup water, the slaves continue their daily routine during the quasi-lynching. The carpenter's actions are for the purpose of scolding and demeaning Northup, but are also a way of "reminding them of the consequences of self-assertion"; therefore other slaves' survival depends on becoming desensitized to one another's pain.[102] Sadly, in order to survive emotionally, numbness to state-sanctioned violence is the plantation way of life. Thus, in the case of Solomon and Patsey, the institution of slavery substantiates the rights of whites to force a slave to punish another. Yet when whites choose to punish a slave with their own hand, slaves are conversely forced by law to avoid protecting the victimized slave.

Another element of the film emphasizes the tenuous space between freedom and slavery. As Northup tries to avoid death, the sight of his twitching feet symbolizes the fragile state of antebellum life; at any moment, a white person could claim ownership over a free person's black body; and in one instant, a freed black person could lose their citizenship, deeming them chattel instead of a human being. Admittedly, Smith imagines that many people would find it difficult to relate to a movie about black freedom; nevertheless, based on the worldwide response, people in the twenty-first century have found a black male character that they can identify with in their everyday lives. Blacks who live "in the US and across the African diaspora—at least those with some measure of financial stability—are able to inhabit and move within identities, communities, nations, professions, and indeed in their own bodies"; therefore Smith links Northup's confidence as a freedman with their contemporary ease and mobility.[103] Furthermore, *12 Years a Slave* provides a unique glance at "the racial, gender, class, and power dynamics that underwrote and enabled the system of slavery."[104] McQueen provides this unique view through Solomon Northup's authentic text, and via "the casting of actors from across the diaspora, the film reminds viewers of the national and global reach of the institution."[105] In addition to the American historical context, by featuring actors from the African diaspora, McQueen's *12 Years* reimagines blackness and freedom with its global implications as well.

As previously mentioned, Smith links the middle-class and proud life of Northup to upwardly mobile blacks living in the United States and across the African diaspora. Poignantly, she follows that line of comparison and contrast in her final thought in her essay: "Northup's twitching foot calls to mind as well Trayvon Martin, Renisha McBride, Jonathan Ferrell, and the hosts of other African Americans, largely invisible in the media, gunned down each year and whose shooters (whether law enforcement officers or civilians) go unpunished. How fragile indeed is black life in the Age of Obama."[106] As stated earlier in this chapter, delusional visions of a postracial America and the cultural reimagining of contemporary America, prompted by the election of Obama, have not come to pass for many Americans. *Fruitvale Station* depicts a modern example of how freedom and survival in the Age of Obama has deteriorated for many black males and their female counterparts. Perhaps this cinematic preoccupation with slavery, during the early 2010s, reflects a desire to understand the contemporary issues in American culture. Tarantino offers an opportunity to express aggression by depicting a valiant ex-slave, hell bent on justifiable rage in *Django Unchained*. But then there is *Lincoln*, which offers an alternate narrative that implies that blacks failed to participate in their own emancipation. Lastly, *12 Years a Slave* juxtaposes the life of black freedman and enslaved man in the embodiment of Solomon Northup.

The recent films starring blacks as superheroes demonstrate a desire to reframe black male identity and freedom. In this process of superhero reinvention, the black male identity becomes one that is not only transformative and exceptional, but beyond inspection and surveillance. Black actors who play superheroes, such as Will Smith's *Hancock*, rise above all human transgressions: vestiges of slavery, fear of the black male body, and suspicion of a black male's motives. Most recently, there are black superheroes, such as Oscar winner Jamie Foxx who stars as Electro in *The Amazing Spider-Man 2* (2014); two-time Oscar nominee Djimon Hounsou as Korath in *Guardians of the Galaxy* (2014) and costar Vin Diesel (Groot) in *Guardians of the Galaxy* (2014); and Dwayne Johnson who stars as the lead actor in *Hercules* (2014).[107] In this reimagining of the compromised positioning of black male characters, Hollywood is featuring many black British actors, such as David Oyelowo as Martin Luther King Jr. in *Selma* (2014). Perhaps this is an attempt to restart old and popular themes in American cinema: equality, justice, and opportunity for all. More importantly, projecting diverse black images on the big screen expresses a desire to realize the deferred promises of American ideals. Nevertheless, for black male actors, who have played the roles of slaves, servants, God (Morgan Freeman in 2003's *Bruce Almighty*), superheroes (Anthony Mackie in 2014's *Captain America: The Winter Soldier*), and/or the president (Jamie Foxx in 2013's *Whitehouse Down* and Samuel L. Jackson in 2015's *Big Game*), their passage both in American life and in the movies has been a problematic and epic quest for full citizenry and recognition of their humanity.

Conclusion

In 2015, a week before the Martin Luther King Jr. holiday, the Academy Award nominations were announced; however, many Americans were disappointed by the lack of Oscar nods for people of color or women—especially, fans of *Selma* (2014) who felt slighted by the movie's receiving only a best picture nomination, and a best original song nomination for John Stephens, better known as the R & B singer John Legend, and Lonnie Lynn, better known as rapper/actor Common. John Legend and Common went on to win the award for the best song "Glory." Nevertheless, many critics considered black British David Oyelowo's performance as the embodiment of the civil rights leader Martin Luther King Jr. Moreover, if Ava DuVernay, the director, had received a nomination for *Selma*, she would have been the first African American woman to garner an Academy Award nomination. On the surface, the absence of color on Hollywood's biggest night is discouraging. Yet in reality, Hollywood's interest in black topics, themes, and performers is cyclical and temperamental. The Academy's sporadic failure to recognize African Americans does not diminish the efforts of black actors, directors, writers, and producers. Instead, the frequency with which blacks are gaining roles in mainstream films, while also producing black-themed films with black casts, is inspiring. Even when the Academy chooses not to acknowledge some of the greatest performers to ever live, diverse audiences are paying to see black stories on film.

As a matter of fact, black filmmakers demonstrate their ferocity when they cinematically respond to unequal and unbalanced treatment. During the 1910s, D. W. Griffith created his blockbuster film depicting mandingo, Uncle Tom, the enraged mulatto, and black male rapist archetypes as sociopolitical threats to America's social, political, and economic hierarchy. In his racist portrayal of white Southern culture, Griffith used white actors as blackface performers. By glorifying the Ku Klux Klan and disparaging the Reconstruction era, Griffith used the power of movies to incite whites' fear of miscegenation, black sexuality, and black autonomy. But when Oscar Micheaux became the first major black filmmaker in the 1920s, he proved that African American males could appropriate their own image and gain economic agency despite the exploitation of white filmmakers such as D. W. Griffith. Traditionally, African Americans have transformed negative depictions to reconstruct black identity for black audiences. As an answer to *The Birth of a Nation*'s blackface, Micheaux consistently features strong black male characters of diverse skin tones and temperaments who are middle-class, professional, and educated. Thus Micheaux deconstructs Griffith's perverted notions of blackness with his own authenticity; therefore *Within Our Gates*, among his other films, mocks blackface performers as ridiculous and distinct from actual black culture. Moreover, Micheaux engaged his black actors in whiteface performance by placing powder on light-skinned African American actors when they played white characters. As a result, the lack of racial authenticity in *The Birth of Nation* is preeminent for most viewers. In fact, Micheaux's *Body and Soul* features Paul Robeson who was one of the greatest black actors and social activists in Hollywood's history. When Robeson starred in dual roles as the black rapist preacher and loving black inventor, he demonstrated the ability to manipulate black stereotypes, while exhibiting incredible acting range. Even now, audiences are unable to think of a famous singer, stage and film actor who was also a former two-time All-American football player, Rutgers class valedictorian, licensed attorney, published writer, as well as a globally known social and political activist. Unfortunately, his association with Communists and love for the Russian people have overshadowed his amazing performances as the stage lead in *Othello* and in films such as *The Emperor Jones* in the 1930s. Even Margaret Mitchell, the author of *Gone with the Wind*, recognized Robeson's influence; he wrote the preface to her book three years after the original publication date in 1936. Of course, Robeson's endorsement of *Gone with the Wind* does not negate the classic film's dehumanized depictions of black males as submissive and willing participants in the black subjugation caused by the vestiges of slavery and Southern white hierarchy. With that said, the popular portrayal of blacks as slaves and servants continues into the 1940s.

With the popularity of Bill "Bojangles" Robinson and Lincoln "Stepin Fetchit" Perry, American audiences preferred black actors best when playing slaves and servants in musicals and comedies. In the 1940s, Bojangles and Stepin Fetchit advanced their careers by representing black archetypes of Uncle Toms and coons, which are as offensive as the Sambo stereotype. Both actors grew up poor, but rose to national prominence as highly paid superstars because audiences, both black and white, were captivated by their performances. Unfortunately, the songs and dances of Bojangles on stage and film and Stepin Fetchit's performances in over 50 films are overshadowed by their history of minstrelsy, legal troubles, and lack of social and political activism. By the 1950s, America was ready for African American actors who could perform on stage but exhibited black social consciousness on stage, film, and in social and political realms. As Canada Lee's mentor, Paul Robeson became Lee's close friend. Although America was ready to view black actors with incredible range and artistic mastery, Lee's and Robeson's affiliation with Communists caused devastation to their acting careers. Under the circumstances of racial oppression, social injustice, and economic inequality, neither Lee nor Robeson were able to subdue their discontent. Their sociopolitical crusade for fairness in terms of labor practices in Hollywood, on the stage, and in American society led to blacklisting from HUAC and surveillance from the FBI. But Lee remains one of the greatest stage performers and producers; his former status as a prize-winning boxer subverted efforts to make him submit to the blacklist by naming Robeson. If not for Lee and Robeson, there would have been no cinematic greats, such as Sidney Poitier and Harry Belafonte. During the 1960s, Poitier's and Belafonte's humanitarian causes and civil rights efforts transformed the nation and Hollywood. Poitier and Belafonte modeled their artistic views after Robeson and Lee with regard to playing positive black characters. Robeson, Lee, Poitier, and Belafonte refused to star in films that degraded black males or the black community. At one point, Poitier became the highest-grossing actor, black or white, in Hollywood, and Belafonte became the top black male singer—even though they both were outspoken social activists. Early in Poitier's career, when he refused to denounce Robeson, he demonstrated his self-autonomy, determination to shape his own image, and unwavering loyalty to the black community. In addition, for King's March on Washington, Belafonte along with Poitier spearheaded their star power and influence to unite black and white stars in America's fight for social justice.

After the progress made by the social and political activism of the 1960s, African Americans were dismayed by the lack of black-themed films. Thus the 1970s welcomed a new wave of black cinema known as blaxploitation. Unlike films starring Poitier in the 1950s and 1960s, black sexuality was a major highlight of the blaxploitation era. Furthermore, archetypes of the black mandingo arose again in a film called *Mandingo*. With that said, almost every negative archetype of the black male was featured during this era: Calvin Lockhart as the scandalous preacher in *Cotton Comes to Harlem*, Ron O'Neal as the drug pusher in *Super Fly*, Max Julien as the glorified pimp in *The Mack*, and Fred Williamson as a vengeful gangster in *Black Caesar*. Even though these charismatic black males exploited the streets, both black and white women, for their own monetary gain, audiences loved these rebellious movies. These black cinematic heroes confronted authority, such as racist politicians, police officers, and white gangsters, with verbal disregard, physical aggression, or armed resistance. Blaxploitation stars were unafraid of white retribution in their films or from American society in their private lives; their characters paid reverence only to those who respected their preeminence in the streets and in the black community. Although black filmmakers, such as Melvin Van Peebles, Ossie Davis, Gordon Parks, Sr., Gordon Parks Jr., Michael Schultz, and Sidney Poitier, economically helped to save various white studios with their black-themed films, African Americans become nearly invisible in the 1980s. With the exception of Bill Cosby, Richard Pryor, and Eddie Murphy, black images were rarely seen. Both Cosby and Pryor transcended their appearances in 1970s blaxploitation films into prominence in the 1980s. However, Cosby is best known for his sit-com *The Cosby Show* rather than his work in film. Meanwhile, Pryor's and Murphy's comedic talents resulted in Pryor's production deal with Columbia and Murphy's production deal with Paramount. Although their stage performances issued social critiques against black and white social norms, their most popular movies presented sanitized black leads, interracial buddy humor, and elements of buffoonery. Nevertheless, once Pryor and Murphy became filmmakers, they genuinely sought black actors to star in their black-themed films. In essence, they engaged in the commodification of black culture and understood the necessity for black actors, writers, directors, and producers to market, profit, and capitalize from their own cinematic representations.

With the exception of Pryor and Murphy, after the near erasure of black images in the 1980s, America was ready for a new era of black films. During the 1990s, directors such as Spike Lee, Richard Townsend, and Keenen Ivory Wayans were trailblazers for blacks seeking mainstream recognition with their independent films. Though Townsend's *Hollywood Shuffle* and Wayans's *I'm Gonna Git You Sucka* were comical, they challenged Hollywood establishment and blaxploitation-era characterizations with their satirical commentary on popular black stereotypes. Nevertheless, the 1990s was the era of the black gangsta film. This era transformed rap stars, such as Ice Cube, Ice-T, DMX, Nas, and 2Pac, into movie stars.

With relatable performances, they played characters who were emotionally, mentally, and economically invested in street life. Still, the prevailing message of black gangsta films, such as *Boyz N the Hood*, *New Jack City*, *Belly*, and *Juice*, is the hope to rise from humble beginnings and elevate oneself beyond the streets. Consequently, audiences both black and white, excused the criminality exhibited by black gangstas. Since survival was the motive for destructive behavior, audiences were drawn to malignant characters and toward benign characters who thrived despite their disparate circumstances. As in the 1970s, some critics were troubled by these 1990s movies that paid homage to ghetto life. With that said, director John Singleton's *Boyz N the Hood* and director Mario Van Peebles's *New Jack City* remain two of the most significant films of this era. Due to the cinematic realism of *Boyz N the Hood* and the negative consequences of capitalism in *New Jack City*, the black criminal thug manifested complexity and disillusionment not seen since the murderous Bigger Thomas in Richard Wright's *Native Son* and the movie sharing the same name.

As movie producers, Spike Lee, Tyler Perry, and Will Smith reject the nihilistic portrayals of blacks with their critically acclaimed and profitable films in the 2000s. Since the 1980s, with his groundbreaking film *She's Gotta Have It*, Lee has continued to subvert Hollywood's negative notions of blackness. Meanwhile, Perry's films willingly exhibit buffoonery for the purposes of promoting black middle-class values and appealing to black female audiences. Although Smith is not a director, Smith's Overbrook Entertainment produces films starring Smith. Thus Lee, Perry, and Smith are black filmmakers who have made millions from their carefully constructed black images. When Lee, Perry, or Smith are involved in a film, audiences are comfortable experiencing black heritage and black masculinity on film. Even though Perry became popular with his cross-dressing performance of Madea, black heteronormative love is the highlight of his films. With regard to Lee, his commitment to social commentary is evident by the classics *Do the Right Thing*, *Get on the Bus*, and *Inside Man* and in his documentaries about the Alabama church bombing in *4 Little Girls* and Hurricane Katrina in *When the Levees Broke*. Even Smith exhibited his social consciousness with his Academy Award–nominated performance in *Ali*. Since Overbrook Entertainment produced this film, this demonstrates his desire to shape black male images in an authoritative and positive manner. During the 2010s, the prominent theme became historical fiction, featuring the humanity of black servants and slaves in oppressive eras. Lee Daniels's *The Butler* offered intergenerational conflict and black divisions within the fight for civil rights; Quentin Tarantino's *Django Unchained* presented a black avenging cowboy prior to the Civil War; Steven Spielberg's *Lincoln* credits the Congress as the sole emancipators of slavery; and *12 Years a Slave* strikes a clear social and legal distinction between status as a freedman or slave, when a talented black musician is fraudulently sold into bondage. In their respective years, both *Lincoln* and *12 Years a Slave* won many Academy nominations and several Academy awards, such as the Best Motion Picture Award for producer Steve McQueen. However, whereas a few of the whites associated with the film *Django Unchained* were nominated, the lead actor Jamie Foxx and supporting actor Samuel L. Jackson were both snubbed by the Academy.

Based on Hollywood's history, the Oscars will continue to withhold nominations or awards for black male performances that are both powerful and positive, such as Idris Elba as the lead in *Mandela*, Jamie Foxx as Django in *Django Unchained*, and Chiwetel Ejiofor as Solomon Northup in *12 Years a Slave*. For some reason, Denzel Washington wins an Academy Award for his criminal performance in *Training Day*, yet he does not win for his lead performance in *Malcolm X*. Even though Americans claim to love Muhammad Ali, Mandela, Malcolm X, and Martin Luther King Jr., Hollywood has a tendency to reject strong male performances by actors who charismatically individualize these roles. Furthermore, black male pioneers or characters who rebel from white social norms, question white hegemony, and subvert notions of black inferiority remain a threat to white social hierarchy in America and in Hollywood. As a result, in the future black filmmakers will maintain complex representations, explore social injustice, and condemn structural racism in the social, political, and entertainment realms. Thus African American actors will continue responding to the lack of critical recognition with mainstream roles as God, superheroes, or the president in blockbuster films.

Audiences respect the acting range of an African American actor, such as Morgan Freeman who can win Oscar nominations as both a chauffeur in *Driving Miss Daisy* and Nelson Mandela in *Invictus* but still enrapture audiences by playing the president in *Deep Impact* and portraying God in *Bruce Almighty*. Meanwhile, Jamie Foxx can play a slave in *Django Unchained*, the president in *Whitehouse Down*, and a superhero named Electro in *The Amazing Spider-Man 2*. Then there is Samuel L. Jackson who can act as an Uncle Tom slave in *Django*; transform into Marvel Comics superhero Nick Fury in the *Iron Man* series, *Thor* series, *The Avengers* series, and *Captain America* series; and play the president in *Big Game*. Lastly, Will Smith, who played a caddy in the *Legend of Bagger Vance*, transcends the negatively criticized character by alternating between action hero in *Bad Boys*, *Bad Boys II*, *Men in Black*, its sequels *Men in*

Black II and *III*, and superhero in *Hancock*. Black filmmakers will continue to respond to snubs by the Academy with black images that reflect their own authentic and intimate knowledge of the black experience. Furthermore, rejections by mainstream society only spark an internal fire among African American performers and filmmakers to reappropriate their own images and exhibit control and agency when the industry refuses to fully acknowledge their contributions. Traditionally, blacks have always surpassed the social, political, and economic constraints of the industry to create classic and popular pictures for mass entertainment.

Lastly, whether black males are playing slaves, butlers, president, God, or superheroes, globally they are altering the perception of black males with their artistic skill, ingenuity, and charismatic screen performances. In actuality, when African Americans play superheroes, American audiences reimagine a world without racial and cultural limitations. Furthermore, when black males act as God, superheroes, and the president, this symbolizes the black male's longing to navigate between infinite spaces without physical boundaries, rigid restrictions, and unlawful surveillance. At this time, America's postracial desires for equality are only aspirational. But in the Age of Obama, the profitability of films depicting African Americans as rebellious and subversive characters demonstrates Americans' willingness to accept diverse black males as lead performers and as black filmmakers. When the Academy still refuses to regularly nominate black actors, this demonstrates actualized fear of black prowess and autonomy. But when audiences patronize mainstream movies with black males acting as God, superheroes, or the president, the evidence of an inclusive pluralistic society is becoming realized. Even if the multifarious abilities of black males are not consistently acknowledged by critics or award shows, American audiences will continue to patronize films that feature black male stars who demonstrate self-possession, autonomy, and artistic brilliance.

Notes

Chapter 1

1. Michael Rogin, "Making America Home: Racial Masquerade and Ethnic Assimilation in the Transition to Talking Pictures," *The Journal of American History* 79, no. 3 (December 1992): 1052.

2. Ralph Ellison, *Shadow and Act* (New York: Vintage, 1995), 47.

3. Ibid., 48.

4. Ibid.

5. Salamishah Tillet, *Sites of Slavery Citizenship and Racial Democracy in the Post–Civil Rights Imagination* (Durham, NC: Duke University Press), 55.

6. Rogin, "Making America Home," 1051-2.

7. Ibid.

8. Ibid.

9. Ibid.

10. Ellison, *Shadow and Act*, 47.

11. Ibid., 47.

12. Ibid., 48.

13. Ibid.

14. Ibid.

15. Eric Lott, *Love and Theft: Blackface Minstrelsy and the American Working Class* (New York: Oxford University Press, 2013), 115.

16. Ibid., 116.

17. Ibid., 117.

18. Ibid.

19. Ibid.

20. Ibid.

21. Ibid.

22. Ibid., 119. See figure 4, "Juba (William Henry Lane)," courtesy of the Harvard Theatre Collection performing as "Juba," at Vauxhall Gardens.

23. Lott, *Love and Theft*, 118.

24. Ibid.

25. Ibid.

26. Ibid., 120.

27. Ibid.

28. Ibid.

29. Michele Faith Wallace, "The Good Lynching and *The Birth of a Nation*: Discourses and Aesthetics of Jim Crow," *Cinema Journal* 43, no. 1 (Autumn 2003): 96.

30. Ibid., 97.

31. Ibid.

32. Ibid., 98.

33. Ibid.

34. James Monaco, *How to Read a Film: Movies, Media, and Beyond* (New York: Oxford University Press, 2009), 262.

35. Ibid.

36. Ibid., 299–300.

37. Ibid., 300.

38. Donald Bogle, *Toms, Coons, Mulattoes, Mammies, and Bucks: An Interpretive History of Blacks in American Films*, 4th ed. (New York: Bloomsbury, 2001), 10.

39. Ibid.

40. Ibid.

41. Ibid.

42. Ibid.

43. Wallace, "The Good Lynching and *The Birth of a Nation*," 86.

44. Ibid.

45. Bogle, *Toms, Coons, Mulattoes, Mammies, and Bucks*, 12.

46. Wallace, "The Good Lynching and *The Birth of a Nation*," 93.

47. Bogle, *Toms, Coons, Mulattoes, Mammies, and Bucks*, 12.

48. Wallace, "The Good Lynching and *The Birth of a Nation*," 89.

49. Ibid., 91.

50. Ibid., 90.

51. Bogle, *Toms, Coons, Mulattoes, Mammies, and Bucks*, 12.

52. Ibid.

53. Wallace, "The Good Lynching and *The Birth of a Nation*," 97.

54. Ibid., 98.

55. Bogle, *Toms, Coons, Mulattoes, Mammies, and Bucks*, 13.

56. Ibid.

57. Ibid.

58. Ibid.

59. Ibid., 13–14.

60. Ibid., 14.

61. Ibid.

62. Ibid., 13.

63. Ibid., 15.

64. Ibid., 17.

65. Lott, *Love and Theft*, 6.

66. Ibid., 6.

67. Lott, *Love and Theft*, 6–7.

68. Wallace, "The Good Lynching and *The Birth of a Nation*," 86.

69. Ibid., 101.

Chapter 2

1. Pearl Browser, Jane Gaines, and Charles Musser, eds., *Oscar Micheaux and His Circle: African-American Filmmaking and Race Cinema of the Silent Era* (Bloomington: Indiana University Press, 2001), 58–59.

2. Ibid., 59.

3. Ibid.

4. Jane M. Gaines, *Fire and Desire: Mixed-Race Movies in the Silent Era* (Chicago: University of Chicago Press, 2001), 132.

5. Ibid.

6. Ibid., 45.

7. Nsenga Burton, "Celebrating 100 Years of Black Cinema," *The Root*, February 3, 2010, accessed June 20, 2014, http://www.theroot.com/articles/ culture/2010/02/100_years_of_black_cinema_oscar_micheaux_melvin_van_ peebles_spike_lee_kasi_lemmons.html. This article provides a century's worth of information on black directors who transformed black cinema. *The Root* was founded in 2008 by the award-winning scholar Henry Louis Gates Jr. As of 2014, he continues to lead this diverse online magazine. *See also* Gaines, *Fire and Desire*, 95, for more information on William Foster's career. Gaines sets the date of *The Railroad Porter* as 1913. Various other sources, including *The Root*, date the release of the film as 1912.

8. Burton, "Celebrating a 100 Years of Black Cinema."

9. J. Ronald Green, "Introduction," *Straight Lick: The Cinema of Oscar Micheaux* (Bloomington: Indiana University Press, 2000), xi.

10. Ibid.

11. Ibid.

12. Ibid.

13. Ibid., xii.

14. Ibid., xv.

15. Ibid.

16. J. Ronald Green, *With a Crooked Stick : The Films of Oscar Micheaux* (Bloomington: Indiana University Press, 2004), 39.

17. Ibid., 39–40.

18. Ibid., 40.

19. Ibid.

20. Ibid., 41.
21. Ibid.
22. Ibid.
23. Ibid.
24. Ibid.
25. Ibid., 53.
26. Ibid.
27. Ibid., 54.
28. Ibid.
29. Ibid.
30. Ibid., 55.
31. Ibid.
32. Ibid., 55–56.
33. Ibid., 56.
34. Ibid.
35. Ibid., 59.
36. Ibid., 66.
37. Ibid.
38. Ibid., 67.
39. Ibid.
40. Ibid., 70.
41. Ibid.
42. Ibid., 75.
43. Ibid.
44. Ibid., 73.
45. Ibid., 75.
46. Gaines, *Fire and Desire*, 251.
47. Green, *Straight Lick*, 5.
48. Ibid.
49. Gaines, *Fire and Desire*, 233.
50. Ibid., 234.
51. Ibid.
52. Ibid.
53. Ibid., 234–35.
54. Ibid., 235.
55. Ibid., 236. The banned scenes consist of (1) reducing the chase scene by the treacherous Gus as he pursues a white girl; (2) the footage that shows the castration scene with Gus; and (3) reducing the intensity of the forced marriage between Sylas Lynch, the mulatto who forces Elsie Stoneman into marrying him.
56. Gaines, *Fire and Desire*, 241.
57. Ibid.
58. Ibid., 242.
59. Ibid., 126.
60. Ibid., 245.

61. Browser, Gaines, and Musser, *Oscar Micheaux and His Circle*, 34.

62. Ibid.

63. Ibid., 36.

64. Ibid., 37.

65. Ibid.

66. Ibid.

67. Ibid., 38.

68. Ibid., 40–41.

69. Ibid., 41. See also Gaines, *Fire and Desire*, 98–99. Gaines discusses how the rise of Noble Johnson (George P. Johnson's brother), president of the Lincoln Motion Picture Company, rose and fell as a black race star. In 1916, the company produced *The Realization of a Negro's Ambition* starring Noble Johnson. Johnson was featured in 34 movies between 1915 and 1918. Due to Noble Johnson's racially ambiguous features and "his own ingenious makeup," he was able to play various ethnic parts. As a successful actor for Universal Pictures, he played everyone from "Mexicans to Native Americans." In a few instances, he played an African American in Universal films: *The Lion's Ward* and Topsy and Uncle Tom in *Topsy and Eva* (1927).

70. Browser, Gaines, and Musser, *Oscar Micheaux and His Circle*, 42.

71. Ibid., 43.

72. Ibid., 43–44.

73. Ibid., 44–45.

74. Ibid., 46.

75. Ibid., 48.

76. Gaines, *Fire and Desire*, 133.

77. Ibid., 134.

78. Ibid.

79. Ibid., 135.

80. Ibid., 140.

81. Ibid., 100.

82. Ibid., 141.

83. Ibid., 144.

84. Richard Grupenhoff, *The Black Valentino: The Stage and Screen Career of Lorenzo Tucker* (Metuchen, NJ: Scarecrow, 1988), 71. See also Burt A. Folklart, "Lorenzo Tucker, 'Black Valentino,' Dies," *Los Angeles Times*, August 21, 1986, accessed July 28, 2014, http://articles.latimes.com/1986-08-21/news/mn-17620_1_oscar-micheaux. Lorenzo Tucker starred "as a prime love interest opposite several black beauties" in 11 of Micheaux's films including the *Wages of Sin, Daughter of the Congo, Harlem Big Show, Temptation*, and *Veiled Aristocrats*. Due to his handsome features, Micheaux promoted him as the "Black Valentino." As the years passed, Tucker discusses the racism in Hollywood. He earnestly believed that his "light skin worked as a reverse prejudice in finding film work." Much to Tucker' dismay, he stated that there was no reason why one prototype was used to represent the entire race.

85. Gaines, *Fire and Desire*, 102–3.

86. Browser, Gaines, and Musser, *Oscar Micheaux and His Circle*, 48.
87. Gaines, *Fire and Desire*, 120.

Chapter 3

1. Gregory D. Black, *Hollywood Censored: Morality Codes, Catholics, and the Movies* (New York: Cambridge University Press, 1994), 6.
2. Ibid., 8–9.
3. Ibid., 9.
4. Thomas Doherty, *Pre-Code Hollywood: Sex, Immorality, and Insurrection in American Cinema 1930–1934* (New York: Columbia University Press, 1999), 276.
5. Ibid., 246.
6. Ibid., 275.
7. Ibid., 286.
8. Ibid., 341.
9. Black, *Hollywood Censored*, 26.
10. Ibid., 31.
11. Ibid.
12. Ibid., 33.
13. Ibid., 34.
14. Ibid.
15. Ibid., 35.
16. Ibid., 35–36.
17. Ibid., 37.
18. Ibid., 38.
19. Ibid.
20. Ibid., 38–39.
21. Ibid., 1.
22. Ibid.
23. Ibid.
24. Ibid., 39.
25. Ibid., 40.
26. Ibid., 2.
27. Ibid.
28. Ibid.
29. Ibid.
30. Ibid.
31. Ibid., 299.
32. Doherty, *Pre-Code Hollywood*, 222.
33. Ibid., 226.
34. Ibid., 222.
35. Ibid.
36. Ibid., 223.

37. Ibid., 224.

38. Ibid., 246.

39. Ibid., 245–46.

40. Ibid., 246.

41. Ibid., 249.

42. Ibid., 250–51.

43. Ibid., 253.

44. Ibid.

45. Ibid., 254.

46. Ibid.

47. Ibid.

48. Ibid.

49. Ibid., 255.

50. Paul Robeson, *Here I Stand*, 1958 (Boston: Beacon Press, 1988), 30.

51. Ibid.

52. Ibid., 31.

53. Ibid., 18.

54. Ibid., 31.

55. Ibid., 18.

56. Ibid.

57. Ibid., 18–19.

58. Ibid.

59. Ibid., 25.

60. Ibid., 21.

61. Ibid., 23.

62. Doherty, *Pre-Code Hollywood*, 284.

63. Ibid.

64. Ibid.

65. Philip S. Foner, ed., *Paul Robeson Speaks* (New York: Citadel Press, 1978), 28.

66. Ibid.

67. Ibid., 77.

68. Ibid., 79.

69. Ibid.

70. Ibid.

71. Ibid., 80.

72. Ibid.

73. Ibid.

74. Ibid., 79.

75. Robeson, *Here I Stand*, 32.

76. Ibid.

77. Ibid., 33.

78. Ibid.

79. Ibid.

80. Ibid., 34.

81. Ibid., 35.

82. Ibid.

83. Doherty, *Pre-Code Hollywood*, 285.

84. Ibid.

85. Robeson, *Here I Stand*, 28.

86. Ibid.

87. Ibid.

88. Ibid., 32.

89. Doherty, *Pre-Code Hollywood*, 285.

90. Ibid.

91. Ibid., 286.

92. Ibid.

93. Ibid.

94. Ibid.

95. Ibid.

96. Ibid., 287.

97. Ibid.

98. Ibid.

99. Ibid., 288.

100. Ibid.

101. Ibid.

102. Foner, *Paul Robeson Speaks*, 128.

103. Ibid., 70.

104. Donald Bogle, *Bright Boulevards, Bold Dreams: The Story of Black Hollywood* (New York: Random House, 2005), 81.

105. Doherty, *Pre-Code Hollywood*, 289.

106. Ibid.

107. Foner, *Paul Robeson Speaks*, 126.

108. Ibid., 128.

109. Ibid., fn5, 518.

110. Ibid.

111. Molly Haskell, " 'Gone with the Wind' Still Raises Fuss after 70 Years," *CNN Opinion*, December 15, 2009, http://www.cnn.com/2009/OPINION/12/15/haskell.gone.with.the.wind/ (accessed July 18, 2014). In 2009, Yale University published Haskell's book entitled *Frankly, My Dear: "Gone with the Wind" Revisited*. While promoting the book, she says in her CNN special that she "was struck by how the film continues to raise tempers and inflame feelings."

112. Haskell, " 'Gone with the Wind.' "

113. James Monaco, *How to Read a Film: Movies, Media, and Beyond* (New York: Oxford University, 2009), 270.

114. Ibid., 270–71.

115. Ibid., 271.

116. Doherty, *Pre-Code Hollywood*, 341.

117. Bogle, *Bright Boulevards, Bold Dreams*, 178.

118. Leonard J. Leff, " 'Gone with the Wind' and Hollywood's Racial Politics," *The Atlantic Monthly* 99.12, 284, no. 6 (December 1999): 106–14, Accessed July 18, 2014, http://www.theatlantic.com/past/docs/issues/99dec/9912leff.htm (July 18, 2014).

119. Ibid.

120. Ibid., Part 2.

121. Bogle, *Bright Boulevards, Bold Dreams*, 180.

122. "Race and Hollywood Black Images on Film," Lenny Bluett on Clark Gable (TCM Featurette), TCM Turner Classic Movies, 2014, Turner Entertainment Networks, accessed July 18, 2014, http://www.tcm.com/mediaroom/video/135939/Lenny-Bluett-on-Clark-Gable-A-TCM-Featurette-.html.

123. Bogle, *Bright Boulevards, Bold Dreams*, 180.

124. Bluett, "Race and Hollywood Black Images on Film."

125. Bogle, *Bright Boulevards, Bold Dreams*, 181.

126. Leff, " 'Gone with the Wind,' " Part 2.

127. Ibid.

128. Ibid.

129. Marcus Greil and Werner Sollors, eds., *A New Literary History of America* (Cambridge, MA: Belknap Press of Harvard University Press, 2009), 788.

130. Bogle, *Bright Boulevards, Bold Dreams*, 181.

131. Leff, " 'Gone with the Wind,' " Part 2.

132. Bogle, *Bright Boulevards, Bold Dreams*, 181.

133. "*Gone with the Wind*: Full Cast and Crew," *IMDb.com*, Amazon Company (1990–2014), accessed July 18, 2014, http://www.imdb.com/title/tt0031381/fullcredits?ref_=tt_ov_st_sm.

134. Bogle, *Bright Boulevards, Bold Dreams*, 177.

135. Leff, " 'Gone with the Wind,' " Part 2.

136. Ibid.

137. Bogle, *Bright Boulevards, Bold Dreams*, 183.

138. Haskell, " 'Gone with the Wind.' "

139. Ibid.

140. Black, *Hollywood Censored*, 299.

141. Ibid., 40.

Chapter 4

1. Mel Watkins, *Stepin Fetchit: The Life and Times of Lincoln Perry* (New York: Vintage, 2006), 289.

2. Ibid.

3. "Lincoln Theodore (=Stepin Fetchit) Perry," *The Black Perspective in Music* 14, no. 3 (Autumn 1986): 326.

4. Jim Haskins and N. R. Mitgang, *Mr. Bojangles: The Biography of Bill Robinson* (New York: Morrow, 1988), 25.

5. Ibid., 65. This chapter is entitled "Bill Robinson on Trial." See also Haskins and Mitgang, *Mr. Bojangles*, 83. Robinson was acquitted of the crime, which he claimed he did not commit.

6. Haskins and Mitgang, *Mr. Bojangles*, 27–28.

7. Ibid., 17. See the list of celebrities and politicians who attended and spoke at Bill Robinson's funeral in the chapter entitled "Everything Is Copasetic."

8. Watkins, *Stepin Fetchit*, 284. Watkins spells the name "Sonny Craver" as "Sunny Craver." However, further research determined that the name of the actor/singer is spelled with a "u" instead of an "o." Also, Watkins spells the performer's last name as "Craver" four times on page 284. One time, he refers to Sunny using the last name "Graver." Therefore this buffers my previous assertion that Watkins misspelled Mr. Craver's first name as well.

9. Haskins and Mitgang, *Mr. Bojangles*, 9.

10. Ibid., 10.

11. Ibid., 11.

12. Ibid., 17. See also Haskins and Mitgang, *Mr. Bojangles*, 16, where it states that over a two-day period, "people of Harlem ... filed past the body." Bojangles was a household name for many of "the thirty-two thousand people." They remembered and "gossiped about his latest show, or gambling exploit, or award, or relationship with whites." Lastly, Robinson's impact was so widespread that he "counted presidents, governors, mayors, and the biggest names in the show business and sports worlds among his friends."

13. Haskins and Mitgang, *Mr. Bojangles*, 17.

14. Ibid., 25.

15. Ibid., 21.

16. Ibid., 25.

17. Ibid., 25–26.

18. Ibid., 26.

19. Ibid., 26–27.

20. Ibid., 28.

21. Ibid., 29.

22. Ibid.

23. Ibid., 31.

24. Ibid.

25. Ibid., 33.

26. Ibid., 41.

27. Ibid., 42.

28. Ibid., 45.

29. Donald Bogle, *Toms, Coons, Mulattoes, Mammies, and Bucks: An Interpretive History of Blacks in American Films*, 4th ed. (New York: Bloomsbury, 2001), 4.

30. Ibid.

31. Ibid., 35.

32. Ibid.

33. Ibid., 37.
34. Ibid.
35. Ibid.
36. Ibid., 47.
37. Ibid.
38. Ibid.
39. Ibid., 47–48.
40. Ibid., 48.
41. Ibid.
42. Ibid., 50.
43. Ibid.
44. Ibid., 52.
45. Ibid., 131.
46. Ibid.
47. Ibid., 132.
48. Ibid., 135.
49. Ibid.
50. Ibid., 136.
51. Ibid.
52. "Stepin Fetchit (1902–1985)," Filmography, *IMDb.com*, 2014, accessed August 3, 2014, http://www.imdb.com/name/nm0275297/.
53. Watkins, *Stepin Fetchit*, 284.
54. Ibid., 276.
55. Ibid.
56. Ibid., 277.
57. Ibid., 278.
58. Ibid.
59. Ibid., 9.
60. Ibid., 10.
61. Ibid., 11.
62. Ibid., 17.
63. Ibid., 28.
64. Ibid., 28–29.
65. Ibid., 281.
66. Ibid., 282.
67. Ibid.
68. Ibid., 286–87.
69. Ibid., 282.
70. Ibid., 283–84.
71. Ibid., 284.
72. Ibid., 285.
73. Ibid., 285–86.
74. Ibid., 288.
75. Ibid., 290.

76. Ibid.

77. Ibid.

78. Ibid.

79. Charlene Regester, "Stepin Fetchit: The Man, the Image, and the African American Press," *Film History* 6, no. 4 (Winter 1994): 502.

80. Ibid.

81. Ibid.

82. Ibid., 504.

83. Ibid., 505.

84. Ibid., 506.

85. Ibid.

86. Ibid., 507.

87. Ibid.

88. Ibid.

89. Ibid., 508.

90. Ibid., 509.

91. Ibid., 509–10.

92. Ibid., 511.

93. Ibid.

94. "Bill 'Bojangles' Robinson Biography: Film Actor, Dancer (1878–1949)," *Biography.com*, A&E Television, 2014, accessed August 4, 2014, http://www.biography.com/people/bill-bojangles-robinson-9460594#dancing-and-acting-career.

95. Ibid.

96. Watkins, *Stepin Fetchit*, 195.

97. Regester, "Stepin Fetchit," 513.

98. Watkins, *Stepin Fetchit*, 197.

99. Ibid., 198.

100. Ibid., 199.

101. Ibid.

Chapter 5

1. Mona Z. Smith, *Becoming Something: The Story of Canada Lee* (New York: Faber & Faber, 2004), 70.

2. Ibid., 270–71 (see the caption of Canada Lee and Sidney Poitier in minister's garment).

3. Smith, *Becoming Something*, 343.

4. Ibid., 344.

5. Ibid., 348.

6. Ibid., 350.

7. Ibid., 271.

8. Ibid.

9. Ibid., 283.

10. Ibid., 284.

11. Ibid., 282–83.

12. Ibid., 285.

13. Ibid., 290.

14. Ibid.

15. Ibid.

16. Ibid., 291.

17. Ibid., 40.

18. Bruce Weber, "Murrey Marder, Early McCarthy Skeptic, Dies at 93," *New York Times*, March 19, 2013, accessed August 6, 2014, http://www.nytimes.com/2013/03/20/us/murrey-marder-reporter-who-took-on-joe-mccarthy-dies-at-93.html?_r=1&.

19. Thomas C. Reeves, "McCarthyism: Interpretations since Hofstadter," *The Wisconsin Magazine of History* 60, no. 1 (Autumn 1976): 42.

20. Bernard Weinraub, "Ideas and Trends; The Blacklist Era Won't Fade to Black," *New York Times*, October 5, 1997, accessed August 5, 2014, http://www.nytimes.com/1997/10/05/weekinreview/ideas-trends-the-blacklist-era-won-t-fade-to-black.html.

21. Ibid.

22. Ibid.

23. Gary Baum and Daniel Miller, "The Most Sinful Period in Hollywood History," *Hollywood Reporter*, November 17, 2012, accessed August 5, 2014, http://www.hollywoodreporter.com/news/sinful-period-hollywood-history-391707. See also Gary Baum and Daniel Miller, "The Hollywood Reporter, after 65 Years, Addresses Role in Blacklist," *Hollywood Reporter*, November 19, 2012, accessed August 5, 2014, http://www.hollywoodreporter.com/news/blacklist-thr-addresses-role-65-391931?page=1.

24. Baum and Miller, "The Most Sinful Period in Hollywood History."

25. Ibid.

26. Ibid.

27. Ibid.

28. Ibid.

29. Ibid.

30. Ibid.

31. Ibid.

32. Ibid.

33. Ibid.

34. Ibid.

35. Ibid.

36. Ibid.

37. Ibid.

38. Weber, "Murrey Marder."

39. Ibid.

40. Ronald Kessler, "Hoover's Secret Files," *The Daily Beast*, August 2, 2011, accessed August 9, 2014, http://www.thedailybeast.com/articles/2011/08/

02/fbi-director-hoover-s-dirty-files-excerpt-from-ronald-kessler-s-the-secrets-of
-the-fbi.html. This is an exclusive excerpt from the book *The Secrets of the FBI*
authored by Kessler. In the book, Kessler mentions how Hoover had files on
Martin Luther King Jr., John F. Kennedy, and Marilyn Monroe. Not since
Hoover has another FBI director yielded so much influence and power over
the bureau, Hollywood, or the nation.

41. Smith, *Becoming Something*, 139.

42. Ibid., 120.

43. Ibid., 4.

44. Ibid., 5.

45. Ibid.

46. Ibid., 6.

47. Ibid., 7.

48. Ibid., 13.

49. Ibid., 20–21.

50. Ibid., 22.

51. Ibid., 32.

52. Ibid., 40.

53. Ibid., 367.

54. *Lifeboat*, TCM: Turner Classic Movies, *TCM.com*, 2014, accessed
August 9, 2014, http://www.tcm.com/tcmdb/title/81373/Lifeboat/notes.html.

55. Smith, *Becoming Something*, 165.

56. Ibid., 166.

57. Ibid.

58. Ibid., 167–68.

59. Ibid., 147.

60. Ibid.

61. Ibid., 148.

62. Ibid., 149.

63. Ibid., 149–50.

64. Jonathan J. Cavallero, "Hitchcock and Race: Is the Wrong Man a White
Man?," *Journal of Film and Video* 62, no. 4 (Winter 2010): 10.

65. Ibid.

66. Ibid.

67. Ibid.

68. John Nickels, "Disabling African American Men: Liberalism and Race
Message Films," *Cinema Journal* 44, no. 1 (Fall 2004): 26.

69. Ibid.

70. Ibid., 26–27.

71. Ibid., 30.

72. Ibid.

73. Ibid.

74. Ibid.

75. Karen M. Bowdre, "Passing Films and the Illusion of Racial Equality," *Black Camera* 5, no. 2 (Spring 2014): 22.
76. Ibid.
77. Ibid.
78. Ibid.
79. Ibid., 30.
80. Ibid., 32.
81. Ibid., 32–33.
82. Ibid., 33.
83. Ibid.
84. Ibid.
85. Ibid., 31.
86. Ibid., 33.
87. Ibid.
88. Smith, *Becoming Something*, 367.
89. Ibid., 297.
90. Ibid., 302.
91. Ibid., 304.
92. Ibid.
93. Ibid., 367.
94. Ibid., 366.
95. Ibid., 367.
96. Ibid., 368.
97. Ibid., 348.
98. Ibid., 351.
99. Ibid., 354.
100. Ibid., 353.
101. Ibid.
102. Ibid., 357.
103. Ibid., 295.
104. Ibid., 295–96.

Chapter 6

1. Harry Belafonte and Michael Shnayerson, *My Song* (New York: Knopf, 2011), 208.
2. Ibid., 5.
3. Ibid., 208.
4. Ibid.
5. Ibid., 242.
6. Ibid., 5.
7. Ibid., 6.
8. Ibid., 6–8.

9. Ibid., 8.

10. Ibid., 9.

11. Ibid., 264.

12. Ibid.

13. Ibid., 265.

14. Ibid., 266.

15. Ibid. See also "A Raisin in the Sun," *IMDb.com*, 2014, http://www.imdb.com/title/tt0055353/.

16. Belafonte and Shnayerson, *My Song*, 267.

17. Ibid., 233.

18. Ibid., 261.

19. Henry Louis Gates Jr., "Foreword," in *Civil Rights in America: The Road to Equality and the Dream Today*, ed. Radhika Jones and Stephen Koepp (New York: Time, 2014), 5.

20. Ibid., 6.

21. Ibid.

22. Ibid.

23. Ibid.

24. Ibid.

25. Jon Meacham, "The Man and the March That Changed America," in *Civil Rights in America: The Road to Equality and the Dream Today*, ed. Radhika Jones and Stephen Koepp (New York: Time, 2014), 27.

26. Ibid., 30.

27. Ibid.

28. Ibid., 33.

29. Katie Pickert, "We Were There," in *Civil Rights in America: The Road to Equality and the Dream Today*, ed. Radhika Jones and Stephen Koepp (New York: Time, 2014), 38.

30. Ibid., 42.

31. Ibid., 44–45.

32. Ibid., 47.

33. Ibid.

34. Ibid., 60.

35. Ibid.

36. Richard Norton Smith, "The Pulpit," in *Civil Rights in America: The Road to Equality and the Dream Today*, ed. Radhika Jones and Stephen Koepp (New York: Time, 2014), 73.

37. "The Dignity of Sidney Poitier," interview with *CBS News*, May 12, 2013, accessed August 23, 2014, http://www.cbsnews.com/news/the-dignity-of-sidney-poitier/.

38. Ibid.

39. Ibid.

40. "Sidney Poitier: Full Biography," *New York Times*, 2010, accessed August 18, 2014, http://www.nytimes.com/movies/person/531681/Sidney -Poitier/biography.

41. Ibid.

42. Ibid.

43. Ibid.

44. Ibid.

45. Ibid.

46. Sidney Poitier, *The Measure of a Man: A Spiritual Autobiography* (New York: HarperCollins, 2000), 88.

47. Ibid., 61.

48. Ibid., 62.

49. Ibid., 61.

50. Ibid., 86.

51. Ibid., 87.

52. Ibid., 98.

53. Ibid., 88.

54. Ibid.

55. Ibid., 89.

56. Ibid.

57. Ibid., 91.

58. Ibid., 94.

59. Ibid., 94–95.

60. Ibid., 95.

61. Ibid., 96.

62. Ibid., 76.

63. Ibid., 100.

64. Ibid., 100–101.

65. Ibid., 102.

66. "The Dignity of Sidney Poitier."

67. Poitier, *The Measure of a Man*, 102.

68. Ibid.

69. Ibid.

70. Ibid., 103.

71. Ibid., 104–5.

72. Ibid., 105.

73. Ibid.

74. Ibid.

75. "Sidney Poitier: Full Biography."

76. "*Porgy and Bess* (1959): Full Cast & Crew," *IMDb.com*, 1999–2014, accessed August 18, 2014, http://www.imdb.com/title/tt0053182/fullcredits?ref _=tt_ov_st_sm.

77. Bosley Crowther, "*Lilies of the Field* (1963)," movie review, *New York Times*, 2010, accessed August 18, 2014, http://www.nytimes.com/movies/movie/29373/Lilies-of-the-Field/overview.

78. "The Dignity of Sidney Poitier."

79. John Nickels, "Disabling African American Men: Liberalism and Race Message Films," *Cinema Journal* 44, no. 1 (Fall 2004): 28.

80. Ibid.

81. Ibid., 29.

82. Ibid.

83. Ibid.

84. Ibid., 33.

85. Ibid.

86. "*In the Heat of the Night* (1967)," *New York Times*, Movies, 2014, accessed August 23, 2014, http://www.nytimes.com/movies/movie/24638/In-the-Heat-of-the-Night/overview.

87. "*In the Heat of the Night* (1967)," *New York Times*, Awards, 2014, accessed August 23, 2014, http://www.nytimes.com/movies/movie/24638/In-the-Heat-of-the-Night/awards.

88. "In the Heat of the Night (1967)," *New York Times*, Movies.

89. Ibid.

90. Ibid.

91. "Sidney Poitier: Full Biography."

92. "Sidney Poitier," The Kennedy Center, Kennedy-center.org, accessed on August 24, 2014, http://www.kennedy-center.org/explorer/artists/?entity_id=3785.

93. Billy Goodykoontz, "Oscar Win Proved Sidney Poitier Was Second to None," *USA Today*, February 25, 2014, accessed August 23, 2014, http://www.usatoday.com/story/life/movies/2014/02/25/black-history-month-poitier-oscar/5817735/.

94. Ibid.

95. Ibid.

96. "The Dignity of Sidney Poitier."

97. Ibid.

98. Ibid.

99. Ibid.

100. Ibid.

101. Belafonte and Shnayerson, *My Song*, 128. According to Belafonte, *Carmen Jones* is "the first black film to make serious money, not just in the United States but in Europe, where it played nearly a year in London and Berlin."

102. Belafonte and Shnayerson, *My Song*, 351.

103. Ibid., 352.

Chapter 7

1. James Monaco, *How to Read a Film: Movies Media and Beyond* (New York: Oxford University Press, 2009), 376.

2. Ibid.

3. Ibid., 300.

4. Ibid., 298.

5. Ibid.

6. Mikel J. Koven, *Blaxploitation Films* (Harpenden, UK: Kamara, 2010), 15–16.

7. Ibid., 16.

8. Ibid., 15.

9. Monaco, *How to Read a Film*, 376.

10. Ibid.

11. Roger Ebert, "Baadasssss!," movie review, *Rogerebert.com*, June 11, 2004, accessed August 31, 2014, http://www.rogerebert.com/reviews/baadasssss-2004.

12. Ibid.

13. Donald Bogle, *Toms, Coons, Mulattoes, Mammies, and Bucks: An Interpretive History of Blacks in American Films* (New York: Bloomsbury, 2013), 235.

14. Josiah Howard, *Blaxploitation Cinema: The Essential Reference Guide* (Godalming, UK: FAB Press, 2008), 10.

15. Ibid., 10.

16. Bogle, *Toms, Coons, Mulattoes, Mammies, and Bucks*, 235.

17. Ebert, "Baadasssss!"

18. Howard, *Blaxploitation Cinema*, 10.

19. Ebert, "Baadasssss!"

20. Ibid.

21. Ibid.

22. Ibid.

23. Ibid.

24. Ibid.

25. Ibid.

26. Ibid.

27. Monaco, *How to Read a Film*, 376.

28. Ebert, "Baadasssss!"

29. Bogle, *Toms, Coons, Mulattoes, Mammies, and Bucks*, 238.

30. Monaco, *How to Read a Film*, 376.

31. Ibid., 408.

32. Ebert, "Baadasssss!"

33. Vincent Canby, "Ossie Davis' 'Cotton Comes to Harlem,' " movie review of *Cotton Comes to Harlem* (1970), *New York Times*, June 11, 1970, accessed August 31, 2014, http://www.nytimes.com/movie/review?res=9C0CEFD61 439E63BBC4952DFB066838B669EE.

34. Ibid.

35. Ibid.

36. Howard, *Blaxploitation Cinema*, 123.

37. Monaco, *How to Read a Film*, 376.

38. Bogle, *Toms, Coons, Mulattoes, Mammies, and Bucks*, 226.

39. Ibid.

40. Monaco, *How to Read a Film*, 376–77.

41. Ibid., 377.

42. Ibid.

43. Bogle, *Toms, Coons, Mulattoes, Mammies, and Bucks*, 17.

44. Ibid., 238.

45. Ibid., 239.

46. Howard, *Blaxploitation Cinema*, 10.

47. Ibid.

48. Bogle, *Toms, Coons, Mulattoes, Mammies, and Bucks*, 239.

49. Ibid.

50. Howard, *Blaxploitation Cinema*, 10.

51. Bogle, *Toms, Coons, Mulattoes, Mammies, and Bucks*, 239.

52. Monaco, *How to Read a Film*, 377.

53. Koven, *Blaxploitation Films*, 17.

54. Ibid.

55. Ibid., 17.

56. Ibid., 17.

57. Ibid. Please see the chapter entitled "BAADASSSSS" for a complete discussion of the movies mentioned in this section. Here are the various prototypes: ORIGINAL BAADASSSSSES, VIGILANTES, FIGHTERS, INDEPENDENT BUSINESSMEN, GANGSTERS, and PIMPS & DRUGDEALERS.

58. Koven, *Blaxploitation Films*, 76.

59. Ibid.

60. Ibid.

61. Ibid. Please see the chapter entitled "THE MAN" for a complete discussion of the movies mentioned in this section. Here are the various prototypes: COPS, DETECTIVES, and AGENTS, SPECIAL AND OTHERWISE.

62. Ibid., 114.

63. Ibid. Please see the chapter entitled "GENRE FILMS" for a complete discussion of the movies mentioned in this section. Here are the various prototypes: HORROR, KUNG-FU, and WESTERNS.

64. Howard, *Blaxploitation Cinema*, 11.

65. Ibid.

66. Ibid.

67. Ibid., 12.

68. Bogle, *Toms, Coons, Mulattoes, Mammies, and Bucks*, 239.

69. Howard, *Blaxploitation Cinema*, 12.

70. Ibid.

71. Bogle, *Toms, Coons, Mulattoes, Mammies, and Bucks*, 239.

72. Howard, *Blaxploitation Cinema*, 12.

73. Ibid.

74. Ibid.

75. Ibid., 13.

76. Ibid.

77. Gerald Martinez, Diana Martinez, and Andres Chavez, *What It Is ... What It Was!: The Black Film Explosion of the '70s in Words and Pictures* (New York: Miramax, 1998), 206.

78. Ibid.

79. Ibid.

80. Ibid., 166.

81. Ibid.

82. Ibid., 168.

83. Ibid.

84. Ibid.

85. Ibid.

86. Ibid., 168, 170.

87. Ibid., 170.

88. Ibid.

89. Ibid.

90. Ibid., 171.

91. Ibid.

92. Howard, *Blaxploitation Cinema*, 92.

93. Ibid., 93.

94. Ibid.

95. Ibid.

96. Koven, *Blaxploitation Films*, 114.

97. Ibid., 114–15.

98. Ibid., 115.

99. Ibid.

100. Ibid.

101. Ibid., 116.

102. Ibid.

103. Ibid., 105.

104. Howard, *Blaxploitation Cinema*, 92.

105. Ibid.

106. Ibid.

107. Koven, *Blaxploitation Films*, 106.

108. Ibid.

109. Howard, *Blaxploitation Cinema*, 169.

110. Martinez, Martinez, and Chavez, *What It Is ... What It Was!*, 206.

111. Koven, *Blaxploitation Films*, 37.

112. Howard, *Blaxploitation Cinema*, 169.

113. Ibid.

114. Ibid.

115. Howard, *Blaxploitation Cinema*, 170.

116. Ibid.

117. Koven, *Blaxploitation Films*, 39.

118. Ibid., 40.

119. Ibid., 49.

120. Howard, *Blaxploitation Cinema*, 210.

121. Ibid., 210–11.

122. Howard, *Blaxploitation Cinema*, 211.

123. Ibid. See also Koven, *Blaxploitation Films*, 49.

124. Koven, *Blaxploitation Films*, 41.

125. Ibid.

126. Ibid.

127. Ibid.

128. Howard, *Blaxploitation Cinema*, 161, 166.

129. Ibid., 114.

130. Ibid., 121.

Chapter 8

1. Mike Pearson, "Are Minorities Changing Hollywood's Status Quo?," *Black Camera* 1, no. 1 (Summer 1985).

2. "Eddie Murphy Biography: Film Actor, Television Actor, Comedian, Director (1961–)," accessed August 11, 2014, *bio*, A&E Television Networks, 2014, http://www.biography.com/people/eddie-murphy-9418676 #on-the-big-screen. *See also* Pearson, "Are Minorities Changing Hollywood's Status Quo?," 1: "Paramount Pictures Signed Murphy to a $25 Million Deal to Star in Four Movies." However, most other secondary sources agree with *biography.com*.

3. Pearson, "Are Minorities Changing Hollywood's Status Quo?," 1.

4. Ibid. See also Ned Geeslin, "From Eastwood to Pavarotti, the Money Machines' Theme Is Cold Cash for Hot Stars," *People* Archive, November 14, 1983, accessed August 11, 2014, http://www.people.com/people/archive/article/ 0,,20086391,00.html. This popular magazine source contradicts the literary journal *Black Camera* by stating instead that Richard Pryor "signed a $40-million, five-year, seven-picture 'production arrangement' with Columbia Pictures—complete artistic freedom on four of the pictures (as long as he stays within the budget), the other three 'major' Columbia releases to star Pryor." Furthermore, most sources cite this deal as occurring in 1983, not 1982 as reported by *Black Camera*.

5. Allen Johnson, "A Year in Review," *Black Camera* 4, no. 1 (Spring 1989): 4.

6. Ibid.

7. Ibid.

8. Albert Johnson, "Moods Indigo: A Long View," *Film Quarterly* 44, no. 2 (Winter 1990–91): 13.

9. Ibid.

10. Ibid.

11. Ibid.

12. Ibid.

13. Ibid.

14. Ibid., 14.

15. Ibid.

16. Ibid.

17. Donald Bogle, *Toms, Coons, Mulattoes, Mammies, and Bucks: An Interpretive History of Blacks in American Films* (New York: Bloomsbury, 2013), 281.

18. Johnson, "Moods Indigo," 14.

19. Ibid.

20. Ibid.

21. James Monaco, *How to Read A Film: Movies, Media and Beyond* (New York: Oxford University Press, 2009), 400.

22. Johnson, "Moods Indigo," 14–15.

23. Ibid., 14.

24. Ibid., 15.

25. Ibid.

26. Ibid.

27. Ibid.

28. Crystal L. Keels, "The Richard Pryor Film Retrospective," *Black Camera* 16, no. 2 (Fall/Winter, 2001): 9.

29. Ibid.

30. Ibid.

31. Bogle, *Toms, Coons, Mulattoes, Mammies, and Bucks*, 257.

32. Ibid.

33. Keels, "The Richard Pryor Film Retrospective," 9.

34. Ibid.

35. Bogle, *Toms, Coons, Mulattoes, Mammies, and Bucks*, 231.

36. Ibid., 246.

37. Keels, "The Richard Pryor Film Retrospective," 9.

38. Bogle, *Toms, Coons, Mulattoes, Mammies, and Bucks*, 263.

39. Keels, "The Richard Pryor Film Retrospective," 9.

40. Ibid.

41. Bogle, *Toms, Coons, Mulattoes, Mammies, and Bucks*, 277.

42. Ibid.

43. Keels, "The Richard Pryor Film Retrospective," 10.

44. Bogle, *Toms, Coons, Mulattoes, Mammies, and Bucks*, 264.

45. Ibid., 277.

46. Ibid.

47. Keels, "The Richard Pryor Film Retrospective," 10.

48. Ibid.

49. Ibid.

50. Ibid.

51. Bogle, *Toms, Coons, Mulattoes, Mammies, and Bucks*, 283.

52. Ibid., 284.

53. Ibid.

54. Tejumola Olaniyan, " 'Uplift the Race!': *Coming to America*, *Do the Right Thing*, and the Poetics and Politics of 'Othering,' " *Cultural Critique*, 34 (Autumn 1996): 91–113.

55. Ibid., 92.

56. Bogle, *Toms, Coons, Mulattoes, Mammies, and Bucks*, 279.

57. Olaniyan, " 'Uplift the Race!,' " 92.

58. Ibid., 94.

59. Ibid., 95.

60. Bogle, *Toms, Coons, Mulattoes, Mammies, and Bucks*, 286–87.

61. Olaniyan, " 'Uplift the Race!,' " 94–95.

62. Ibid., 96.

63. Ibid., 95–96.

64. Ibid., 96.

65. Ibid., 97–98.

66. Ibid., 99.

67. Ibid., 104.

68. Johnson, "Moods Indigo," 16.

69. Bogle, *Toms, Coons, Mulattoes, Mammies, and Bucks*, 317.

70. Johnson, "Moods Indigo," 16.

71. Ibid.

72. Ibid.

73. Ibid.

74. Ibid., 17.

75. Ibid.

76. Bogle, *Toms, Coons, Mulattoes, Mammies, and Bucks*, 318.

77. Johnson, "Moods Indigo," 17.

78. Bogle, *Toms, Coons, Mulattoes, Mammies, and Bucks*, 281.

79. Monaco, *How to Read a Film*, 400.

80. Bogle, *Toms, Coons, Mulattoes, Mammies, and Bucks*, 280.

81. Ibid.

82. Ibid., 280–81.

83. Ibid.

84. "Richard Pryor: Actor, Comedian, Screenwriter (1940–2005)," *bio.*, 2014, A&E Television Networks, accessed September 20, 2014, http://www .biography.com/people/richard-pryor-9448082#synopsis.

85. Bogle, *Toms, Coons, Mulattoes, Mammies, and Bucks*, 281.

86. Dorothy Pomerantz, "Eddie Murphy Tops Our List of the Most Overpaid Actors in Hollywood," *Forbes*, December 4, 2012, accessed September 20, 2014, http://www.forbes.com/sites/dorothypomerantz/2012/12/04/eddie-murphy-is-the -most-overpaid-actor-in-hollywood/.

87. Ibid.

88. Kim Masters, "How Much Will Eddie Murphy's Oscar Exit Hurt His Career? (Analysis)," *Hollywood Reporter,* August 9, 2011, accessed September 20, 2014, http://www.hollywoodreporter.com/news/eddie-murphy-oscars-career-brett-ratner-259479.

89. Henry Barnes, "Eddie Murphy to Return in Beverly Hills Cop 4," *Guardian*, July 30, 2013, accessed September 20, 2014, http://www.theguardian .com/film/2013/jul/30/eddie-murphy-beverly-hills-cop-4.

Chapter 9

1. Kenneth Chan, "The Construction of Black Male Identity in Black Action Films of the Nineties," *Cinema Journal* 37, no. 2 (Winter 1998): 35–48.

2. Ibid., 35.

3. Andrew Ross, Manthia Diawara, Alexander Doty, Wahneema Lubiano, Tricia Rose, Ella Shohat, Lynn Spigel, Robert Stam, and Michele Wallace, "A Symposium on Popular Culture and Political Correctness," *Social Text* 36 (Autumn 1993): 1–39.

4. Ibid., 3.

5. Ibid.

6. Chan, "The Construction of Black Male Identity in Black Action Films of the Nineties," 36.

7. Valerie Smith, Camille Billops, and Ada Griffin, "Introduction: [Black Film]," *Black American Literature Forum* 25, no. 2, *Black Film Issue* (Summer 1991): 217.

8. Ibid.

9. Ibid.

10. Chan, "The Construction of Black Male Identity in Black Action Films of the Nineties," 35–36.

11. Ibid., 36.

12. Bakari Kitwana, *The Hip Hop Generation* (New York: Basic Civitas Books, 2002), 121.

13. Ibid., 122.

14. Ibid.

15. Ibid.

16. Ibid.

17. Ibid.

18. Ibid.

19. Ibid., 123.

20. Ibid.

21. Ibid.

22. Ibid.

23. Ibid.

24. Ibid., 124.

25. Ibid.

26. Ibid.

27. Ibid.

28. Ibid., 125.

29. Ibid., 126.

30. Ibid.

31. Ibid.

32. Ibid.

33. Ibid., 127.

34. Ibid.

35. Chan, "The Construction of Black Male Identity in Black Action Films of the Nineties," 37.

36. Ibid., 37–38.

37. See Mikel J. Koven, *Blaxploitation Films* (Harpenden, UK: Kamera, 2010). Koven discusses in Chapters 1 and 2 of his book that there are two main archetypal figures in Blaxploitation films: Baadasssssses and The Man. "The Baadasssss" rebels and works outside the law; meanwhile, "The Man" works within the law to achieve his goals.

38. Melvin Donalson, *Hip Hop in American Cinema* (New York: Peter Lang, 2007), 36.

39. Ibid., 36–37.

40. Ibid., 37.

41. Ibid.

42. Ibid.

43. Ibid.

44. Ibid., 34.

45. Ibid., 34–35.

46. Ibid., 37.

47. Chan, "The Construction of Black Male Identity in Black Action Films of the Nineties," 38.

48. Ibid.

49. Ibid.

50. Ibid.

51. Ibid.

52. Ibid.

53. Ibid.

54. Ibid.

55. Donalson, *Hip Hop in American Cinema*, 89.

56. Ibid.

57. Ibid.

58. Ibid., 90

59. Ibid.

60. Ibid.
61. Ibid.
62. Ibid., 91.
63. Ibid.
64. Ibid.
65. Ross et al., "A Symposium on Popular Culture and Political Correctness," 6.
66. Donalson, *Hip Hop in American Cinema*, 92.
67. Ibid.
68. Ibid.
69. Ibid.
70. Ibid.
71. Ibid., 93.
72. Ibid.
73. Ibid.
74. Ross et al., "A Symposium on Popular Culture and Political Correctness," 6.
75. Ibid.
76. Ibid.
77. Kitwana, *The Hip Hop Generation*, 137.
78. Donalson, *Hip Hop in American Cinema*, 43–44.
79. Ibid., 43.
80. Kitwana, *The Hip Hop Generation*, 137.
81. Donalson, *Hip Hop in American Cinema*, 43.
82. Kitwana, *The Hip Hop Generation*, 137.
83. Ibid., 138.
84. Donalson, *Hip Hop in American Cinema*, 43.
85. Kitwana, *The Hip Hop Generation*, 138.
86. Ibid.
87. Donalson, *Hip Hop in American Cinema*, 43.
88. Kitwana, *The Hip Hop Generation*, 139.
89. Donalson, *Hip Hop in American Cinema*, 43.
90. Kitwana, *The Hip Hop Generation*, 139.
91. Donalson, *Hip Hop in American Cinema*, 141–52.
92. Ibid., 41.
93. Ibid.
94. Ibid.
95. Ibid., 35.
96. Ibid.
97. Ibid.
98. Ibid., 35–36.
99. Ibid., 36.
100. Nelson George, *Hip Hop America* (New York: Penguin, 1998), 208.
101. Jeff Chang, *Can't Stop Won't Stop* (New York: Picador, 2005), 2.

Chapter 10

1. Michael T. Martin and Julie Dash, " 'I Do Exist': From 'Black Insurgent' to Negotiating the Hollywood Divide—a Conversation with Julie Dash," *Cinema Journal* 49, no. 2 (Winter 2010): 11.

2. Ibid.

3. Aaron Barlow, ed., *Star Power: The Impact of Branded Celebrity* (Santa Barbara, CA: Praeger, 2014): 201.

4. Ibid.

5. Ibid.

6. Ibid., 201–2.

7. Ibid., 202.

8. Kimberly Fain, "Spike Lee: Rise, Success, and Doin' the Right Thing," in *Star Power: The Impact of Branded Celebrity*, ed. Aaron Barlow (Santa Barbara, CA: Praeger, 2014): 219.

9. Barlow, *Star Power*, 202.

10. Fain, "Spike Lee," 221–22.

11. Barlow, *Star Power*, 202.

12. Ibid.

13. Ibid.

14. Julee Wilson, "*Ebony* 'Trayvon' Covers: The Martins, Spike Lee, Boris Kodjoe, Dwyane Wade and Their Sons for September Issue (Photos)," *Huff Post Black Voices*, August 6, 2013, accessed October 2, 2014, http://www.huffingtonpost.com/2013/08/06/ebony-trayvon-covers-sons-photos_n_3715134.html.

15. Fain, "Spike Lee," 209.

16. Ibid.

17. Maurice E. Stevens, "Dis/Identification: Subject to Countermemory: Disavowal and Black Manhood in Spike Lee's *Malcolm X*," *Signs* 28, no. 1, *Gender and Cultural Memory, Special Issue*, ed. Marianne Hirsch and Valerie Smith (Autumn 2002): 277.

18. Ibid.

19. Ibid.

20. Ibid., 278.

21. Ibid.

22. Ibid.

23. Ibid., 278–79.

24. Ibid., 279.

25. Ibid., 280.

26. Ibid., 281.

27. Ibid.

28. Ibid., 281–82.

29. Ibid., 284.

30. Ibid.

31. Ibid., 298.

32. Ibid.

33. Ibid., 299.

34. Ibid., 301.

35. Lori Harrison-Kahan, "Inside 'Inside Man': Spike Lee and Post 9/11-Entertainment," *Cinema Journal* 50, no. 1 (Fall 2010): 39.

36. Ibid.

37. Ibid.

38. Ibid., 40.

39. Ibid.

40. Ibid., 51.

41. Ibid., 47.

42. Ibid.

43. Ibid.

44. Ibid.

45. Ibid.

46. Ibid., 40.

47. Ibid.

48. Ibid.

49. Ibid.

50. Ibid.

51. Ibid.

52. Ibid., 51.

53. Ibid.

54. Ibid., 50.

55. Ibid.

56. Ibid.

57. Ibid.

58. Ibid.

59. Ibid., 51.

60. Ibid., 53.

61. Ibid.

62. Ibid.

63. Ibid.

64. Ibid., 54.

65. Ibid., 55.

66. Ibid.

67. Ibid.

68. Regina Kimbell and Mary Huelsbeck, "A Black Camera Interview: Nappy or Straight: Must We Choose? Regina Kimbell on Black Hair-Itage," *Black Camera* 22/23, 22, nos. 2–23, no. 1 (Spring 2008): 53.

69. Nick Stillman and Kalup Linzy, "Kalup Linzy," *BOMB* 104 (Summer 2008): 51.

70. Robert J. Patterson, " 'Woman Thou Art Bound': Critical Spectatorship, Black Masculine Gazes, and Gender Problems in Tyler Perry's Movies," *Black Camera* 3, no. 1 (Winter 2011): 9.

71. Timothy Lyle, " 'Check with Yo' Man First; Check with Yo' Man': Tyler Perry Appropriates Drag as a Tool to Re-circulate Patriarchal Ideology," *Callaloo* 34, no. 3 (Summer 2011): 943.

72. Ibid., 944.

73. Ibid.

74. Ibid.

75. Patterson, " 'Woman Thou Art Bound,' " 16.

76. Ibid.

77. Lyle, " 'Check with Yo' Man First; Check with Yo' Man,' " 945.

78. Ibid.

79. Ibid., 946.

80. Ibid.

81. Ibid., 947.

82. Ibid.

83. Ibid., 948.

84. Ibid.

85. Patterson, " 'Woman Thou Art Bound,' " 10.

86. Ibid.

87. Ibid.

88. Ibid., 11.

89. Ibid.

90. Ibid., 12.

91. Ibid.

92. Matt Doeden, *Will Smith: Box Office Superstar* (Minneapolis, MN: Twenty-First Century Books, 2010), 4.

93. Ibid., 5.

94. Ibid., 27.

95. Ibid., 38. See also Tom Green, "Will Smith's Exponential Leap: 'Six Degrees' Elevates Rapper and TV Star," *USA Today*, December 8, 1993.

96. Doeden, *Will Smith*, 39.

97. Ibid.

98. Ibid., 42.

99. Ibid., 46.

100. Ibid., 47.

101. Ibid., 92.

102. Ibid.

103. Ibid., 93.

104. Ibid.

105. Ibid.

106. Ibid., 12.

107. Ibid., 13.

108. "About Overbrook," *overbrookent.com*, 2011, accessed October 4, 2014, http://www.overbrookent.com/about/.

109. Ibid.

110. Ibid.

111. Ibid.

112. Ben Fritz, "Will Smith's 'After Earth' Flops at Box Office," *Wall Street Journal*, June 2, 2013, accessed October 4, 2014, http://www.wsj.com/articles/ SB10001424127887324423904578521542174762344.

113. Ibid.

114. "After Earth," Box Office Mojo, accessed October 7, 2014, http://www .boxofficemojo.com/movies/?id=1000ae.htm.

115. Fritz, "Will Smith's 'After Earth' Flops at Box Office."

116. Doeden, *Will Smith*, 65; see also "Lee Slams Smith for 'Driving Mr. Damon,' " *ABC News*, November 10, 2000, accessed October 4, 2014, http://abcnews.go.com/Entertainment/story?id=113438.

117. Doeden, *Will Smith*, 64.

118. Ibid., 65.

119. Susan Gonzalez, "Director Spike Lee Slams 'Same Old' Black Stereotypes in Today's Films," *Yale Bulletin and Calendar* 29, no. 21 (March 2, 2001), accessed October 4, 2014, http://www.yale.edu/opa/arc-ybc/v29.n21/ story3.html.

120. "Our Work: Film," *overbrookent.com*, 2011, accessed October 4, 2014, see http://www.overbrookent.com/film/; see http://www.overbrookent .com/film/page/2/; see http://www.overbrookent.com/film/page/3/.

121. Doeden, *Will Smith*, 76.

122. Ibid., 77.

123. Darren Frinch, "Samuel L. Jackson Is the Highest Grossing Actor of All Time, and by God, He's Worth Every Penny," *Entertainment Weekly* October 27, 2011, accessed October 5, 2014, http://popwatch.ew.com/2011/10/ 27/samuel-l-jackson-highest-grossing-actor/.

124. Ibid.

125. Sean Thompson, "Beyoncé to Star Alongside Will Smith in 'Hancock 2'?," *Vibe*, June 2014, accessed October 2, 2014, http://www.vibe.com/article/ beyonce-hancock-2-will-smith-rumors.

126. "Spike Lee on Tyler Perry: 'One Day We Might Work Together' (VIDEO)," *Huff Post Own Videos*, November 14, 2013, accessed October 14, 2014, http://www.huffingtonpost.com/2013/11/14/spike-lee-tyler-perry-feud_n _4269317.html; see also "Tyler Perry to Spike Lee: 'Go Straight to Hell,'" *Huff Post Entertainment*, April 20, 2011, accessed October 14, 2014, http://www .huffingtonpost.com/2011/04/20/tyler-perry-spike-lee-go-to-hell_n_851344.html.

127. "Spike Lee on Tyler Perry."

Chapter 11

1. Henry A. Giroux, "The Disimagination Machine and the Pathologies of Power," *Symploke* 21, nos. 1–2 (2013): 258.

2. Chris Vognar, "He Can't Say That, Can He?: Black, White, and Shades of Gray in the Films of Tarantino," *Transition* 112 (2013): 22.

3. Ibid.

4. Ibid., 30.

5. Solomon Northup, *Twelve Years a Slave*, ed. Henry Louis Gates Jr. (New York: Penguin, 2012). See also Paula Byrne, *Belle* (New York: Harper Perennial, 2014).

6. "10 Black British Actors Taking Hollywood by Storm (PHOTOS)," *Huff Post Black Voices*, March 5, 2014, http://www.huffingtonpost.com/2014/02/28/9-black-british-actors-you-need-to-know-_n_4875041.html.

7. Ibid.

8. Paterson Joseph, "Why Were the Baftas So White? Because There Aren't Enough Black People on TV," *Guardian*, May 16, 2013, accessed October 5, 2014, http://www.theguardian.com/commentisfree/2013/may/16/baftas-black-actors-tv. See also Tim Walker, "Baftas Were a Disgrace for Not Celebrating Black Talent, Says Lenny Henry," *Telegraph*, ed. Richard Eden, May 2013, accessed October 8, 2014, http://www.telegraph.co.uk/culture/tvandradio/10057059/Baftas-were-a-disgrace-for-not-celebrating-black-talent-says-Lenny-Henry.html.

9. Joseph, "Why Were the Baftas So White?"

10. Ibid.

11. Ibid.

12. Ibid.

13. A. O. Scott, "A New Year, and a Last Day Alive: 'Fruitvale Station' Is Based on the Story of Oscar Grant III," *New York Times*, July 11, 2013, accessed October 8, 2014, http://www.nytimes.com/2013/07/12/movies/fruitvale-station-is-based-on-the-story-of-oscar-grant-iii.html?_r=0.

14. Michael Phillips, "Movie Review: 'Red Tails,'" *Los Angeles Times*, January 20, 2012, accessed October 5, 2014, http://articles.latimes.com/2012/jan/20/entertainment/la-et-red-tails-20120120-1. The article states that "George Lucas' production takes a comic book approach to the exploits of World War II's Tuskegee Airmen."

15. Phillips, "'Movie Review: 'Red Tails.'"

16. Sophie Schillaci, "'42' Star Chadwick Boseman: Jackie Robinson's Widow 'Overjoyed' by Biopic," *Hollywood Reporter*, April 10, 2013, accessed October 4, 2014, http://www.hollywoodreporter.com/news/42-star-chadwick-boseman-jackie-436901.

17. Mark D. Cunningham, "No Getting around the Black," *Cinema Journal* 53, no. 4 (Summer 2014): 143.

18. Ibid., 141.

19. Ibid.

20. Ibid.

21. Ibid.

22. Ibid.

23. Ibid., 144.

24. Glenda R. Carpio, " 'I Like the Way You Die, Boy': Fantasy's Role in *Django Unchained*," *Transition* 112 (2013): 1.

25. Ibid.

26. Ibid.

27. Ibid.

28. Ibid., 2.

29. Ibid., 4.

30. Ibid.

31. Ibid.

32. Ibid., 5.

33. Ibid.

34. Ibid.

35. Ibid.

36. Ibid., 6.

37. Ibid.

38. Ibid.

39. Ibid.

40. Ibid.

41. Ibid., 7.

42. Ibid.

43. Ibid.

44. Ibid.

45. Ibid.

46. Vognar, "He Can't Say That, Can He?," 31.

47. Carpio, " 'I Like the Way You Die, Boy,' " 8.

48. Ibid.

49. Ibid., 9.

50. Ibid.

51. Vognar, "He Can't Say That, Can He?," 31.

52. Ibid.

53. Carpio, " 'I Like the Way You Die, Boy,' " 9.

54. Ibid.

55. Ibid., 10.

56. Ibid., 12.

57. Vognar, "He Can't Say That, Can He?," 31.

58. Walter Johnson, "Allegories of Empire: Django/Dorner/Blackness/Blowback," *Transition* 112 (2013): 17.

59. Ibid., 17.

60. Ibid., 18.

61. Ibid., 19.

62. Vognar, "He Can't Say That, Can He?," 22.

63. "Film Roundtable: *Lincoln*," *Civil War History* 59, no. 3 (September 2013): 358. This article lists no author, yet it lists Brian Craig Miller as the facilitator. Thus the information from this discussion is derived from the introduction to the roundtable discussion on *Lincoln*. This source refers to one of *Lincoln*'s Academy awards as the "Best Achievement in Production Design." However, most sources refer to the award as the "Best Production Design Award."

64. "Film Roundtable: *Lincoln*."

65. Jon Wiener, "The Trouble with Spielberg's 'Lincoln,' " *The Nation*, November 26, 2012, accessed October 14, 2014, http://www.thenation.com/blog/171461/trouble-steven-spielbergs-lincoln.

66. Ibid.

67. Ibid.

68. Ibid.

69. Eric Foner, "Lincoln's Use of Politics for Noble Ends," *New York Times*, November 26, 2012, accessed October 4, 2014, http://www.nytimes.com/2012/11/27/opinion/lincolns-use-of-politics-for-noble-ends.html?_r=0.

70. Kate Masur, "In Spielberg's 'Lincoln,' Passive Black Characters," *New York Times*, November 12, 2012, accessed October 5, 2014, http://www.nytimes.com/2012/11/13/opinion/in-spielbergs-lincoln-passive-black-characters.html?_r=0#p[IftSwa],h[IftSwa].

71. Ibid.

72. Ibid.

73. Ibid.

74. Ibid.

75. Ibid.

76. Ibid.

77. Ibid.

78. Ibid.

79. Ibid.

80. Jasmine Nichole Cobb, "Directed by Himself: Steve McQueen's *12 Years a Slave*," *American Literary History* 26, no. 2 (Summer 2014): 339.

81. Ibid.

82. Ibid.

83. Ibid.

84. Ibid., 340.

85. Ibid.

86. Ibid.

87. Ibid.

88. Ibid.

89. Ibid., 343.

90. Ibid., 344.

91. Ibid.

92. Valerie Smith, "Black Life in the Balance: *12 Years a Slave*," *American Literary History* 26, no. 2 (Summer 2014): 362.

93. Ibid.

94. Ibid.

95. Ibid.

96. Ibid.

97. Ibid.

98. Ibid.

99. Ibid.

100. Ibid., 363.

101. Ibid.

102. Ibid.

103. Ibid., 364.

104. Ibid.

105. Ibid., 365.

106. Ibid.

107. Kristen Paige Kirby, "Jamie Foxx's Electro in 'The Amazing Spider-Man 2' Is a Badly Drawn Baddie," *Washington Post*, May 1, 2014, accessed October 8, 2014, http://www.washingtonpost.com/express/wp/2014/05/01/jamie-foxx-electro-amazing-spider-man-2/; Richard L. Eldredge, "Q&A: Djimon Hounsou at the Atlanta Screening of Guardians of the Galaxy," *The Atlanta Magazine*, July 31, 2014, accessed October 5, 2014, http://www.atlantamagazine.com/news-culture-articles/qa-djimon-hounsou-at-the-atlanta-screening-of-guardians-of-the-galaxy/#sthash.7R2KHrxW.dpuf; Catherine Shoard, "Vin Diesel on Guardians of the Galaxy: 'I Didn't Realise How Much I Love Trees,' " *Guardian*, July 31, 2014, accessed October 5, 2014, http://www.theguardian.com/film/2014/jul/31/vin-diesel-groot-guardians-of-the-galaxy-interview; Bryan Alexander, "Dwayne Johnson's Heroic 'Hercules' Transformation," *USA Today*, July 23, 2014, accessed October 5, 2014, http://www.usatoday.com/story/life/movies/2014/07/23/rock-hercules-diet-dwayne-johnson/12616221/.

Bibliography

"About Overbrook." Overbrook Entertainment. Overbrookent.com, 2011, accessed October 4, 2014, http://www.overbrookent.com/about/.

"After Earth." Box Office Mojo, accessed October 7, 2014, http://www.boxofficemojo.com/movies/?id=1000ae.htm.

Alexander, Bryan. "Dwayne Johnson's Heroic 'Hercules' Transformation." *USA Today*, July 23, 2014, http://www.usatoday.com/story/life/movies/2014/07/23/rock-hercules-diet-dwayne-johnson/12616221/.

"ATL (2006)." *IMDb.com*, accessed October 4, 2014, http://www.imdb.com/title/tt0466856/.

Barlow, Aaron, ed. *Star Power: The Impact of Branded Celebrity*. Santa Barbara, CA: Praeger, 2014.

Barnes, Henry. "Eddie Murphy to Return in Beverly Hills Cop 4." *Guardian*, July 30, 2013, accessed September 20, 2014, http://www.theguardian.com/film/2013/jul/30/eddie-murphy-beverly-hills-cop-4.

Baum, Gary, and Daniel Miller. "The Hollywood Reporter, after 65 Years, Addresses Role in Blacklist." *Hollywood Reporter*, November 19, 2012, http://www.hollywoodreporter.com/news/blacklist-thr-addresses-role-65-391931?page=1.

Baum, Gary, and Daniel Miller. "The Most Sinful Period in Hollywood History." *Hollywood Reporter*, November 17, 2012, http://www.hollywoodreporter.com/news/sinful-period-hollywood-history-391707.

Belafonte, Harry, and Michael Shnayerson. *My Song*. New York: Knopf, 2011.

"Bill 'Bojangles' Robinson Biography: Film Actor, Dancer (1878–1949)." Biography.com, A&E Television, 2014, accessed August 4, 2014, http://www.biography.com/people/bill-bojangles-robinson-9460594#dancing-and-acting-career.

Black, Gregory D. *Hollywood Censored: Morality Codes, Catholics, and the Movies*. New York: Cambridge University Press, 1994.

Bogle, Donald. *Bright Boulevards, Bold Dreams: The Story of Black Hollywood.* New York: Random House, 2005.

Bogle, Donald. *Toms, Coons, Mulattoes, Mammies, and Bucks: An Interpretive History of Blacks in American Films.* 4th ed. New York: Bloomsbury, 2001.

Bowdre, Karen M. "Passing Films and the Illusion of Racial Equality." *Black Camera* 5, no. 2 (Spring 2014): 21–43.

Browser, Pearl, Jane Gaines, and Charles Musser, eds. *Oscar Micheaux and His Circle: African-American Filmmaking and Race Cinema of the Silent Era.* Bloomington: Indiana University Press, 2001.

Burton, Nsenga. "Celebrating 100 Years of Black Cinema." *The Root*, February 3, 2010, http://www.theroot.com/articles/culture/2010/02/100_years_of _black_cinema_oscar_ micheaux_melvin_van_peebles_spike_lee_kasi _lemmons.html.

Byrne, Paula. *Belle.* New York: Harper Perennial, 2014.

Canby, Vincent. "Ossie Davis' 'Cotton Comes to Harlem.' " Movie review of *Cotton Comes to Harlem* (1970), *New York Times*, June 11, 1970, http://www.nytimes.com/movie/review?res=9C0CEFD61439E63BBC495 2DFB066838B669EDE.

Carpio, Glenda R. " 'I Like the Way You Die, Boy': Fantasy's Role in *Django Unchained*." *Transition* 112 (2013): iv–12,.

Cavallero, Jonathan J. "Hitchcock and Race: Is the Wrong Man a White Man?" *Journal of Film and Video* 62, no. 4 (Winter 2010): 3–14.

Chan, Kenneth. "The Construction of Black Male Identity in Black Action Films of the Nineties." *Cinema Journal* 37, no. 2 (Winter 1998): 35–48.

Chang, Jeff. *Can't Stop Won't Stop.* New York: Picador, 2005.

Cobb, Jasmine Nichole. "Directed by Himself: Steve McQueen's *12 Years a Slave*." *American Literary History* 26, no. 2 (Summer 2014): 339–46.

Crowther, Bosley. "Lilies of the Field (1963)." Movie review, *New York Times*, 2010, accessed August 18, 2014, http://www.nytimes.com/movies/movie/ 29373/Lilies-of-the-Field/overview.

Cunningham, Mark D. "No Getting around the Black." *Cinema Journal* 53, no. 4 (Summer 2014): 140–46.

"The Dignity of Sidney Poitier." Interview with *CBS News*, May 12, 2013, http:// www.cbsnews.com/news/the-dignity-of-sidney-poitier/.

Doeden, Matt. *Will Smith: Box Office Superstar.* Minneapolis, MN: Twenty-First Century Books, 2010.

Doherty, Thomas. *Pre-code Hollywood: Sex, Immorality, and Insurrection in American Cinema 1930–1934.* New York: Columbia University Press, 1999.

Donalson, Melvin. *Hip Hop in American Cinema.* New York: Peter Lang, 2007.

Ebert, Roger. "Baadasssss!" Movie review, *Rogerebert.com*, June 11, 2004, http://www.rogerebert.com/reviews/baadasssss-2004.

"Eddie Murphy Biography: Film Actor, Television Actor, Comedian, Director (1961–)." *bio.com.* A&E Television Networks, 2014, http://www.biography .com/people/eddie-murphy-9418676#on-the-big-screen.

Eldredge, Richard L. "Q&A: Djimon Hounsou at the Atlanta Screening of *Guardians of the Galaxy*." *The Atlanta Magazine*, July 31, 2014, http://www.atlantamagazine.com/news-culture-articles/qa-djimon-hounsou-at-the-atlanta-screening-of-guardians-of-the-galaxy/.

Ellison, Ralph. *Shadow and Act*. New York: Vintage, 1995.

Fain, Kimberly. "Spike Lee: Rise, Success, and Doin' the Right Thing." In *Star Power: The Impact of Branded Celebrity*, ed. Aaron Barlow. Santa Barbara, CA: Praeger, 2014, 205–31.

"Film Roundtable: Lincoln." *Civil War History 59*, no. 3 (September 2013): 358–75.

Foner, Eric. "Lincoln's Use of Politics for Noble Ends." *New York Times*, November 26, 2012, accessed October 4, 2014, http://www.nytimes.com/2012/11/27/opinion/lincolns-use-of-politics-for-noble-ends.html?_r=0.

Foner, Philip S., ed. *Paul Robeson Speaks*. New York: Citadel Press, 1978.

Frinch, Darren. "Samuel L. Jackson Is the Highest Grossing Actor of All Time, and by God, He's Worth Every Penny." *Entertainment Weekly*, October 27, 2011, http://popwatch.ew.com/2011/10/27/samuel-l-jackson-highest-grossing-actor/.

Fritz, Ben. "Will Smith's 'After Earth' Flops at Box Office." *Wall Street Journal*, online.wsj.com, June 2, 2013, accessed October 4, 2014, http://online.wsj.com/news/articles/SB10001424127887324423904578521542174762344.

Gaines, Jane M. *Fire and Desire: Mixed-Race Movies in the Silent Era*. Chicago: University of Chicago Press, 2001.

Gates, Henry Louis, Jr. "Foreword." In *Civil Rights in America: The Road to Equality and the Dream Today*, ed. Radhika Jones and Stephen Koepp. New York: Time, 2014.

Geeslin, Ned. "From Eastwood to Pavarotti, the Money Machines' Theme Is Cold Cash for Hot Stars." *People* Archive, November 14, 1983, http://www.people.com/people/archive/article/0,,20086391,00.html.

George, Nelson. *Hip Hop America*. New York: Penguin, 1998.

Giroux, Henry A. "The Disimagination Machine and the Pathologies of Power." *Symploke* 21, nos.1–2 (2013): 257–69.

"*Gone with the Wind*: Full Cast and Crew." *IMDb.com*. Amazon Company (1990–2014). http://www.imdb.com/title/tt0031381/fullcredits?ref_=tt_ov_st_sm.

Gonzalez, Susan. "Director Spike Lee Slams 'Same Old' Black Stereotypes in Today's Films." *Yale Bulletin and Calendar* 29, no. 21 (March 2, 2001), http://www.yale.edu/opa/arc-ybc/v29.n21/story3.html.

Goodykoontz, Billy. "Oscar Win Proved Sidney Poitier Was Second to None." *USA Today*, February 25, 2014, http://www.usatoday.com/story/life/movies/2014/02/25/black-history-month-poitier-oscar/5817735/.

Green, J. Ronald. "Introduction." *Straight Lick: The Cinema of Oscar Micheaux*. Bloomington: Indiana University Press, 2000.

Green, J. Ronald. *With a Crooked Stick : The Films of Oscar Micheaux.* Bloomington: Indiana University Press, 2004.

Green, Tom. "Will Smith's Exponential Leap: 'Six Degrees' Elevates Rapper and TV Star." *USA Today*, December 8, 1993.

Greil, Marcus, and Werner Sollors, eds. *A New Literary History of America.* Cambridge, MA: Belknap Press of Harvard University Press, 2009.

Grupenhoff, Richard. *The Black Valentino: The Stage and Screen Career of Lorenzo Tucker.* Metuchen, NJ: Scarecrow, 1988.

Harrison-Kahan, Lori. "Inside 'Inside Man': Spike Lee and Post 9/11-Entertainment." *Cinema Journal 50*, no. 1 (Fall 2010): 39–58.

Haskell, Molly. " 'Gone with the Wind' Still Raises Fuss after 70 Years." *CNN Opinion*, December 15, 2009, http://www.cnn.com/2009/OPINION/12/15/haskell.gone.with.the.wind/.

Haskins, Jim, and N. R. Mitgang, *Mr. Bojangles: The Biography of Bill Robinson.* New York: Morrow, 1988.

Howard, Josiah. *Blaxploitation Cinema: The Essential Reference Guide.* Godalming, UK: FAB Press, 2008.

In the Heat of the Night (1967). *New York Times*, Awards, 2014, accessed August 23, 2014, http://www.nytimes.com/movies/movie/24638/In-the-Heat-of-the-Night/awards.

In the Heat of the Night (1967). *New York Times*, Movies, 2014, http://www.nytimes.com/movies/movie/24638/In-the-Heat-of-the-Night/overview.

Johnson, Albert. "Moods Indigo: A Long View." *Film Quarterly* 44, no. 2 (Winter 1990–91): 13–27.

Johnson, Allen. "A Year in Review." *Black Camera* 4, no. 1 (Spring 1989): 4–5.

Johnson, Walter. "Allegories of Empire: Django/Dorner/Blackness/Blowback." *Transition* 112 (2013): 13–21.

Joseph, Paterson. "Why Were the Baftas So White? Because There Aren't Enough Black People on TV." *Guardian*, May 16, 2013, accessed October 5, 2014, http://www.theguardian.com/commentisfree/2013/may/16/baftas-black-actors-tv.

Keels, Crystal L. "The Richard Pryor Film Retrospective." *Black Camera* 16, no. 2 (Fall/Winter, 2001): 9–10.

Kessler, Ronald. "Hoover's Secret Files." *Daily Beast.com*, August 2, 2011, http://www.thedailybeast.com/articles/2011/08/02/fbi-director-hoover-s-dirty-files-excerpt-from-ronald-kessler-s-the-secrets-of-the-fbi.html.

Kimbell, Regina, and Mary Huelsbeck. "A Black Camera Interview: Nappy or Straight: Must We Choose? Regina Kimbell on Black Hair-Itage." *Black Camera* 22/23, 22, nos. 2–23, no.1 (Spring 2008): 49–59.

Kirby, Kristen Paige. "Jamie Foxx's Electro in 'The Amazing Spider-Man 2' Is a Badly Drawn Baddie." *Washington Post*, May 1, 2014, http://www.washingtonpost.com/express/wp/2014/05/01/jamie-foxx-electro-amazing-spider-man-2/.

Kitwana, Bakari. *The Hip Hop Generation.* New York: BasicCivitas Books, 2002.

Koven, Mikel J. *Blaxploitation Films*. Harpenden, UK: Kamara, 2010.

Leff, Leonard J. " 'Gone with the Wind' and Hollywood's Racial Politics." *The Atlantic Monthly* 99.12, 284, no. 6 (December 1999): 106–14, http://www.theatlantic.com/past/docs/issues/99dec/9912leff.htm, http://www.theatlantic.com/past/docs/issues/99dec/9912leff2.htm.

Lifeboat. TCM: Turner Classic Movies. TCM.com, 2014, accessed August 9, 2014, http://www.tcm.com/tcmdb/title/81373/Lifeboat/notes.html.

"Lincoln Theodore (=Stepin Fetchit) Perry." *The Black Perspective in Music* 14, no. 3 (Autumn 1986).

Lott, Eric. *Love and Theft: Blackface Minstrelsy and the American Working Class*. New York: Oxford University Press, 2013.

Lyle, Timothy. " 'Check with Yo' Man First; Check with Yo' Man': Tyler Perry Appropriates Drag as a Tool to Re-circulate Patriarchal Ideology." *Callaloo* 34, no. 3 (Summer 2011): 943–58.

Martin, Michael T., and Julie Dash. " 'I Do Exist': From 'Black Insurgent' to Negotiating the Hollywood Divide—a Conversation with Julie Dash," *Cinema Journal* 49, no. 2 (Winter 2010): 1–16.

Martinez, Gerald, Diana Martinez, and Andres Chavez. *What It Is . . . What It Was!: The Black Film Explosion of the '70s in Words and Pictures*. New York: Miramax, 1998.

Masters, Kim. "How Much Will Eddie Murphy's Oscar Exit Hurt His Career? (Analysis)." *Hollywood Reporter*, August 9, 2011, http://www.hollywoodreporter.com/news/eddie-murphy-oscars-career-brett-ratner-259479.

Masur, Kate. "In Spielberg's 'Lincoln,' Passive Black Characters." *New York Times*, November 12, 2012, http://www.nytimes.com/2012/11/13/opinion/in-spielbergs-lincoln-passive-black-characters.html?_r=0#p[IftSwa],h[IftSwa] and http://www.nytimes.com/2012/11/13/opinion/in-spielbergs-lincoln-passive-black-characters.html?pagewanted=2&_r=0.

Meacham, Jon. "The Man and the March That Changed America." In *Civil Rights in America: The Road to Equality and the Dream Today*, ed. Radhika Jones and Stephen Koepp. New York: Time, 2014.

Monaco, James. *How to Read a Film: Movies, Media, and Beyond*. New York: Oxford University Press, 2009.

Nickels, John. "Disabling African American Men: Liberalism and Race Message Films." *Cinema Journal* 44, no. 1 (Fall 2004): 25–48.

Northup, Solomon. *Twelve Years a Slave*, ed. Henry Louis Gates Jr. New York: Penguin, 2012.

Olaniyan, Tejumola. " 'Uplift the Race!': *Coming to America*, *Do the Right Thing*, and the Poetics and Politics of 'Othering.' " *Cultural Critique* 34 (Autumn 1996): 91–113.

"Our Work: Film." *Overbrook Entertainment*. Overbrookent.com, 2011, accessed October 4, 2014, http://www.overbrookent.com/film/; http://

www.overbrookent.com/film/page/2/; see http://www.overbrookent.com/film/page/3/.

Patterson, Robert J. " 'Woman Thou Art Bound': Critical Spectatorship, Black Masculine Gazes, and Gender Problems in Tyler Perry's Movies." *Black Camera* 3, no. 1 (Winter 2011): 9–30.

Pearson, Mike. "Are Minorities Changing Hollywood's Status Quo?" *Black Camera* 1, no. 1 (Summer 1985).

Phillips, Michael. "Movie Review: 'Red Tails.' " *Los Angeles Times*, January 20, 2012, accessed October 5, 2015, http://articles.latimes.com/2012/jan/20/entertainment/la-et-red-tails-20120120-1.

Pickert, Katie "We Were There." *Civil Rights in America: The Road to Equality and the Dream Today*, ed. Radhika Jones and Stephen Koepp. New York: Time, 2014.

Poitier, Sidney. *The Measure of a Man: A Spiritual Autobiography*. New York: HarperCollins, 2000.

Pomerantz, Dorothy. "Eddie Murphy Tops Our List of the Most Overpaid Actors in Hollywood." *Forbes*, December 4, 2012, http://www.forbes.com/sites/dorothypomerantz/2012/12/04/eddie-murphy-is-the-most-overpaid-actor-in-hollywood/.

"*Porgy and Bess* (1959): Full Cast and Crew." *IMDb.com*, 1999–2014, accessed August 18, 2014, http://www.imdb.com/title/tt0053182/fullcredits?ref_=tt_ov_st_sm.

"Race and Hollywood Black Images on Film." Lenny Bluett on Clark Gable (TCM Featurette), TCM Turner Classic Movies, 2014, Turner Entertainment Networks, http://www.tcm.com/mediaroom/video/135939/Lenny-Bluett-on-Clark-Gable-A-TCM-Featurette-.html.

A Raisin in the Sun. IMDb.com, 2014, http://www.imdb.com/title/tt0055353/.

Reeves, Thomas C. "McCarthyism: Interpretations since Hofstadter." *The Wisconsin Magazine of History* 60, no. 1 (Autumn, 1976): 42–54.

Regester, Charlene. "Stepin Fetchit: The Man, the Image, and the African American Press." *Film History* 6, no. 4 (Winter 1994): 502–21.

"Richard Pryor: Actor, Comedian, Screenwriter (1940–2005)." *bio*, 2014. A&E Television Networks, accessed September 20, 2014, http://www.biography.com/people/richard-pryor-9448082#synopsis.

Robeson, Paul. *Here I Stand*. 1958. Boston: Beacon Press, 1988.

Rogin, Michael. "Making America Home: Racial Masquerade and Ethnic Assimilation in the Transition to Talking Pictures." *The Journal of American History* 79, no. 3 (December 1992): 1050–77.

Ross, Andrew, Manthia Diawara, Alexander Doty, Wahneema Lubiano, Tricia Rose,

Scott, A. O. "A New Year, and a Last Day Alive: 'Fruitvale Station' Is Based on the Story of Oscar Grant III." *New York Times*, July 11, 2013, http://www.nytimes.com/2013/07/12/movies/fruitvale-station-is-based-on-the-story-of-oscar-grant-iii.html?_r=0.

Shoard, Catherine. "Vin Diesel on Guardians of the Galaxy: 'I Didn't Realise How Much I Love Trees.' " *Guardian*, July 31, 2014, http://www.theguardian.com/film/2014/jul/31/vin-diesel-groot-guardians-of-the-galaxy-interview.

Shohat, Ella, Lynn Spigel, Robert Stam, and Michele Wallace. "A Symposium on Popular Culture and Political Correctness." *Social Text* 36 (Autumn 1993): 1–39.

"Sidney Poitier." Kennedy Center, Kennedy-center.org, http://www.kennedy-center.org/explorer/artists/?entity_id=3785.

"Sidney Poitier: Full Biography." *New York Times*, 2010, accessed August 18, 2014, http://www.nytimes.com/movies/person/531681/Sidney-Poitier/biography.

Smith, Mona Z. *Becoming Something: The Story of Canada Lee*. New York: Faber & Faber, 2004.

Smith, Richard Norton. "The Pulpit." In *Civil Rights in America: The Road to Equality and the Dream Today*, ed. Radhika Jones and Stephen Koepp. New York: Time, 2014.

Smith, Valerie. "Black Life in the Balance: *12 Years a Slave*." *American Literary History* 26, no. 2 (Summer 2014): 362–66.

Smith, Valerie, Camille Billops, and Ada Griffin. "Introduction: [Black Film]." *Black American Literature Forum* 25, no. 2, *Black Film Issue* (Summer 1991): 217–19.

"Spike Lee on Tyler Perry: " 'One Day We Might Work Together' (VIDEO)," *Huffington Post Own Videos*, November 14, 2013, accessed October 14, 2014, http://www.huffingtonpost.com/2013/11/14/spike-lee-tyler-perry-feud_n_4269317.html.

"Stepin Fetchit (1902–1985)." Filmography, IMDb.com, 2014, http://www.imdb.com/name/nm0275297/.

Stevens, Maurice E. "Dis/Identification: Subject to Countermemory: Disavowal and Black Manhood in Spike Lee's *Malcolm X*." *Signs* 28, no. 1, *Gender and Cultural Memory*, Special Issue, eds. Marianne Hirsch and Valerie Smith (Autumn 2002): 277–301.

Stillman, Nick, and Kalup Linzy. "Kalup Linzy." *BOMB* 104 (Summer 2008): 44–51.

"10 Black British Actors Taking Hollywood by Storm (PHOTOS)." *Huff Post Black Voices*, March 5, 2014, http://www.huffingtonpost.com/2014/02/28/9-black-british-actors-you-need-to-know-_n_4875041.html.

Thompson, Sean. "Beyoncé to Star Alongside Will Smith in 'Hancock 2'?" *Vibe*, June 2014, http://www.vibe.com/article/beyonce-hancock-2-will-smith-rumors.

Tillet, Salamishah. *Sites of Slavery: Citizenship and Racial Democracy in the Post–Civil Rights Imagination*. Durham, NC: Duke University Press, 2012.

"Tyler Perry to Spike Lee: 'Go Straight to Hell,' " *Huffington Post Entertainment*, April 20, 2011, accessed October 14, 2014, http://www.huffingtonpost.com/2011/04/20/tyler-perry-spike-lee-go-to-hell_n_851344.html.

Vognar, Chris. "He Can't Say That, Can He?: Black, White, and Shades of Gray in the Films of Tarantino." *Transition* 112 (2013): 22–31.

Walker, Tim. "Baftas Were a Disgrace for Not Celebrating Black Talent, Says Lenny Henry." *Telegraph*, ed. Richard Eden, May 2013, accessed October 8, 2014, http://www.telegraph.co.uk/culture/tvandradio/10057059/Baftas-were-a-disgrace-for-not-celebrating-black-talent-says-Lenny-Henry.html.

Wallace, Michelle Faith. "The Good Lynching and 'The Birth of a Nation': Discourses and Aesthetics of Jim Crow." *Cinema Journal* 43, no. 1 (Autumn 2003): 85–104.

Watkins, Mel. *Stepin Fetchit: The Life and Times of Lincoln Perry.* New York: Vintage, 2006.

Weber, Bruce. "Murrey Marder, Early McCarthy Skeptic, Dies at 93." *New York Times*, March 19, 2013, http://www.nytimes.com/2013/03/20/us/murrey-marder-reporter-who-took-on-joe-mccarthy-dies-at-93.html?_r=1&.

Wiener, Jon. "The Trouble with Spielberg's 'Lincoln.' " *The Nation*, November 26, 2012, accessed October 14, 2014, http://www.thenation.com/blog/171461/trouble-steven-spielbergs-lincoln.

Weinraub, Bernard. "Ideas and Trends; The Blacklist Era Won't Fade to Black." *New York Times*, October 5, 1997, http://www.nytimes.com/1997/10/05/weekinreview/ideas-trends-the-blacklist-era-won-t-fade-to-black.html.

Wilson, Julee. "*Ebony* 'Trayvon' Covers: The Martins, Spike Lee, Boris Kodjoe, Dwyane Wade and Their Sons for September Issue (Photos)." *Huff Post Black Voices*, August 6, 2013, http://www.huffingtonpost.com/2013/08/06/ebony-trayvon-covers-sons-photos_n_3715134.html.

Index

About the Author

KIMBERLY FAIN, JD, MA, is a licensed attorney who has taught English at Texas Southern University and Houston Community College. Fain holds a juris doctor degree from Thurgood Marshall School of Law, a master of arts degree from Texas Southern University, and a bachelor's degree from Texas A&M University at College Station. In 2007 and 2008, she won a Houston Teachers Institute Fellowship at the University of Houston's Honors College. She received the Rice University Center for the Study of Women, Gender, and Sexuality Scholarly Award of 2012. And in 2013, she received a Norman Mailer creative nonfiction semifinalist award for a personal narrative, "Reinvention," centering on her paternal grandfather and the Great Migration.